Servants of Allah

Servants of Allah

African Muslims Enslaved in the Americas

Sylviane A. Diouf

NEW YORK UNIVERSITY PRESS

New York and London

NEW YORK UNIVERSITY PRESS
New York and London

© 1998 by New York University
All rights reserved

Library of Congress Cataloging-in-Publication Data
Diouf, Sylviane A., 1952–
Servants of Allah : African Muslims enslaved in the Americas /
Sylviane A. Diouf.
p.   cm.
ISBN 0-8147-1904-X (acid-free paper)
ISBN 0-8147-1905-8 (pkb. : acid-free paper)
1. Slaves—Religious life—United States—History.
2. Slaves—Religious life—America—History. 3. Muslims, Black—United
States—History. 4. Muslims, Black—America—History.
5. Afro-Americans—History—To 1863. I. Title.
E443 .D56   1998
305.6'971073—ddc21   98-19768
                                      CIP

New York University Press books are printed on acid-free paper,
and their binding materials are chosen for strength and durability.

Manufactured in the United States of America

10 9 8 7 6 5

To my son, Sény Fakaba Kamara

Contents

Acknowledgments   *ix*

Introduction: An Understudied Presence and Legacy   1

1   African Muslims, Christian Europeans, and the
Atlantic Slave Trade   4

2   Upholding the Five Pillars of Islam in a Hostile World   49

3   The Muslim Community   71

4   Literacy: A Distinction and a Danger   107

5   Resistance, Revolts, and Returns to Africa   145

6   The Muslim Legacy   179

Notes   211

Select Bibliography   235

Index   247

About the Author   254

Acknowledgments

For her enthusiastic support and encouragement from the start, when it really mattered, I express my deepest gratitude to Martine Sambe in Dakar. Heartfelt thanks to Karen Gravelle for continual support and crucial assistance. Kessy Sambe in Paris, who helped with the research: *merci.*

I am particularly grateful to my son, Sény, whose loving support and understanding, smart comments, and daily encouragement have made this work so much easier.

All translations from French, Portuguese, and Spanish documents are from the author. For clarity, African names appear as they were spelled in primary sources and not as they would now be transcribed.

Introduction

An Understudied Presence and Legacy

For three hundred and fifty years, Muslim men, women, and children, victims of the general insecurity that the Atlantic slave trade and the politico-religious conflicts in West Africa fostered, were sold in the New World. They were among the very first Africans to be shipped, and among the very last. When they reached the other side of the Atlantic Ocean, after a horrific journey, they introduced a second monotheistic religion (after the arrival of Catholicism and before Protestantism) into post-Columbian America. Islam was also the first revealed religion freely followed—as opposed to imposed Christianity—by the Africans who were transported to the New World.

The American story of these Muslims starts in Africa. It has its roots in the aftermath of the dislocation of the Jolof Empire, the politico-religious wars in Futa Toro, Bundu, Kayor, Futa Jallon, the northwest part of the Gold Coast, northern Dahomey, and central Sudan. The story starts with religious men and women, dedicated to their faith, who were willing to take chances in a time of insecurity to pursue education and knowledge and to find the best possible religious guidance, wherever it was. It starts in peasant resistance to the raids of warlords and corrupt monarchies. It also has its origins in the violent reaction of so-called unbelievers, who had become a reservoir of captives whom the Muslims sold to the Europeans and Americans and who, in turn, got rid of their captors.

Literate, urban, and in some cases well traveled, the Muslims realized incomparable feats in the countries of their enslavement. They came as Muslims and they lived as Muslims. The preservation of their faith and the maintenance of their lifestyle in a hostile Christian environment were in themselves no small accomplishments. Yet many historians and writers have not acknowledged their presence, much less their success at upholding their religion. The most widely held opinion among writers on slavery and on Islamic issues in the Americas is that "what Muslim faith they brought with them was quickly absorbed in their new Christian milieu and disappeared."[1] A few scholars in the United States have recently recognized some famous Muslims and published their stories, but these figures have remained individuals, not part or representatives of a wider community, whose presence and achievements remain unknown.

That Islam as brought by the African slaves has not survived does not mean that the Muslim faith did not flourish during slavery on a fairly large scale. On the contrary, systematic research throughout the Americas shows that, indeed, the Muslims were not absorbed into the cultural-religious Christian world. They chose to remain Muslims, and even enslaved, they succeeded in following most of the precepts of their religion. With remarkable determination they maintained an intellectual life in mentally sterile surroundings. Through hard work and communality they improved their situation while building a tradition of resistance and revolt. Despite being far outnumbered by Christians, polytheists, and animists, they preserved a distinctive lifestyle built on religious cohesiveness, cultural self-confidence, and discipline.

Standing out in the slave community, a few individuals were identified by their owners and by other Christians as men of stature and became the subjects or the authors of testimonies and narratives. The educated and cosmopolitan Africans whose life stories have been preserved put a personal, intimate face on the brutal experience of being uprooted from home, taken away from family, marched to the coast, branded, loaded aboard a slave ship, shackled naked to the floor, thoroughly examined by strangers, and put to infernal work in degrading conditions in an unknown, distressing world. Few Africans have left personal accounts of their life under slavery, but among those who did are a disproportionate number of Muslims.

In freedom as in enslavement, Islam was the hope of the Muslims, their strength and their comfort. But for most, Islam and its complex relationship with the Atlantic slave trade were also what had brought them in chains to the West, as chapter 1 of this book illustrates.

As Muslims in Christian lands, these involuntary immigrants had to overcome particularly daunting obstacles to maintain and express their faith. Notwithstanding the limits imposed on them by their subordinate status, many succeeded in following, to the letter, the principles of Islam. How they upheld the Five Pillars of Islam in their new world is the subject of chapter 2.

A double minority—religious and ethnic—in the colonial world, as well as in the enslaved community, the West African Muslims did not succumb to acculturation but strove hard to maintain their traditions, social values, customs, and particular identity. At the same time, paradoxically, Islam was the engine of upward mobility within the structure of slavery. The Muslims' mode of survival and their success in the preservation of their tradition, as well as their relations with the non-Muslim slaves and the slaveholders, are explored in chapter 3.

African Muslims arrived in the Americas with a tradition of Arabic literacy that they struggled to preserve. After years of study in Koranic schools and centers of higher learning, they refused to let enslavement turn them into mere beasts of burden. They kept on reading the Koran and writing in Arabic, and they even established schools. Their literacy not only set them apart from most slaves and many slaveholders but became the basis of their disproportionate influence in slave communities and, in some instances, their key to freedom. In the world of slavery, literacy was a distinction and a danger, as is explained in chapter 4.

Well organized and a galvanizing force, Islam in America was the catalyst of revolt and insubordination. It played a major part in the most elaborate slave uprisings and was the motivating force that sent freed men and women back to Africa. These areas are studied in chapter 5.

Despite the efforts of its followers, African Islam did not survive in the Americas in its orthodox form. Yet its mark can be found in certain religions, traditions, and artistic creations of the peoples of African descent. But for all their accomplishments and contributions to the cultures of the African Diaspora, the Muslims largely have been ignored. They have received scant attention at best, despite a wealth of material: from autobiographies and biographies to letters, newspaper articles, mentions in travelers' chronicles, and notices in plantation records and colonial correspondence. Chapter 6 of this book examines the Muslims' legacy and ponders their disappearance from collective memory and their neglect by scholarly research.

Because Islam as brought by the Africans did not outlive the last slaves, one might think that the Muslims failed, that their story in the Americas speaks of defeat and ultimate subjugation. Through examining their history, their stories, and their legacy, however, this book reveals that what they wrote on the sand of the plantations is a successful story of strength, resilience, courage, pride, and dignity.

1

African Muslims, Christian Europeans, and the Atlantic Slave Trade

When the first Africans were shipped to the New World, beginning in 1501, Islam was already well established in West Africa. The religion revealed to the Arabian trader Muhammad between 609 and 632 C.E. had been introduced to North Africa as early as 660. South of the Sahara it had been known since the eighth century through contacts with merchants from the north. Islam in its orthodox Sunni form started to spread, however, after the conversion of the two rulers War Diaby, from Takrur in northern Senegal—which, by applying the *sharia*, or Islamic law, became the first West African Muslim state—and Kosoy, from Gao in present-day Mali. Both conversions occurred at the beginning of the eleventh century. Within fifty years, Islam had expanded from the banks of the Senegal River in the west to the shores of Lake Chad in the east. Malian traders and clerics introduced it to northern Nigeria—where the Muslims became known as *Malé*, or people coming from Mali—in the fourteenth century.

In contrast to its arrival in North Africa, where it had been brought by the invading Arabs, the spread of Islam in sub-Saharan Africa followed a mostly peaceful and unobtrusive path. Religious wars or *jihad*, came late—in the eighteenth and especially the nineteenth century—and Islam was diffused not by outsiders (except in the early years) but by indigenous traders, clerics, and rulers. These carriers of the faith were natives and therefore identified culturally and socially as well as ethnically with the potential converts. Some fundamental features of traditional religions and customs, such as the ritual immolation of animals, circumcision, polygamy, communal prayers, divination, and amulet making, also were present in Islam. Such affinities facilitated conversion as well as accommodation and tolerance of others' rituals and beliefs. Africans themselves considered Islam an African religion.

Islam and Islamic populations quickly became an integral part of the West African landscape; but Islam was not the religion of the majority, and its followers coexisted with non-Muslims. Some Muslim rulers governed largely non-Muslim populations, while animist or polytheist kings often had Muslim subjects. Muslim minorities could be found in practically every town, Muslim majorities in many. Islam was initially the religion of traders and rulers, but depending on the time and place, it also became the religion of the masses in opposition to their "pagan" leaders. As with any religion, Islam in Africa had a variety of followers—the devout, the sincere, the casual believers, the fundamentalists, the lightly touched, and the mystics.

Starting in the fifteenth century, Islam in West Africa gradually became associated with the Sufi orders. The Sufis stress the personal dimension of the relationship between Allah and man, as embodied in *surah* 2:115: "Wherever you turn, there is Allah's Face." They emphasize rituals and devotional practices such as the recitation of the Koran, incantations (*dhikr*), music to attain spiritual ecstasy (*sama*), meditation, acts of devotion, asceticism, retreats (*khalwa*), and fasting as techniques to get closer to God. Their leaders offer a mystic path (*tariqah*) to the believer that is more personal, more immediate, and more "human" than the intellectual and legalistic way of the *ulama* (learned men). The Sufi brotherhood also serves as a social organization that links its members over geography, ethnicity, and social class. They recite the Koran together and have their particular holy days and pilgrimages. There is usually much cohesion and support among the members of the brotherhood. The most extensive Sufi order in West Africa until the mid nineteenth century was the Qadiriyah, founded by Qadir al Gilani, who lived in Baghdad from 1078 to 1166. With the transportation of Africans across the Atlantic, Sufism, which was dominant in West Africa, took hold in the New World; the traces it left can still be detected today, as is assessed in later chapters.

Just as they were part of a local milieu, the West African Muslims belonged to a much larger sphere—an Islamic world with pockets of followers from Spain to China. The West African Muslim world had direct economic, religious, and cultural ties to the Maghreb, Egypt, and the Middle East and was evolving in what today would be called a global market of ideas and goods. Kingdoms and empires such as Kanem and Mali had established diplomatic relations with Morocco, Tunisia, Egypt, and Algeria. Pilgrims on their way to Mecca spent time in Egypt. The sultan of Kanem, Dunama Dibbalemi (1210–1248), built a school in Cairo for his subjects who were studying there. Mansa Musa of Mali—who, on a pilgrimage to Mecca in 1324, spent so much gold that he single-handedly drove the gold market down—brought back to his country lawyers and descendants of the prophet Muhammad, as well as a Spanish-born Muslim architect, and sent numerous students to North Africa. There was a constant exchange of religious commentators, scholars, lawyers, and theologians between black Africa, the Maghreb, and the Middle East. "Natives of Cairo, of the great desert, of Medina and Mecca . . . even the imperial Sherfa tribe [descendants of the prophet Muhammad]"[1] visited the region, stopping over in "heathen" lands such as Ashanti, as reported by Joseph Dupuis, a British consul who met some of these travelers at the court of the *asantehene*. Because they introduced new ideas, perspectives, and goods, the Muslims were the catalysts of change and modernization in West Africa.

Literacy among African Muslims

One invaluable innovation these Muslims brought, which would later be important to the Muslims shipped to the New World, was literacy. In a continent whose civilizations relied on oral tradition and where no writing system was available, only the Muslims were literate. Islam emphasizes literacy, though Muhammad himself could not read or write, and the Koran is very explicit about the need to study. The second *surah*, "The Heifer," states: "Those to whom We have given the Book study it as it should be studied" (v. 121). In West Africa, literacy and the spread of Islam went hand in hand, as the historian John Hunwick stresses:

> Wherever Islam spread encouragement was given to the learning of Arabic and to the foundation of both small schools for teaching the reading of the Koran and higher schools for deeper study of the Arabic language and the literature of Muslim peoples—more especially the theological and legal literature which was to form the basis of both the spiritual and temporal life of the new converts. Once established in an area as the language of the religion, Arabic was soon put to other more worldly ends, for purposes of trade, politics and family records.[2]

Literacy in Arabic is of primary importance in Islam, because believers rely on the Koran not only to understand the religion but also to guide them in their daily life, to provide them with the right prayers for different circumstances, and to instruct them on legal matters and proper social behavior.

Contrary to the norm in Europe at the time, both peasants and girls were taught how to read and write. Concerning female literacy, French slave dealer Theophilus Conneau mentioned in his memoirs that while he was visiting the region of Timbo (Guinea), at the beginning of the nineteenth century, he saw "many elderly females . . . soon in the morning and late at evening, reading the Koran."[3] Lamine Kebe, a former Koranic teacher enslaved in the United States, made a point of mentioning that he had a few girls (7 percent) in his school in Futa Jallon (Guinea) and that his own aunt "was much more learned than himself, and eminent for her superior acquirements and for her skills in teaching."[4] He further gave his interlocutor the names of "women who have been devoted teachers for life, and have rivaled some of the most celebrated of the other sex in success and reputation for talent and extraordinary acquisitions."[5] This is not an isolated case; women in other parts of the Muslim world, including Africa, were recognized for their knowledge. Miriam, a daughter of Usman dan Fodio, the leader of the *jihad* in central Sudan (Nigeria), was so reputed, as was his mother, Ladi. Nevertheless, female literacy was not as extensive as male literacy—usually girls form about 20 percent of the students in Koranic schools—and one of Usman dan Fodio's grievances against the old order was that it did not do enough to encourage girls to go to school. He strongly denounced the men who treated women "like household implements which become broken after long use . . . this is an abominable crime. Alas—how can they shut up their wives, their daughters, and their captives in the darkness of ignorance while daily they impart knowledge to their students."[6]

Not only were the Koranic schools accessible to boys and girls in a coed setting, but they were also open to non-Muslims. Some parents sent their children to the *marabout* (teacher, cleric) because literacy was prestigious and useful and those schools were the only educational structures available. This phenomenon is mentioned by Mungo Park, who visited Senegambia, Guinea, and Mali from 1795 to 1797, and by French explorer Gaspard Theodore Mollien, who was in the same area in 1818.

The striving for literacy was quite strong in West Africa. When Al-Maghili, the Algerian scholar and counselor of King Rumfa, left Kano, Nigeria, at the end of the fifteenth century, the city boasted three thousand teachers, as Al-Maghili stressed in his accounts. One hundred years later, the West African town Timbuktu in Mali had 150 schools. Among the first acts of the religious leaders who founded the theocracies of Bundu, Futa Jallon, Futa Toro, and Sokoto, was to build more schools and encourage higher learning. It is telling that European visitors were quite surprised by the number of schools in West Africa compared to the norm in their own countries. Mungo Park, for example, noted that the Fulani of Bundu in Senegal had established little schools in every city. A director of the French trading company, La Compagnie du Sénégal who was very impressed with the Mandingo emphasized that almost all could read and write and that they had public schools in which *marabout*s taught Arabic to the children.[7] Baron Roger, a governor of Senegal, remarked as late as 1828 that "there are villages in which we find more Negroes who can read and write the Arabic, which for them is a dead and scholarly language, than we would find peasants in our French countryside who can read and write French!"[8]

Even if only basic, literacy was widespread in Muslim West Africa, so much so that by the end of the nineteenth century the French estimated that 60 percent of all Senegalese were literate in Arabic. In the 1880s, a French traveler remarked that "though Timbuktu is no longer a great center of erudition, the population is schooled, the majority of its inhabitants can read and write and know a large part of the Koran by heart, and they can discuss it."[9] By the end of the nineteenth century, Futa Jallon had three thousand Koranic schools and northern Nigeria twenty-five thousand, as reported by the French and British colonial administrations.[10]

A large proportion of the Muslims could read and write in Arabic and in *ajami*, the generic name given to their own language transcribed in the Arabic alphabet. They were avid readers of the Koran, and many knew it by rote. Among these were hundreds of thousands who ended their lives as slaves in the Americas, where their literacy played a significant role in their individual development, the shaping of their community, their relations with non-Muslims, their pursuit of freedom, and the rebellious movements they led or participated in.

Slavery and Islamic Law

Islam in Africa had a definite influence on governance, the administration of justice, and the institution of slavery. The Muslims who were enslaved in America, like their non-Muslim neighbors, were familiar with slavery. Some had already been slaves while others had been slaveholders, and those who were neither had nevertheless experienced life in slave societies. How the Muslims viewed slavery, what form it had in Africa, how one became a slave, and how a slave could become free offer important clues to understanding how Muslims would live and react to their own enslavement in a foreign, Christian land.

African slavery did not follow one model; the institution varied according to region, people, time, and religion. There were, however, similarities among the different African systems and huge differences with American slavery. Whereas kidnapping and straight purchase were the methods by which the Americans and Europeans acquired their African slaves, wars were the principal sources of captives in West Africa. The Africans' viewpoint on the matter is of particular interest. When Frenchman Gaspard Mollien told a group of Senegalese in 1818 that the European battlefields were covered "with thousands of dead, they could not conceive that the Europeans could massacre men since it would be more profitable and humane to sell them than to kill them."[11]

Besides war captives, in non-Muslim states criminals were enslaved, as, sometimes, were debtors who had first pawned themselves or members of their family to their creditor and could not repay their debt. With the development of the trans-Atlantic slave trade, penal slavery increased very rapidly in these regions. Rulers added new categories of crimes punishable by enslavement as they saw fit. On this point British slave dealer Francis Moore emphasized, "Since the slave-trade has been used, all punishments are changed into slavery; there being an advantage on such condemnation, they strain for crimes very hard, in order to get the benefit of selling the criminal."[12]

African slaves were used as porters, soldiers, palace guards, domestics, and concubines but mostly as agricultural laborers. They either lived with their owner's family and worked partly for their master and partly for themselves or were settled in slave villages to work as sharecroppers. In these arrangements, their status resembled that of the European serf, as historian John Thornton points out: "African slaves were often treated no differently from peasant cultivators, as indeed they were the functional equivalent of free tenants and hired workers in Europe." In addition, "slaves were often employed as administrators, soldiers, and even royal advisors, thus enjoying great freedom of movement and elite lifestyles."[13] The absolute chasm that existed between the slave and the slaveholder in the Americas was unknown in Africa. Several European travelers who were familiar with the American system expressed surprise at the "leniency" of the African model. Francis Moore noted in the 1730s that "some of the Negroes [in Gambia] have many house slaves, which are their greatest glory; those slaves live so well and easy, that it is sometimes a hard matter to know slaves from their masters or mistresses."[14] In Senegal, noted another European, they were "treated so well, eating with their masters, working along with them, and being as well clothed . . . that it is impossible to distinguish them from free men."[15] Furthermore, African slaveholders did not mete out the horrendous punishments that were the lot of the American slave. A British traveler to Senegal remarked, "I never saw any whip or instrument of torture used on that part of the coast, nor do I believe, from the enquiries I made, that Slaves are treated with severity."[16] His assertions were correct; however, a small number of West African peoples—notably in present-day Ghana and Benin—who practiced human sacrifices killed prisoners of war and slaves on certain occasions. Finally, the selling of slaves born in the family was generally considered unacceptable and shameful, and only slaves who had been bought could be sold.

The adoption of Islamic law had a decisive effect on slavery in West Africa, for it significantly reduced the causes for enslavement while at the same time encouraging manumission. Islam neither condemned nor forbade slavery but stated that enslavement was lawful under only two conditions: if the slave was born of slave parents or if he or she had been a "pagan" prisoner of war. Captives could legally be made slaves if the prisoner was a *kafir* (pagan) who had first refused to convert and then declined to accept the protection of the Muslims. In theory, a freeborn Muslim could never become a slave; therefore, judicial process led to death for those who had committed a capital crime—since prisons did not exist—while the perpetrators of smaller offenses, including debtors, saw their property seized or received corporal punishment.

In areas where Islamic law prevailed, it was applied to the Muslims but not to the "unbelievers." Slave dealer Theophilus Conneau, who was familiar with the Islamic state of Futa Jallon, described this situation: "Slaves and Caffrees are considered by the Mahometans as unbelievers, therefore as mere ignorants. Their punishment is applied with less vigor but with more contempt, and a crime which would be visited by death on a Mahometan is only considered a case of slavery on an unbeliever."[17]

The West African Muslims largely followed the rule that prohibited them from selling their brethren, as was unanimously noticed by the European traders. As a result, in principle no condemned debtors, offenders, or criminals were among the Muslims who landed in the New World. Swedish naturalist Carl Bernhard Wadstrom, who visited Sierra Leone, Guinea, and Senegal in 1787, noticed that "no Foulahs are ever sold as slaves, for debts or crimes, and kidnapping seldom occurs."[18] The same phenomenon was observed by Jean Baptiste Léonard Durand, a former director of the slave dealing La Compagnie du Sénégal, who wrote about the Mandingo, "They love one another and help each other: one does not hear that they make captives; this punishment is given by the king only and only reserved to those who are guilty of something extremely serious."[19] The historian Paul Lovejoy has gathered data concerning Muslims from the central Sudan that confirm the exceptionality of sentences of enslavement for criminal Muslims. Out of Lovejoy's sample of 108 slaves, most of whom were Muslims shipped to Bahia in the nineteenth century, only one had been condemned to slavery as a result of judicial process.[20] In contrast, up to 11 percent of a sample of diverse recaptives (Africans freed from the slave ships when Great Britain and the United States abolished their international trade in 1807 and 1808) forced by the Europeans to settle in Sierra Leone had been condemned to slavery for crimes ranging from murder to adultery, theft, and sorcery.[21]

A common rule among the Muslims was to redeem their coreligionists. Such redemption was widely practiced, but with the development of the trans-Atlantic trade, old customs were often conveniently overridden. Slave captors, both local and foreign, transported their prisoners swiftly to avoid having them redeemed by family members, especially when the captives were deemed a political or religious "nuisance." Sometimes, time was against the captives. Ayuba Suleyman Diallo, a Senegalese from Bundu who was sold to a British slaver in the Gambia in 1731, informed the slaver that his father would redeem him. Diallo dispatched an acquaintance to his hometown, but when several slaves sent by his father arrived to take his place, the ship had already left for Maryland, where the young husband and father of four was to spend some eventful months.[22]

Sometimes redemptions were successful. The transaction might involve exchanging one person for two or three; in other cases, the slave dealer was given money. Wadstrom reported three cases of the latter sort: a slave factor in Granville Town, Sierra Leone, seized two men because one man who had once lived in their town had defaulted on a debt. It did not matter that the men were not related to the debtor and did not even know him. But "a Mahometan chief . . . took compassion on them, advanced about 50 pound sterlings for their redemption, and sent them home. The same chief having lately sent a favourite free boy, with a message to a factor to whom he was in debt, the boy was seized by way of payments. The chief . . . endeavoured to trace the child from factory to factory."[23] The little boy was ultimately redeemed with the same fifty pounds that the penniless man went to claim back from the governor and gave to the factor. Wadstrom does not say why the Muslim was in debt to the factor, but it is possible that he had exchanged a slave or slaves for European goods and still owed the dealer some captives. He did not hesitate to redeem other Muslims and went to great lengths to do so, but he may very well have been involved in selling "pagans." This practice was common among Muslims. Because the enslavement of unbelievers was lawful they were engaged in the slave trade, both trans-Saharan and trans-Atlantic. Some of the men who were eventually shipped to the Americas had been involved in this type of commerce, either as traders or as providers of prisoners of war. Such was the case with Ayuba Suleyman Diallo (who later was given the name Job ben Solomon), Ibrahima abd al Rahman, and others whose life stories are explored in this book.

Although Islam prohibited the selling of free believers, the practice did not always follow the principle. African Muslims did sell their coreligionists, especially in times of war. The civil wars and the *jihad* of nineteenth-century central Sudan, for instance, sent many Muslims sold by other Muslims to the Americas. Muslim rulers such as the Askia Muhammad of Songhai, Alooma of Bornu, Al-Kanemi of Kanem, or Muhammad Bello of Sokoto often released their Muslim prisoners of war and kept as slaves only the "unbelievers."[24] However, there are also examples of Muslims who knowingly sold fellow Muslims. Arabs and Middle Easterners did so routinely. One of the schemes used to circumvent the Islamic legal prohibition was to declare that the other Muslims were lax in their practices and beliefs, even to being borderline *kafir*. Men from Bornu who went to war against other Muslims declared to British travelers, "They were kaffering, and not saying their prayers! The dogs."[25] The charge was not uncommon. Heretics and apostates, real or not, could also be sold, since even more than atheists and polytheists they are considered the perpetrators of a heinous crime in Islam. Conneau reported the case of one apostate who was sent to America: among the forty slaves brought on November 30, 1826, to the brutal and hated dealer John Ormond by Ama-De-Bella (Amadou Billo), the son of the *almami* of Timbo, was a Muslim who had abjured his religion and set fire to a dwelling, endangering the population. As a Muslim he would have been condemned to death, but since he was an apostate, he was sold to the Europeans—a fate that was considered worse than death.

The application of Islamic law concerning slavery had a profound effect on manumission. The Koran makes ample provisions for the freeing of slaves, as a mark of piety or charity or for expiation. Therefore, the manumission rate in the Islamic world was systematically higher than anywhere else.[26] Conversion to Islam was a prerequisite for emancipation, though it did not result automatically in liberation. However, once a Muslim, the slave could use the channels of liberation defined by Islamic law: ransom, self-redemption, exchange, or manumission. The children of slave concubines by their masters were born free, and the women, who could not be sold, usually became free at least after their owner's death. In some circumstances, slaves and masters exchanged status: if both were taken as prisoners of war, a slave who had become a Muslim while his master remained a "pagan" could become free while his owner became a slave.

Overseas, the Muslims were confronted with a completely different situation. There children inherited the status of their mother, so that even if their father was a free man, they remained slaves, unless their white father emancipated them (mostly done in French colonies). In the New World, there was absolutely no way by which a former master could become a slave. Manumission was rare; redemption by family members was out of the question for first-generation Africans, and self-redemption was a long process. Conversion to Catholicism was not a prerequisite for emancipation but, on the contrary, was the justification for enslavement, with the logic that, through slavery, the Europeans were "civilizing" the Africans and introducing them to the one true faith.

Among the other fundamental differences between the African and American systems was the basic feature of American slavery, that is, its linkage of race, color, and servitude, which was foreign to the African Muslims. Islam has never linked slavery to a particular group except the unbelievers. The Koran and the *Hadith* (the sayings and deeds of Muhammad) do not differentiate among men of various colors but stress that the most pious are the most loved by God. Some of Muhammad's earliest, most prominent, and most respected companions were black, such as Bilali, a former slave who became the first muezzin; the khalif Omar; Amr ibn al-As, who conquered Egypt and Palestine; Abu Bakra, also a former slave, whose son became a governor; Shuqran and Mihja, who fought at the famous battle of Badr. Although there was no color prejudice in pre-Islamic and early Islamic Arabia, a debate arose by the end of the seventh century between Islamic writers who expressed antiblack prejudice[27] and others who vigorously defended the dark-skinned Africans.[28] Yet even at a late stage, slavery in the Muslim world was never a purely black phenomenon. White slaves were purchased by the Arabs until the abolition of slavery, though in many cases they enjoyed a higher status than the black slaves.[29] Olaudah Equiano, an African who intimately knew American slavery because he had been a slave and had visited fifteen American and Caribbean countries, believed that religion, rather than color, was the decisive factor in Islamic countries. He wrote about the Turks, "In general I believe they are fond of black people, and several of them gave me pressing invitations to stay among them, although they keep the Franks, or Christians, separate, and do not suffer them to dwell immediately amongst them."[30]

For obvious reasons, among West African Muslims color and slavery did not have any linkage; the only criterion that determined who should or could be enslaved was, in accordance with Islamic principles, based on religion. The West African Muslims shared the view expressed by Ahmed Baba, the prolific scholar and jurist from sixteenth-century Timbuktu: "Let it be known that infidelity, whether on the part of Christians, Jews, idolaters, Berbers, Arabs, or any other individual notoriously rebellious to Islam, is the only justification for slavery; there is no distinction to be made between miscreants, Sudanese [black] or not."[31] People from Bornu, Kano, Songhai, and Mali were not to be enslaved, Baba maintained, because they were recognized Muslims; "as for the Djilfos [Wolof] they are Muslims according to what we have learnt, this has been proved; there are among them *tolba* and *fuqaha* [specialists in law] and people who know the Koran by heart." The rule, then, was not to trade in people whose provenance was unknown, warned the scholar, who added, "This commerce is one of the calamities of our time." Concerning the treatment of the slaves, Baba stressed that God commands they be treated with humanity, as stated in the Koran and the *Hadith,* and he concluded, "One must pity their sad fate and not treat them harshly because the fact of becoming the property of somebody else breaks the heart, because servitude is inseparable from the idea of violence and domination, especially when it concerns a slave taken far from his country."[32]

Asked about the biblical "curse of Ham," which vows that Ham's descendants will be slaves of his brothers' progeny (Gen. 9:20–25), Ahmed Baba answered that there was no difference between the human races in the Koran, and that even if Ham was the father of the Sudanese, God was too merciful to make millions of men pay for the mistake of one.

In Africa, a social stigma was attached to the condition of slave but not an ethnic or racial one, so that when a slave became free, he or she could become a full member of society. Many monarchs were the sons of slave concubines or were former slaves themselves, but the condition of their birth had carried no negative consequences for their future.

The practice was extremely different in the Americas, where the status of slave was linked to the person's color and, even many generations removed, remained an opprobrium. Thus, freed Africans and their children, who should have been—according to their own culture and religion—fully integrated into American societies, remained the objects of humiliation, segregation, discrimination, and racism, a condition that could have only damaging psychological as well as social repercussions.

Nothing in their cultural and religious background could have prepared the African Muslims for what they encountered in the New World. Those who had never been slaves or who had been slaveholders found a system they certainly would not have condoned at home. Even the former slaves could not have expected what was in store for them. This new world not only was hostile but went contrary to everything the Africans believed in, all they had learned from childhood and seen around them. The system must have been viewed as unacceptable, revolting, inhuman to the slaves but also inhuman on the part of the slaveholders, and this perception certainly shaped the response of the Muslims to their new existence as slaves of the Christians.

The European Approach to Slavery

Kidnapping and enslavement had characterized the earliest contact between European Christians and the Africans. Dinis Dias, the first navigator to reach Senegal in 1444 for the Portuguese crown, abducted four of the men who came to his vessel in their canoes. A year later, a Portuguese expedition captured children. They met fierce hostility, however, and left many dead sailors behind. Because they had encountered organized, structured, and militarized societies that could not simply be pillaged, the Europeans had to negotiate with the authorities. By 1448 they had established commercial relations with the kingdoms along the coast of West Africa for the supply of local goods and captives on the one hand and the distribution of European merchandise on the other.

The development of the European-African slave trade was not unique or unusual; Europeans had been dealing in slaves for centuries. Medieval Europe traded in European slaves on a large scale. Slavs, Irish, Welsh, Greeks, Scandinavians, Russians, and Turks furnished the bulk of the slave population across Europe up to the middle of the fifteenth century. They worked as domestics, in mines, on farms, on the sugar plantations of the Portuguese, and in the harbors. Just as in Africa, most European slaves were obtained through raids and wars. As was also true in Africa, slavery in Europe was justified on the grounds that the slaves were different: they followed a religion other than that of their captors or belonged to a different ethnic group. The Christian Venetians, for example, could not trade in Christian slaves but sold and bought "pagan" Slavs. The Catholic Church forbade the Jews to own Christians but was not concerned with slaves who were not Christians.[33]

The patterns of slavery in medieval Europe and in Africa were similar initially; what became unique was that by the sixteenth century Europeans reserved slavery for the Africans, and the enslavement of whites totally disappeared from the countries they controlled. Slavery and color were linked for the first time, and adherence to Christianity on the part of the Africans did not make any difference. Their evangelization was a priority as a religious duty but served primarily as a justification for the slave trade.

The papal bulls of Nicholas V in 1454 and Calixtus III in 1456 justified Portugal's slave trade as a crusade for Christianity. The Europeans immediately set out to "enlighten" the Africans, among whom, as they soon realized, were many Muslims. Father Barreira, a Portuguese Jesuit who traveled from Sierra Leone to Senegal in 1606, noted that "the *Fulos* . . . follow the sect of Mahomet . . . the *Jalofo* follow the law of Mahomet . . . the *Berbeci* . . . follow the law of Mahomet . . . the *Mandingas* follow the sect of Mahomet."[34] A Spanish priest writing about Senegal in 1646 was happy to report that he had baptized four hundred white children and adults, including twenty-five "white Hebrews"—Jews who had been expelled from Spain and had settled in Senegal—but that "concerning the natives, there is no way for us to convince them."[35] This refusal of conversion on the part of the Muslims was confirmed by a group of Portuguese living in Rufisque, near present-day Dakar, who informed the Spanish Capuchins that "unless God creates a miracle, [they] would obtain no results in the conversion of the natives."[36] He was certainly right; today, 94 percent of the Senegalese are Muslims.[37]

Among other testimonies of failure in Christian missionary endeavors, a letter sent by a Spanish Capuchin to his superior illustrates the Senegalese Muslims' unwillingness even to consider conversion. Father Francisco de Vallecas reported around 1646 that he and other priests "were doing everything possible to attempt to convert these people. We talked to the kings of *Dencallor* and *Lambaya*; we showed them the truth of the Holy Gospel and the falsity of the sect of *Mohama* which is followed by all the natives of these coasts, and after several retorts, they ordered the interpreters to remain silent, and without them it was impossible to do any fruitful work."[38] Portuguese, Spanish, and French missionaries who visited Senegambia noted repeatedly the refusal of the Muslims to convert. The profound impact of Islam on its followers and their rejection of Christianity in Africa is important in view of how the "followers of the sect of *Mohama*" later reacted to forced conversion in the New World and what they did to preserve their own religion, as is discussed in chapter 2.

Senegambians brought to Spain by the Arabs had been known in Europe since the thirteenth century, but by 1447 they were coming directly from Africa to the Iberian markets. Between 1489 and 1497, 2,003 African slaves—they were a minority—were sold in Valencia, Spain, and the majority were said to be Wolof.[39] Many more were offered on the Portuguese markets. All slaves living in Catholic lands were forcibly baptized. A simulacrum of Christian conversion, coupled with nominal religious instruction, was deemed sufficient to turn the "idolaters," and the "zealots of the sect of Mahomet," into Christians called *ladinos*.

These *ladinos* were the first Africans to be introduced into the New World, as early as 1501. Direct trade with the African coast was forbidden for fear that with Africans coming straight from Africa, Islam would find its way into the new colonies. In the context of the period, the Spanish concern was wholly natural. Moorish control over Granada had ended only in 1492, and hostility toward the occupying Muslims and Islam ran deep. Spain was cautious because it knew firsthand the danger that Islam and the Muslims could represent. The Crown's fears were well expressed in a royal order of 1543, which stated that the Muslims should not be introduced to Spain's American possessions because "in a new land like this one where faith is only recently being sowed, it is necessary not to allow to spread there the sect of Mahomet or any other."[40]

Given their different historical experiences, the French and the British never had a second thought about introducing "Mohammedans"—as they erroneously called the Muslims[41]—to their American possessions, and early French sources mention the presence of Muslims, including many *marabout*s.

The Spanish reluctance notwithstanding, *bozales*, or people coming directly from Africa, were imported because the trade in *ladinos* could not meet the demand. Nicholas de Ovando, the governor of Hispaniola, considered trade in *bozales* a bad policy and asked for a complete stop to the importation of Africans in 1503. After the first slave uprising in the New World, led by the Wolof in 1522, a royal decree of May 11, 1526, specifically forbade the introduction of "Gelofes" (Wolof), *negros* (blacks) from the Levant (or Middle East), those who had been raised with the Moors, and people from Guinea without a special license from the Casa de Contratación, which regulated the slave trade and put levies on the slaves.[42] All the groups that the decree prohibited were either completely or mostly Muslim. Within fifty years, five decrees were passed to forbid the importation of African Muslims to the Spanish colonies. This insistent reissuing of the prohibition shows that Muslims nevertheless continued to be imported and to cause concerns and problems in the New World. The colonists claimed that the Muslims incited the other nations to rebellion, and it was feared that they would take Islam to the Indians, as is discussed in chapter 5.

The African Historical Context for Muslim Captivity

These Muslims did not arrive in the New World by accident. There were political, religious, and social reasons that they were victims of the slave trade. America may have demanded generic African laborers, but Africans did not sell other Africans indiscriminately. Specific events led to the deportation of specific peoples, either as individuals or as groups. Understanding the circumstances in Africa that resulted in the Muslims' captivity is of crucial importance for understanding their reaction to enslavement in the Americas and the direction they gave to their new life.

The history of Africa, in all its complexity, cannot be dissociated from the history of the people of African descent in the New World. Who the men and women were who were shipped away, how they had been captured and under which historical circumstances, and why they were sold to the Europeans and Americans are all elements that participated in the development of an African American identity. It is beginning from this African historical context, which has been ignored by most scholars of slavery— who place Africa at the periphery of the Diaspora instead of at its center—that the story of the Muslims in the Americas must be explained, understood, and evaluated.

Muslims in Western Africa were enslaved in a variety of military actions over a period of more than 350 years and across territory ranging from Senegal to Chad and from the southern border of the Sahara to the northern fringes of the tropical forest. It would be impossible to account for all or even many of the conflicts, but some are of particular importance because they sent numerous Muslims, as groups, to the Americas. These wars were not straightforward events; they consisted of many battles of unequal importance, of raids and predatory expeditions, and could last for years. So regardless of who the ultimate winners were, prisoners from both camps were sold, at one point or another, which meant that even when the Muslims were victorious and succeeded in establishing theocracies, they lost men to enslavement over the course of many battles.

A few years after the establishment of a regular slave trade between Africa and the Americas, a series of events led to the shipment overseas of numerous Senegalese, among them many Muslims. This chain of events started in the Jolof Empire, founded in the thirteenth century by a Muslim dynasty originally from Walo on the Senegal River; the empire extended over most of what is today Senegal. Its population of Wolof, Mandingo, Tukulor, Fulani, and Serer was largely Muslim, except for the Serer. Each vassal kingdom—Walo, Takrur, Kayor, Baol, Sine, Salum, Wuli, and Niani—recognized the hegemony of Jolof and paid tribute.

The Fulani launched the first blow to unity. Between 1490 and 1512, they organized the autonomous kingdom of Futa Toro under the leadership of Koli Tenguela Ba, who founded the Denyanke dynasty. Then, in Sine, King Mbegan Ndour, who had benefited from the Atlantic commerce with the Portuguese, had become powerful and wanted his independence. He first successfully repressed a *jihad* launched by a Tukulor *marabout*, Eli Bana, and then established his autonomy from Jolof in the

1510s. Finally Kayor, which also traded with the Portuguese (contrary to landlocked Jolof), took its independence around 1550, and the Jolof Empire was no more.

Every conflict that led to the disintegration of Jolof sent Muslim Wolof, Mandingo, Tukulor, and Fulani to Mexico, Peru, Colombia, and Hispaniola. The presence of these Senegalese prisoners of war had profound repercussions in the Spanish colonies. In 1522 the Wolof of Hispaniola led the first African slave revolt in the history of the Americas, and they also rebelled in Puerto Rico and Panama. Between 1533 and 1580 the majority of the slaves in Cartagena, Colombia, were Wolof and Fulani.[43] According to Father Alonso de Sandoval, a Jesuit who lived in Cartagena from 1605 to 1617, the Wolof, Berbeci,[44] Mandingo, and Fulani were the main groups represented in that city and, despite their different languages and customs, were united through belonging to the "cursed sect of Mahomet."[45]

The Senegambians—*ladinos* and *bozales*—were the first Africans to be sold to the New World. After this first wave, which the Spaniards tried to regulate and limit, African Muslims from a wider area were imported in larger numbers.

One of the early movements that contributed to the deportation of large groups of Muslims to the plantations of the Americas was the so-called *marabouts'* war, or *Tubenan* (from the Arabic and Wolof *tuub*, to convert to Islam) revolution. Its leader was Nasir al-Din, a Berber *marabout* from Mauritania who belonged to the Qadiriyah brotherhood. He launched a *jihad* that reached Senegal in 1673. The movement was directed against the pagan rulers, and its goal was strict religious orthodoxy. Nasir al-Din denounced the animist kings because they sold their subjects to the Europeans under the flimsiest pretext. He stated that "God does not allow kings to raid, kill, or enslave their people, he has them, on the contrary, to guard them from their enemies. The peoples are not made for the kings, but the kings are made for the peoples."[46]

Nasir al-Din was welcomed by a population demoralized and scared at the rapid development of the Atlantic slave trade. With the help of the native and Moorish *marabouts*, he subdued the Senegalese kingdoms of Futa Toro, Jolof, Kayor, and Walo and replaced their rulers with *marabouts*. In Saint-Louis, the slave trading post located at the mouth of the Senegal River since 1659, the French were worried. The captives they bought came from the hinterland and were transported partly on the river. With the four kingdoms in the hands of hostile Muslims, all traffic was stopped. Louis Moreau de Chambonneau, an employee of the Compagnie du Sénégal, summed up the French predicament: "The leading marabouts . . . despise us a lot because of the difference between our religion and their superstition; they tell the people that we trade in captives to eat them; since they became Masters of the country, up to now not one has entered our canoe; without the powerful, it is impossible for us to trade in anything."[47]

Nasir al-Din was not an abolitionist. He was not opposed to domestic slavery but had an interest in reestablishing the status quo that the trans-Atlantic commerce was disrupting. Besides wishing to spread his faith, he was not averse to protecting the trans-Saharan trade in cereals, cattle, gold, and captives, which was declining due to the enormous demand of the French in Saint-Louis for the same goods. In other words, the *marabouts* did not want their coreligionists to be sold to the Christians but—justifiably, in the logic of those times—they were not opposed to selling "infidels" to the Moors.

After Nasir al-Din's death in battle in 1674 the French maneuvered well, playing on internal divisions. Soon the *brak* (king) of Walo, installed by the *marabouts*' party, turned against those who had put him in power and launched campaigns of terror, burning villages and selling, according to contemporary French documents, "quantities of captives" to the Compagnie du Sénégal. By 1677 the *Marabouts*' war was over. The devastation was total: to crush the Muslims, the villages had been destroyed and the crops burnt. The resulting famine was so terrible that men and women were reduced to pawning themselves and their children for food, risking enslavement and sale to the Europeans. Chambonneau, who traveled in Futa in July 1676 for the Compagnie du Sénégal, stated that if he had had enough goods he could have bought six hundred men and women.[48]

The war had particularly devastating consequences for the Muslim clerics. A French traveler, Le Sieur Lemaire, emphasized in 1682, "They have no more marabouts in their country [Walo] and those they can catch, they enslave."[49] The slave dealer Jean Barbot concurred, remarking that the people of Kayor had resolved "never more to entertain any Marabout, but to sell all such as they should find in their country for slaves."[50] Barbot obliged: "The Alquayre of Rio Fresca [Rufisque] sold me a *marabou* sent to him by King Damet on account of some misdeed he had committed. This black priest was abroad for two months before he spoke a word, so deep was his sorrow. I sold him in the American Islands."[51]

The defeat of the *marabouts* sent numerous Muslims to the New

World. Many of those who remained settled in Bundu, a large area between the Senegal River and the Gambia River. In a movement that got its inspiration from Nasir al-Din, Bundu in 1690 became the second (after Takrur) Muslim theocracy in West Africa, under the leadership of the *almami* Malick Sy. Bundu was the home of Ayuba Suleyman Diallo, who was born ten years after the establishment of the theocracy. Under the name Job ben Solomon, he was enslaved on a tobacco plantation in Maryland. His unique and rich life story has been documented by himself and by British officials on both sides of the Atlantic.[52]

As had been the case with the disintegration of the Jolof Empire and the *marabouts*' war, armed conflicts supplied the largest contingents of men from West Africa to the New World. Some conflicts were purely economic in that they were launched for the purpose of rounding up captives for the American markets. The impact of the European demand for slaves on the African wars is no longer a matter of conjecture and has been widely explained and commented on. In the eighteenth century, a female mulatto slave dealer who was described as "the mistress of a large Mandingo town" and sold her captives to the Europeans in Sierra Leone, summed up this relationship very clearly: "She said there had been no wars in the interior country to hers for some time, and that wars do not happen when slaves are not wanted."[53]

Africans had other "commodities" to sell, and they made a brisk business in gold, ivory, gum, hides, cattle, grain, and fabrics with the foreigners; but to get slaves in the quantities they wanted, the factors demanded captives for the most sought-after European products. A "deputy king" of Timbo explained to the Company of Sierra Leone that "the factories would not furnish them with guns, powder and cloth, which he considered as the chief articles, for any thing except slaves."[54] This policy was firmly applied all along the coast, and it locked the Africans into a terrible vicious circle. If a party acquired superior weapons, its potential rivals would have to do the same to avoid becoming its next victims. This meant getting and selling men, women, and children to secure arms in order to protect one's population from enslavement. Weapons and ammunition were exclusively sold to the rulers, not to the peasants, because the trade companies wanted to ensure that the latter could not defend themselves and thus become easy prey.

To arm one side in a conflict was a strategy followed by the European countries to get their cargo of captives. A 1687 French document reveals how the tactic was used:

> [The king of Baol in Senegal] must be told that, having learned he is at war with the Dhamel [king of Kayor], we are disposed to give him arms, powder, lead and other things if he needs them and we will be happy to assist him and be his friends . . . and that with the victory we wish he reaps against King Dahmel, he will get many captives that he could send to Gorée and we will trade them for good merchandise, and we should encourage him to send us a considerable number because we are in great need of them at Gorée.[55]

To arm both sides in a conflict was another scheme. This policy was well illustrated by the British governor O'Hara in Saint-Louis, Senegal, who, in 1773, provided ammunition to King Makodu Kumba Jareng as well as to his rival for the throne. "By pitting one against the other, the English have the exclusivity of the captives," wrote a French official to his minister.[56]

But some wars were not good for commerce, for instance, when the disruption was so great that caravans of captives could not reach the seaboard, or when the opponents were of equal strength and used defense rather than aggression or were too busy to raid their neighbors. A letter dated March 28, 1724, from an employee to his directors at the Compagnie du Sénégal sheds light on the maneuvers of the Europeans who wanted peace to get slaves:

> Whatever we have told . . . King Thin [Baol] and Damel [Kayor] to incite them to peace, has been useless because of the influence that the Maraboux have on Damel. They advise him to continue . . . this is why they only traded little at Gorée and why they do not dare raid their neighbors or their own subjects, as they usually do; they only guard themselves in their respective States, fearing surprise. It seems that this war will not end soon. Without it, the company could benefit from their avidity for our goods in exchange for the captives they could provide us if there was peace, to which I will devote myself entirely as well as to develop commerce in all the posts of the concession.[57]

Not every conflict was provoked by the American demand for slaves. Africa had its own political wars—for succession, control, expansion, consolidation—and politico-religious conflicts, which were completely independent of the European presence. Most wars in West Africa were political or religious, but as with the economic wars, the prisoners were condemned to enslavement and some were sold to the Europeans. A succession conflict in Senegal illustrates how purely local events could be closely linked to the trans-Atlantic slave trade and bring vast numbers of Muslims to the New World.

In the 1730s, Damel Maïsa Teinde Wedj had unified Kayor and Baol and encountered the ire of the French slave factors because, as a Muslim, he refused to sell slaves and to trade his goods for alcohol. When he died, his brother, Mawa, and his son, Maïsa Bige, started a series of civil wars for access to the throne that led to a massive deportation of Wolof. In 1753, Mawa sold four hundred captives, victims of the civil war and of a famine that had been going on for some time. Pruneau de Pommegorge, an employee of the Compagnie du Sénégal, recalled that, in 1754, he "traded the product of one of these wars; close to five hundred *Yolofs*, a war that could be called civil since it was the uncle of the young king who had gathered his people, to whom the discontent rallied. With this force, he entered *Cayor* and attacked his nephew."[58] The five hundred men subsequently conspired on Gorée Island to kill the whites and go back to Kayor, but their plot was discovered. On the ship that transported them to the Americas, they again organized a revolt. Fifteen men who had been unshackled to help the crew gave nails and pieces of metal they had stolen to the other captives, who got rid of their chains. After a fierce battle that left seven sailors dead, the rebels could be reduced only by a cannon fired right in their midst. Two-hundred-thirty Wolof warriors were killed, and the rest disembarked in the French West Indies.

At roughly the same time, in Futa Jallon, the mountainous area in the heart of Guinea, Muslims were also involved in a revolution. Led by Fulani and Mandingo originally from Macina (Mali) and Futa Toro, the movement was, as in Bundu, a reaction partly against the oppression that the Muslims felt at the hands of the animists and partly against the incapacity or unwillingness of the rulers to protect their populations from the European slave traders. In 1725 the *almami* Karamoko Alfa established a Muslim theocracy in Futa Jallon. It was a confederation of nine provinces, with an *alfa* (religious leader) at the head of each one, chosen from among the leaders of the *jihad*. Its political capital was at Timbo.

After Karamoko's death in 1751, the man chosen as the new *almami* was his cousin Ibrahima Sori, also called Sori Mawdo (Sori the Great). With *almami* Ibrahima Sori, the war party triumphed. Though he and the other leaders of the holy war had made the fight against the European slave trade one of the rallying cries of their struggle, their concern extended only insofar as the victims were Muslims. "The people on whom we make war," explained a high-ranking official, "never pray to God: we do not go to war with people who give God Almighty service."[59] Sori Mawdo engaged in military operations against the unbelievers, and under his leadership, Futa Jallon provided record numbers of animist captives to the European dealers.

The interrelationship of religion, war, enslavement, and the Atlantic trade has been well described by Theophilus Conneau, a French captain who bought slaves for Cuba in the 1820s. When he wondered how the *almami* could provide so many slaves from a country

> where a true believer was a free subject, [Amadou Billo's] response was that the Koran permitted the sale of their bondservants, and from that source many were yearly exchanged for European goods, which in turn supplied them with the means of carrying on the wars commanded by the Secret Book—to conquer and subjugate all tribes to the true faith. In order to carry out more fully the commands of a true Mahometan to destroy all unbelievers, they had recourse to the cupidity of the white man, whose milder religion authorized its votaries to enslave the African.[60]

Most wars in Futa Jallon were launched under the pretext of expanding the influence of Islam, but as Conneau pointed out, if the warriors had not expected to take slaves, they might not have attacked the well-fortified "Caffree towns." Amadou Billo's answer was that the Muslims were no better than the Christians: one stole while the other held the bag. He also emphasized that if the whites had not come to tempt the Africans with powder and guns, "the commands of the Great Allah would be followed with milder means."[61]

In Futa Jallon as in the rest of West Africa, a number of slaves kept domestically were put to work in the fields to grow the grain, yams, and cassavas that were sold to the Europeans, which were to be the food distributed to the Africans during the Middle Passage. Thus as the demand for slaves to be shipped overseas increased, the "need" for more domestic slaves saw a parallel increase. With this influx of captives, the Muslim population as a whole had more time to devote to study and religious affairs. Mosques and Koranic schools flourished. The Koran was translated into Pulaar, the language of the Fulani, and as the holy book became more accessible, Islam grew deeper roots. Because trade in Muslims was forbidden, the kingdom experienced peace and security.

Ibrahima Sori had several sons. One of them, Ibrahima abd al Rahman, was a colonel in his father's army. In January 1788, at age twenty-six, he was sent with a contingent of two thousand to fight a population that had destroyed the vessels that came to the coast and had prevented the trade between the Europeans and Futa Jallon. In a bitter twist of fate, as Ibrahima was actively protecting the Atlantic slave trade, he was captured by those who were fighting against the infamous commerce. Remembering his ordeal forty years later, the Pulo prince wrote that his captors "pulled off my shoes, and made me go barefoot one hundred miles, and led my horse before me. . . . They carried me to the Mandingo country, on the Gambia. They sold me directly, with fifty others, to an English ship. They took me to the Island of Dominica. After that I was taken to New Orleans. Then they took me to Natchez."[62] For four decades, "Prince," as he was nicknamed by his owner, planted and chopped cotton in Mississippi. Among the fifty warriors who went through the Middle Passage with him, one, Samba, ended up living on the same plantation. Futa Jallon, with its history of wars, was an active supplier of animist captives, but by the same token, it turned out to be an unwilling provider to the plantations of the New World of Muslim warriors defeated in battle.

The concentration of slaves in Futa Jallon and on the coast in Sierra Leone, where they were put to work while awaiting shipping, led to numerous revolts. Captives also fled and created maroon villages. One major revolt took place in 1785, when maroons allied to the Susu defeated their former Mandingo owners and killed numerous members of the aristocracy. For ten years the maroons conducted raids on Mandingo villages in Guinea and sold their prisoners to the Europeans, before they were defeated by an alliance of Mandingo and Susu.

After Futa Jallon, another Muslim theocracy started to rise, this time located in Senegal. The *Torodo* (the Muslim cleric class of Futa Toro) revolution that gave rise to this theocracy again was in part a consequence of the Atlantic slave trade. Futa Toro, the land of the Muslim Tukulor and Fulani, had been the scene of a succession crisis since the first decade of the eighteenth century, and civil wars had sent numerous prisoners to the Americas. Between 1720 and 1743, the French provided their colony of Louisiana with a great many men and women captured during these conflicts. In 1763, Saint-Louis was ceded to the British by the Treaty of Paris, and the new governor, O'Hara, engaged in large-scale slave raiding. Besides the official commerce of the British, he had established a personal trade. He provided his plantations of the West Indies with Senegalese workers and sold the surplus. He personally took part in raids in Futa Toro and Walo with the Trarza and Brakna Moors from Mauritania. In 1775 O'Hara furnished them enough weapons to attack Walo, which had threatened to cut off Saint-Louis from the Upper Senegal. In six months they destroyed the kingdom and took eight thousand captives, whom O'Hara shipped to the West Indies.

In addition, a terrible famine had swept through the region. It had many causes: an invasion of locusts, cyclical droughts, the constant civil wars, the slave trade that decimated the farming population, the destruction of the crops, and the fact that the merchants in Saint-Louis had bought large quantities of grain to feed their thousands of captives on shore and during the Middle Passage. One of the results of the famine was that Senegalese slaveholders sold their slaves to the Europeans so they no longer would have to feed them, while many people bargained their freedom for food. They pawned themselves and their families and were often sold as slaves.

It is in this context that two Tukulor *marabouts*, Suleyman Bal and Abdel Kader Kane, launched a revolt against the Moors and the animist Denyanke regime that was incapable of assuring the peace and protecting its subjects. Bal and Kane had been students in the *dahira* (Koranic schools) of Koki and Pir in Kayor, which had been influenced by Nasir al-Din; they belonged to the Qadiriyah and had traveled to the Islamic states of Bundu and Futa Jallon. In 1776 they established the independent theocracy of Futa Toro, and Kane was appointed *almami*. In July, as a reprisal against the decimation that slave hunting had brought to Futa and Walo, the *almami* and his council stopped all British trade upriver. As in Bundu and Futa Jallon, the Muslims strictly forbade the selling of their coreligionists and succeeded in imposing this rule on the French when France repossessed Saint-Louis. In 1788, Abdel Kader Kane displayed his determination: he had a French slave convoy searched by his soldiers, who freed the almost ninety men from Futa whom they found among the captives. But this action did not stop the trade, and the *almami* threatened the French in no uncertain terms in a letter to the governor in Saint-Louis, dated March 1789:

> We are warning you that all those who will come to our land to trade [in slaves] will be killed or massacred if you do not send our children back. Would not somebody who was very hungry abstain from eating if he had to eat something cooked with his blood? We absolutely do not want you to buy Muslims under any circumstances. I repeat that if your intention is to always buy Muslims you should stay home and not come to our country anymore. Because all those who will come can be assured that they will lose their life.[63]

With peace, stability, and security Futa Toro developed, and peasants from Jolof and Sine-Salum made their way to the river to escape the exactions of the *ceddo* (animist slave warriors) and the ever-present threat of the slave trade. Abdel Kader Kane, who was a learned man, encouraged the building of mosques and schools all over his country. He invited the kings of Walo, Kayor, Baol, and Jolof to join his Islamic reform, and they agreed. But in 1790, Damel Amari Ngone Ndella, a *ceddo* monarch, was back on the throne of Kayor, after some years of exile in Walo, and strife soon broke out between him and the *marabouts*. His slaves attacked a Muslim village in Ndiambur, and Amari Ngone sold the *marabouts* and their students to the Europeans. This event led the *marabouts* to a violent confrontation with the *damel*. They organized their own army led by cleric warriors, but the *ceddo* defeated them. Bloody battles were waged near the Islamic centers of higher learning at Pir and Koki. The leading *marabouts*, clerics and warriors of the faith, were killed or sold to the Europeans. Those who managed to escape took refuge in the Cap-Vert peninsula, where, with the local Lebu, they organized an independent Islamic state.

The refusal of Amari Ngone Ndella to renew the allegiance of Kayor to the *almami* and the killing and enslavement of the most prominent Muslim families of the kingdom, whom the *almami* knew and had been in school with, led Abdel Kader Kane to his own confrontation with the *damel*. He enjoined Amari Ngone Ndella to embrace Islam or become his vassal. The *damel* refused and continued his repression of the Muslims. Kane counterattacked by gathering an army of thirty thousand, including women and children, and marching on Kayor. The movement was as much religious as it was aimed at putting an end to the selling of Muslims to the Europeans and avenging the death or enslavement of the Muslims of Kayor. Samba Makumba, a Muslim deported to Trinidad as a result of these events, summed up the situation for a visitor about fifty years later:

> He belonged to the tribe Fullah Tauro, which engaged in war with six other tribes in Africa to prevent them, as he said, from carrying on the slave trade. The Mahometans are forbidden to make slaves of those of their own faith, and when any of their people are concerned in this traffic, they believe their religion requires them to put a stop to it by force. It was for this purpose a war was commenced by the Fullahs against these other tribes and in this war Samba was taken prisoner and sold as a slave.[64]

Samba Makumba and his companions were poorly armed, mostly with sticks and faith. Many died of thirst and dysentery as they walked through a landscape of desolation: Amari Ngone and his army had burned every village, every field, and sealed or poisoned every well. This scorched-earth tactic was a success, and the Muslim forces were defeated at Bungoy in 1796. Kane remained a prisoner for three months before being sent back to Futa by a magnanimous *damel*.

For many Muslims, however, the nightmare had just begun. The French, who were opposed to Kane because he had forbidden the trade in Muslims, were waiting for them in the slave depots of Saint-Louis and Gorée where they were brought by the victors. As Baron Roger, the governor of Senegal, explained:

> When the slave dealers in Saint-Louis, Gorée, and Rufisque learned that a war was about to erupt between Caior and Fouta, they rejoiced because whoever was the winner, there would be captives and the trade could only benefit. Damel asked them to provide him with weapons and ammunition to help him defend himself and was obliged to give them, in reimbursement for these advances, the first prisoners to fall into his hands.[65]

One of the prisoners was Kélédor, a young Wolof from Walo who had been sent by his father to study in Futa Toro. He left Gorée Island on a boat with four hundred men, women, and children, almost all of them Muslim victims of the war. Many *marabouts* were among them, Kélédor reported, and several men committed suicide by jumping into the sea while chanting, "Iallah! Iallah!" which is how the Senegalese call God.[66] The survivors landed in Saint-Domingue (present-day Haiti), where the young man later fought alongside the Haitian liberator Toussaint-Louverture, and then moved to Puerto Rico before sailing home with a group of former Muslim slaves. Kélédor told his fascinating story to the French governor, who turned it into a very accurate, if romanticized, novel. Other enslaved Futanke were met by Scottish explorer Mungo Park as he was traveling "in the interior districts of Africa" with a slave caravan.[67] Nine survivors of the Bungoy debacle were on the slave ship Park boarded on Gorée Island. They landed in Antigua after twenty-five days at sea.

This was not the last time Futa Toro turned into a major and unwilling provider of Muslim slaves. In 1804 the French, whose trade on the river had been interrupted by the *almami* between 1801 and 1803, sent twelve boats from Saint-Louis to burn a dozen villages. They took six hundred prisoners, the majority of whom belonged to the ruling class. Three years later internal strife, partly fueled by the French of Saint-

Louis, led to confrontations between Kane and his allies, on the one hand and a coalition of Kaarta and Bundu rulers on the other. Abdel Kader Kane was killed in 1806, with the complicity of a new generation of Futa leaders. These events probably led to the capture in 1807 of Omar ibn Said, a scholar, warrior of the faith, and trader from Futa who was shipped to the United States, where he spent the rest of his life as a slave in North Carolina.[68]

Warriors of the Faith

Throughout eighteenth-century Senegambia and Guinea, Muslim movements and theocracies were associated with the fight against old regimes that had reinforced their power by selling men and women to the Europeans. The Muslim movements appealed to the mass of peasants, who were the main victims of the slave trade. These theocracies became havens not only for the Muslims but for the non-Muslims who accepted their protection. The Islamic "party" was able to expand and consolidate its power beyond the borders of the different kingdoms the Muslims inhabited. Starting with Nasir al-Din, the religious leaders of Futa Toro, Futa Jallon, and Bundu belonged to the Qadiriyah. They were all connected: they had studied in the same schools of Pir and Koki in Kayor; they had family relations; they shared the same vision of Islam and the same political views. Their followers moved from one Muslim area to the other, fought for Islam and against the enslavement of Muslims wherever they were, and sought refuge in their brethren's enclaves when persecuted. Their networks extended throughout West Africa, with men from Futa Toro and Futa Jallon teaching in Kong (Ivory Coast) and Bouna (Ghana.) Islam in general and the Qadiriyah brotherhood in particular united the faithful, whoever and wherever they were. This unity that they experienced in Africa would become significant for the Muslims enslaved in America, who formed a community of men and women linked by Islam, transcending restrictive notions of ethnicity and nationality.

The Muslims who joined the politico-religious wars that swept through West Africa in the eighteenth and nineteenth centuries had learned since their first years of school what was expected of a warrior of the faith. They knew that they must not be the aggressors and that they had to follow strict rules of conduct: "Fight in the cause of Allah those who fight you," enjoins *surah* 2 of the Koran, "but do not transgress limits; for Allah loves not transgressors" (2:190). Those who refused to take part in the war would be disgraced and punished: "And he who turns back, Allah will punish him with a grievous Chastisement" (48:18). But those killed in war "rejoice in the Bounty Provided by Allah: And with regard to those left behind, who have not yet joined them in their bliss, the martyrs glory in the fact that on them is no fear nor have they cause to grieve" (3:170). Because of these teachings and an Islamic tradition of cleric-warriors, the deeply devoted *marabout*s, teachers, *talib* (students, novices), *imam* (prayer leaders); the whole Islamic community of *ulama* (scholars); the *alfa* or *charno* (religious leader), *qadi* (judge), and *hufaz* (memorizers of the Koran) were on the front line. These erudite warriors were numerous among the captives from Senegambia and Guinea who were sent to America.

The year 1804 saw important developments that would bring more of them across the Atlantic. One was a conflict in the Gold Coast (Ghana) that pitted the Muslims against the fetishist Ashanti. The king of Ashanti, the *asantehene* Osei Kwame, had been chased from power and strangled in 1803 because, it was feared, he intended "to establish the Korannic law for the civil code of the empire."[69] The Muslims of the northwest region rebelled and were assisted by their coreligionists from Kong and Bouna. Their coalition was defeated. It was in these circumstances that Abu Bakr al Siddiq, a fifteen-year-old student from an illustrious Muslim family that came originally from Timbuktu and Jenne, was captured. He was shipped to Jamaica, where he spent his next thirty years as a slave.[70]

The most significant events of 1804, however, took place in central Sudan, in what is today Nigeria. From the end of the eighteenth through the nineteenth century, this region went through a series of conflicts. Some had a decisive impact on the formation of the Muslim communities of the Americas and are briefly described here.

The most significant conflict was the *jihad* launched by a devout and purist Pulo, Usman dan Fodio, whose family had emigrated from Futa Toro fourteen generations earlier. He, too, belonged to the Qadiriyah. A former teacher—he had been the personal tutor of Yunfa, the sultan of Gobir in Hausaland—and preacher, the *Shehu (shaykh,* "sheikh"*)*, as the Nigerians call him, was born in 1754. Hausaland had been partly Muslim since before the fourteenth century, and the city of Kano had become a renowned center of higher learning that attracted scholars from Egypt, Algeria, Morocco, Timbuktu, and all over the Sahel, particularly during the reign of Yunfa's grandfather. The Hausa rulers were convinced Muslims who, because they reigned over a diverse population, had to make concessions to traditional practices in order to maintain political stability. Yet to Usman dan Fodio and his reformist movement, Islam appeared in decline, weakened by unorthodox practices. Yunfa was verbally attacked by the reformists, who presented him, in Usman dan Fodio's words, as an "apostate . . . who mingles the observances of Islam with the observances of heathendom."[71]

Feeling his power threatened, Yunfa—like his father, Nafata, who had forbidden the Muslims to wear the turban and the veil as a distinctive mark of their faith and had made conversion to Islam unlawful—resorted to anti-Islamic measures in order to keep the movement from growing. It was to no avail, as the *Shehu* rallied large numbers of followers through not only his vision of what a true Islamic state should be but also his denunciations of widely resented political oppression, heavy taxation, and social injustice. As a defiant gesture, Usman dan Fodio withdrew to the western part of Gobir in a move meant to emulate the *hijra*, the departure of Muhammad from Mecca to Medina. Thousands of Fulani and Hausa followed him in his new autonomous community, including numerous slaves whom he refused to return to the sultan, arguing that they were Muslims and thus free. Meanwhile, Yunfa, in reprisal, started to enslave Fulani pastoralists, hoping that the *Shehu* would stop his activities.

The *jihad* was launched. It lasted four years and pitted the army of Yunfa, made up of one hundred thousand foot soldiers and a ten-thousand-man cavalry, against the few thousand followers of dan Fodio. Vastly outnumbered and underequipped, the Muslims were inspired by their faith, which made them accomplish heroic deeds. At Birnin Konni, after a thirty-two-mile walk during the night, they invaded the city, won the battle under a scorching sun, and walked back to their base in Gudu, all in less than thirty-six hours. The *jihad*ists were victorious. By 1808 most of the Hausa states had been subdued and put under the leadership of the Sokoto caliphate, which lasted a hundred years before being defeated by the British. Kanem and Bornu, two Muslim states in the north, forged an alliance and were able to contain Usman dan Fodio's forces.

During the *jihad* in Hausaland, and later in Kanem and Bornu, Usman dan Fodio's followers suffered heavy losses. As usual, the ranks of the scholars and students were decimated through death and enslavement. At the battle of Tsuntsua in 1804, Muhammad Bello, Usman dan Fodio's son, recalled, we lost about 2,000 martyrs, most of whom were our best soldiers, and of the most pious and virtuous of our men: as the chief Justice Mohammed Thaanbo, the noble Saado, Mahmood Ghordam, Mohammed Jamm, the learned and intelligent poet and reciter Zaid, Aboo-bakr Bingoo, the true diviner Es-sudani, and several others.[72]

The loss was such that when the caliphate was established, there were not enough of the *Shehu*'s scholars left to fill the posts of local *emir*, judge, or *imam*. Of the surviving men—on both sides of the conflict—large numbers ended their life in Brazil, Trinidad, and Cuba. (The impact the Muslims from central Sudan had on the history of Brazil and Bahia in particular is discussed in chapter 5.)

Usman dan Fodio's *jihad* was not the only event that provided the Americas with Muslim slaves from central Sudan. Before and after these events, Hausa were routinely sold by their southern neighbors, the Oyo (or Nago, or Anago)—the name Nago was applied first to western Oyo but later became synonymous with all Oyo in Brazil. They were collectively called Yoruba in the late nineteenth century. The Yoruba acquired their slaves by raids in the north and west and by purchase from the Nupe and Bariba. A large proportion of their domestic slaves were Hausa. As the European demand increased, they sold many overseas. Oyo was overwhelmingly animist, but Islam had made some headway in the sixteenth or seventeenth century, and significant numbers of Muslims inhabited the region.

A major civil war took place in Oyo in 1817, for political reasons but with religious undertones. Afonja, the non-Muslim commander in chief of the army based at Ilorin, fomented a revolt against the king, the *alafin*. In the context of the successful *jihad* of Usman dan Fodio in Hausaland and of the holy war of the Nupe and Fulani in Nupe, Afonja hoped that he could count on the Muslims' support. With the help of a Pulo leader, Alimi, he incited a *jihad* against the *alafin* and rallied the numerous Hausa slaves of the kingdom, the pastoralist Fulani, and the Muslim Yoruba. The slaves were promised their freedom if they joined the ranks of the *jihad*ists. Ali Eisami Gazirmabe, a Muslim Kanuri who had been enslaved at Oyo and later sold to the Europeans, remembered in his memoirs, "A war arose: Now all the slaves who went to the war, became free; so when the slaves heard these good news, they all ran there."[73] Meanwhile, the Muslim troops, composed of ethnically and socially diverse elements united under the flag of Islam, reaped some victories. They brought their fight into the heart of Oyo and burned parts of its capital but were defeated, and some were most probably sold away.

The Muslims ultimately were victorious, and after getting rid of Afonja, who had taken umbrage at their increasing power, they turned the old Oyo into the Ilorin Emirate, under the authority of the caliph of Sokoto. These events in Yorubaland produced prisoners of war who were deported to the Americas. Bahia alone imported about eight thousand slaves a year between 1800 and 1830, the vast majority being Hausa and Yoruba, coming from the ports of Bagadry and Porto-Novo (Benin).

Who the Captives Were

Other, smaller-scale conflicts also were responsible for the deportation of Muslims; but wars alone did not account for all the displaced. Abductions were another method of supply, less costly and less dangerous than war but also less rewarding, because the abducted were individuals or small groups. Like their non-Muslim neighbors, African Muslims were the victims of organized gangs, unscrupulous traders, bandits, roaming soldiers, and occasional kidnappers. There was also, along the coast, a particular type of abduction called "buckra [white] panyaring." It was described by a slave captain:

> If a native there does not pay speedily, you man your boat towards evening, and bid your sailors go to any town, no matter whether your debtor's town or not, and catch as many people as they can. If your debt be large, it may be necessary to "*catch*" two towns. After this your debtor will soon compleat his number of slaves.—But what if he should not?—Why then we carry our prisoners away, to be sure.[74]

Besides panyaring, which could also happen deep inland as the European ships went upriver, there were plain abductions. Nobody was safe: women at the well, men in the fields, children around the village became victims of the kidnappers. Evidently, those who traveled frequently and far were easy targets.

For reasons stemming from their religion, the Muslims were particularly mobile. It was not uncommon for a family to leave its village or town and settle in another area, where, by preaching and through example, they would eventually make converts or bring knowledge and assistance to their coreligionists. Some families actually split, with brothers going in different directions for religious purposes or simply as a result of internal dissension. This situation is well exemplified by Abu Bakr al Siddiq's family's peregrinations. After his grandfather's death, Abu Bakr's father and uncles decided to go their separate ways because of differences between their families. As Abu Bakr recalled in his autobiography, his uncle Ideriza (Idriss) went to Macina and Jenne (Mali); his uncles Ahdriman (Abdalrahmane) settled in Kong (Ivory Coast) and Mahomet in Bouna (Ghana); Abon Becr (Abu Bakr) remained in Timbuktu, as did Abu Bakr's father, Hara Mussa Sharif, whose wife came from Bornu (Nigeria).[75]

Extreme mobility was characteristic of the *marabouts*, who led a nomadic existence based on *qira'ah* (study), *harth* (farming), and *safar* (travel). Richard Jobson, a British trader who observed them in Senegambia, wrote in 1623:

> These Mary-buckes are a people, who dispose themselves in generall, when they are in their able age to travaile, going in whole families together, and carrying along their bookes, and manuscripts, and their boyes or younger race with them, whom they teach and instruct in any place they rest, or repose themselves, for which the whole Country is open before them.[76]

The *marabouts* taught, provided guidance, manufactured protective amulets, recruited students, and sometimes mixed commerce with preaching. Deported *marabouts* were quite numerous in the Americas, as can be deducted from, among other pieces of evidence, the widespread use of gris-gris in the New World, as is discussed in chapter 4. In addition, several chroniclers and travelers acknowledged their presence there.

Other clerics ended their lives as slaves; we find their traces all over the Americas. Mohammed Kaba, from Bouka in the Malinke area of Guinea, was studying to become a lawyer, or *faqi*, like his uncle when he was abducted at age twenty and deported to Jamaica, where he lived in servitude for fifty-six years.[77] Bilali, the slave driver of the Spalding plantation on Sapelo Island, Georgia, from the early 1800s on, was a former cleric originally from Timbo, Guinea. Brazilian authorities made references to *ulama*, whom they called "malomi" (from the Hausa *malam*, a corruption of the Arabic). Abu Bakr, who was captured and taken to Jamaica, was studying to become a cleric like his father and grandfathers. *Ulama, qadi, marabouts*—all these men who had devoted years to studying spent most of their lives performing the most menial and tedious work, which was the lot of slaves on the American plantations.

The Koranic teachers and *talib* were also hardened travelers. Many were attracted by centers of learning such as Timbuktu, Jenne, Kano, and Bouna. In this last town, as Abu Bakr al Siddiq recollected in Jamaica, "there are many teachers for young people: they are not of one country, but come from different parts, and are brought there to dwell for their instruction."[78] The concentration of learned men in some areas led parents to send their children there, even if the school was quite a distance from their homes. Consequently, teenage boys—girls went to the local schools—traveled long distances to acquire a good education. Such travel could have a terrible outcome. Salih Bilali was about fourteen when he rode alone on his horse from Jenne on the Niger River to his hometown of Kianah. He was "seized by a predatory party and carried to Sego and was transferred from master to master, until he reached the coast at Anamaboo"[79] in Ghana. When his owner wrote these lines on Saint Simon's Island, Georgia, Salih Bilali had been a slave for fifty-nine years.

Like the students, the teachers were at risk. Tamerlan, a *marabout* and a teacher, explained to a French colonel in Saint-Domingue that "he used to write books; that the great king of Africa had chosen him as the teacher of his son."[80] One day, as he was traveling with the prince, their convoy was attacked; the young boy was killed, and Tamerlan, after a three-month walk to the sea, was sold to the Europeans and transported to the island. Other teachers were among the slaves and freemen of Bahia who revolted in 1835, and Mohammedu Sisei, from the Gambia, was a teacher when he was captured and shipped to Trinidad.[81]

Muslims traveled to acquire or dispense knowledge but also, more prosaically, to obtain the supplies indispensable to their religion. Paper, for instance, was an essential item for *marabout*s and teachers, who used it for writing letters, books, or gris-gris. Muslim traders traditionally obtained it from their contacts in North Africa and the Middle East, but when the Europeans established trading posts on the African coast, it was often easier to purchase paper directly from them. British trader Richard Jobson stressed in his 1623 memoirs how much paper meant to the "Mary-buckes": though costing three pence, "to them it is a rich reward."[82] Buying paper from the Europeans, however, meant that the teachers and clerics had to travel to the coast or the rivers, an endeavor that could be risky. Teacher Lamine Kebe was kidnapped while he was on a trip to buy paper for his school, and he spent the next thirty years as a slave in the American South. Ayuba Suleyman Diallo (Job ben

Solomon) met the same fate while on a trade mission to the Gambia, where he was buying paper and selling slaves.

In addition to proselytizing families, the teachers, and their students, traders were a peripatetic group. These merchants were a vital, dynamic part of West African societies. Most were Mande (Mandingo, Dyula, Malinke) and had been active in commerce before the advent of Islam in their areas, but the opening up of the wide Islamic market stimulated their activities. The traders became the first representatives of Islam to the non-Muslim populations, reaching deep into animist areas and preparing the way for the religious leaders. They represented the link between the forest area to the south and the Maghreb to the north. They had established and controlled trade routes that crisscrossed the Sahel and the adjacent areas, bringing necessary as well as luxury goods to the southern populations and raw materials to the north. They had set up regional, interregional, and what would be called, in modern terms, "international" networks.

The traders' commerce is well described by Mohammed Ali ben Said, a Muslim from Bornu (northern Nigeria) who was enslaved in the 1830s and eventually became a teacher in Detroit and a soldier in the Union army. "Bornoo, my native country," he wrote, "is the most civilized part of Soodan, on account of the great commerce carried on between it and the Barbary States of Fezzan, Tunis, and Tripoli. They export all kinds of European articles to Central Africa, and take gold-dust, ivory, &c., in return."[83] The merchants, part of what is now called the "Muslim Diaspora," traveled hundreds of miles in every direction, their donkeys and slaves loaded with cotton cloth, gum arabic, musk, kola nuts, hides and leather goods, weapons, silk, books, gold, and ivory. For social, commercial, and security reasons, they traveled in caravans and were, in general, let free to go as they pleased. Nevertheless, they were sometimes the victims of organized bands of thieves.

When the Atlantic slave trade started to devastate Africa, the traders became ideal targets for kidnappers, who killed two birds with one stone: they stole the merchandise and sold the merchants. The merchandise also was sometimes men and women. Many a slave seller ended up in the same ship as his captives. Muslims were no exception. Many Fulani who sold slaves in Sierra Leone were the victims of bands of kidnappers, who made their living by roaming the areas a few miles from the coast. A case witnessed by Carl Wadstrom serves as an illustration of the practice. Wadstrom met an old man in Timbo one year before Ibrahima abd al Rahman was captured, who begged him to inquire about his son,

> who with six others, some of them related to the king, had been seized, in returning from Rio Pongos [where they had sold slaves], about four years ago. They had been sold to the British slave-factor at the Isles of Los, and immediately shipped off to the W. Indies, except one, who was recovered by the Foulah king.[84]

Two Omar, one Bubakar, and three Amadu, one of whom was the old man's son, had joined the ranks of the Muslims in America. Traders were also at risk when they owed merchandise or captives to the European factors. They could be taken as slaves themselves or see their children, neighbors, or whole town pawned and eventually shipped away.

People who lived in Mandingo areas were very much exposed. Wadstrom again explains that "a chief factor attributed the frequency of kidnapping among the Mandingoes to their head men getting in debt to the Europeans, and being then confined by them in which case, their people were obliged to kidnap some persons to redeem them."[85]

Besides the teachers, traders, and clerics, the nobility also seem to have been well represented among the Muslims shipped overseas. Rulers, members of their immediate family or close entourage, any notables and aristocrats ran a particular risk of being enslaved as political prisoners and prisoners of war. Such was the case of Ibrahima abd al Rahman, son of the *al-mami* of Futa Jallon. John Mohammed Bath was a prince deported to Trinidad.[86] Samba Makumba, also of Trinidad, presented himself as an *emir*.[87] Licutan, a sultan from central Sudan was shipped to Bahia.[88] Arouna, a Hausa, came from a royal family and was enslaved in Jamaica.[89] Macandal, in Saint-Domingue, was of an illustrious family.[90] Mohammadou Maguina in Trinidad was "of noble birth,"[91] and Anna Moosa, enslaved in Tortola, Barbados, and Jamaica, was the son of "a lord in the Carsoe [Khassonke from Mali] nation."[92] Abu Bakr al Siddiq mentioned in his autobiography that his father's name was "Kara-Mousa, *Scheriff*." Abu Bakr himself was addressed in the same manner in Jamaica by another Muslim, Mohammed Kaba, who referred to him in a letter as "Bekir Sadiki Scheriffe."[93] After obtaining his freedom, Abu Bakr spent some time in Morocco, where he was acknowledged as a *mulay*, the title given to a sharif. His family was noble indeed: only men who are recognized as descendants of the prophet Muhammad or of his clan bear the name sharif. It is not impossible that other *sherufa* were enslaved in the New World.

Besides their literacy and their dedication to their faith, what distinguished the clerics, teachers, students, rulers, and traders was their contact with the wider world: the intelligentsia of Morocco, Tunisia, Algeria, Iraq, Egypt, and Arabia whom they met in Mecca and Cairo or in their homeland when the foreigners visited. The scholars were familiar with the works of Muslim intellectuals from a wide range of countries who used Arabic as their vehicle of communication. They also had access to books from other religions in their Arabic versions, as confirmed by Mungo Park, who mentions having seen the Pentateuch of Moses, the Psalms of David, and the "New Testament of Jesus" that he called the Book of Isaiah during his travel in Senegambia at the end of the eighteenth century. European philosophers such as Plato, Aristotle, Hippocrates, and Euclid were also known in Arabic translations.[94]

The most dynamic segments of the Muslim population were thus made up of well-read, well-traveled, cosmopolitan, multilingual, resourceful, adaptable men who were prompt to see and seize opportunities, even in unfamiliar surroundings, and who were unafraid of the unknown. They were used to dealing with their coreligionists from diverse ethnic groups and cultures, as well as with non-Muslims. This particular background became very helpful to those who were shipped to the Americas. Not only did it enable them to remain intellectually alert, but it also helped many to ascend the echelons of the slave structure.

There is no doubt that uneducated, poorly educated, semiliterate, and illiterate men and women were among the Muslims of the Americas, but certain facts about Muslim life in this era, as testified in documents of the time, strongly indicate that a large proportion of the deported Africans came from the intellectual elite. In such times of upheaval as the period from the sixteenth to the nineteenth century, with the development of the Atlantic slave trade, the disintegration of major empires and kingdoms, and the founding of Muslim theocracies, the mobility of the educated Muslims made them particularly vulnerable to human predators. In addition, though some clerics shunned wars, Islam has a tradition of the cleric/warrior, following the examples of Muhammad himself and of Ali, his cousin and son-in-law. Omar ibn Said and Lamine Kebe exemplify this heritage: at the same time that they stressed their twenty-five years of study and presented themselves as learned and devout men they also emphasized their warrior past, asserting that they went to the holy war against the "infidels."[95] The ranks of the clerics, high-level students, and *marabouts* became terribly depleted after each military operation, as

Usman dan Fodio painfully discovered. The particularity of the *jihad*, with its exaltation of martyrdom, which appealed to the most devout, reinforces the hypothesis that a high concentration of learned men were indeed among the Muslims deported to the Americas as slaves.

Documentation on the Muslim women, in contrast, is lacking. Because their movements were more restricted than men's and they did not directly participate in wars, they were less likely than their companions to be caught as a result of their activities. They were usually the victims of kidnapping and were also captured, with their children, after the males had been defeated in war. Because of social and religious realities, they were generally less traveled and less educated than the men. They could not hold positions as clerics, but the wives of clerics came from deeply religious families and had had access to schooling; some women were teachers and knew the Koran by heart. The female members of the aristocracy were as likely as the men to be deported in times of political unrest, but in general women were significantly less present than men among the captives; the Atlantic slave trade took away about seven West African men for every three women. Among Muslims the proportion of women was significantly lower because of the modes of enslavement of Muslims, that is, wars and *jihad*. Paul Lovejoy has shown that only 5 percent of the captives from central Sudan deported to the New World were women and girls.[96]

Most Muslims shipped across the Atlantic were young men and women between the ages of eighteen and thirty. The vast majority were certainly husbands and fathers and wives and mothers, as men and women at the time married in their late teens or midtwenties, and African traditions as well as Islam are opposed to celibacy and actively promote marriage and the creation of large families. Job ben Solomon is a perfect example: when he was captured at age thirty-one, he had two wives and four children. Lamine Kebe left a wife and three children in Futa Jallon.

Among the kidnapped were men who had been vulnerable because of the life they had chosen based on their religious beliefs. Without a doubt, some of them had also participated in wars, religious or political, knowing the consequences of their choice. The warriors were men of deep faith. Many had a strong education, and all were aware that their involvement could result in only three alternatives: they could be victorious, they could be enslaved with a possibility of being redeemed, or they could be sold to the Europeans and leave their families and homeland forever for a completely unknown future. They were agents of their own destiny, and this particularity is of extreme importance in explaining the world they created in the places of their enslavement.

Islam, the Muslims, and the Atlantic slave trade were interconnected in a variety of ways. Muslims sold "unbelievers" to the Europeans because Islam allowed it. "Pagan" rulers, for their part, sold Muslims to the Europeans because of their religion. By condemning the trans-Atlantic trade, the Muslims rallied non-Muslims to their cause; Islam expanded in part because it forbade its followers to sell their brethren, and powerless peasants sought its protection against the European trade. By exchanging slaves for firearms, the Muslim theocracies were able to defend their borders and protect their subjects, including non-Muslims who had asked for their protection. The Europeans were opposed to the Muslims, who, as a rule, did not raid their own people and were organized enough to resist them, but were eager to trade with them for pagan captives. Although Muslims were enslaved and, later, colonization—which the Muslim movements opposed—was triumphant, Islam became associated with resistance to foreign rule and protection of the peasants—a distinction that it acquired during the centuries of the slave trade and that gained it support during military colonization. In the end, Islam became the dominant religion of West Africa. The trans-Atlantic slave trade played its part in its success.

The Experience of Captivity

For the Africans who were the direct victims of the trade, whether through abduction or war, life took a dreadful, inconceivably cruel turn. Each experienced a terrible personal tragedy and had to cope, using whatever resources he or she could find within and the support of the group. Little personal documentation about the forced march to the slave ship and the Middle Passage exists, but most of what we know comes from the testimonies of Muslims. Though narratives by African-born slaves are rare, an unusually high percentage are the work of Muslims. Still, few described what they endured in the slave caravans or aboard the ships. Omar ibn Said, Abu Bakr al Siddiq, and Ibrahima abd al Rahman, for instance, mentioned these experiences only briefly. This discretion may have been due to the deep aversion Africans feel at relating personal matters, especially those of an intimate nature. Besides this cultural reason, these men may have gone through the psychological process of shutting off terrible memories and the refusal to open up old wounds that are frequently experienced by survivors of atrocities. A third explanation may lie in the censorship that men who were being helped by whites imposed on themselves. Too-vivid descriptions of the Middle Passage, for example, could only underline the barbarity of the society to which those whose assistance was requested belonged. So the few testimonies that exist are of inestimable value, not only because of their rarity but also because they put human faces on a tragedy of such enormous proportions that the individual too often disappears behind the numbers and the controversy surrounding them.

The first episode in the succession of events that led to the deportation of millions of Africans was the constitution of the slave caravan. Men, women, and children were rounded up in convoys that ultimately could number in the hundreds, as new captives were picked up along the way. Dorugu, a seventeen-year-old Muslim Hausa, described the caravan he was with when taken captive in 1839: "We went along, and passed another town near to our own. They took the people there, and I think we were then about four hundred; so we went together and they set the town on fire."[97]

On the first leg of the journey, a succession of traders led the captives. Some caravans or individuals were destined from the outset for the European dealers on the coast, but others were sold and bought in markets along the way, with no final destination clearly established. Mahommah Gardo Baquaqua, a Muslim from northern Dahomey (present-day Benin) who was deported to Pernambuco, Brazil, in the 1840s experienced a typical situation. He was sold three times before reaching the coast and never knew until he boarded the slave ship that he was to cross the ocean. His first buyer had secured him in the traditional manner: a six-foot branch with two prongs crossed the back of Mohamma's neck and was fastened with an iron bolt. In the caravans each branch was then attached to the neck of the captive in front, so that, as Kélédor recalled his own ordeal, "we formed a single line, a chain in which each one dragged by the head the one who followed him."[98] If a captive tried to escape, he had to carry the long branch in front of him; otherwise, it would get stuck in the ground or the bushes, preventing him from walking, let alone running.

Abu Bakr al Siddiq's recollections of his first moments as a captive are succinctly described in his autobiography, written in Arabic: "As soon as I was made prisoner, they stripped me, and tied me with a cord, and gave me a heavy load to carry."[99] Abu Bakr's experience was typical, since captives were used for carrying the slave dealers' goods. They also carried their own meager rations, recalled a Muslim from South Carolina: "We had nothing to eat on this journey but a small quantity of grain, taken with ourselves. This grain we were compelled to carry on our backs, and roast by the fires which we kindled at nights, to frighten away the wild beasts."[100] Very large caravans sometimes experienced a shortage of goods to carry, but to ensure that all captives would be too exhausted to run away, the merchants gave forty-pound rocks to the captives who had no other load to transport.[101]

The walk to the sea could be very long. The South Carolina Muslim mentioned above walked for three weeks and went down a river for three days. The slave caravan—twenty-five Muslims among them—that Mungo Park traveled with came from Segu (Mali) and boarded a ship at Gorée Island (Senegal) after a two-month walk of more than seven hundred miles. Abu Bakr walked from Bouna to Lago (a few miles west of Accra), a total distance of more than 300 miles, and Mohamma Gardo Baquaqua came to the coast from about 350 miles north. Tamerlan of Saint-Domingue walked for three months.

The Atlantic Ocean, the European vessels, and the Europeans themselves were unknown to many captives. Baquaqua pointed out that he had never seen a ship before and thought it was some object of worship of the white man. He also imagined that they were all to be slaughtered on board. A Danish physician who founded a colony in the Gold Coast relayed the fears of other captives: "I was once asked by a slave, in complete earnest, if the shoes I was wearing had been made of Black skin, since he had observed that they were the same colour as his skin. Others say that we eat the Blacks and make gunpowder of their bones."[102] To the African Muslim from South Carolina, the whites appeared "the ugliest creatures in the world."[103]

Before being loaded on the slave ship, the captives had to go through what captain Theophilus Conneau described as a "disagreeable operation" and a "disgusting duty . . . which cannot be avoided."[104] In Baquaqua's words, the operation went thus:

> The slaves were all put into a pen, and placed with our backs to the fire, and ordered not to look about us, and to insure obedience, a man was placed in front with a whip in his hand ready to strike the first who should dare to disobey orders; another man then went round with a hot iron, and branded us the same as they would the heads of barrels or any other inanimate goods or merchandise.[105]

As Conneau explained, this measure was necessary because the buyer in America had to know which individuals had been bought for him, and when one died at sea, the mark made it clear whose loss it was.

After men and women alike had been shaved, an extreme humiliation awaited them. The sailors took away the pieces of cloth the captives had managed to keep, remembered the recaptive Ali Eisami Gazirmabe, and threw them overboard. Gazirmabe echoes the memories of Mohamma Gardo Baquaqua, who stated that they were thrust naked into the hold of the vessel. The famous 1802 rendition of the slave ship *Brookes* with its men and women wearing white loincloths is a puritanical representation; the Africans were stripped on every ship. The fear of "vermin" was the reason given for such a policy. Paul Isert, the Danish colonist, offered another explanation: the Africans were kept naked so that they would not hang themselves with their clothes, "which has in fact happened."[106] It goes without saying that this state of affairs was terribly mortifying for the captives, but it may have been especially so for the Muslims, who had kept themselves very much covered because their religion demanded physical modesty.

Amid the sheer horror of their new condition, the Africans had to endure still another degrading process: the forced entertainment taking place on the deck, during which they were made to sing and dance in an attempt to keep their spirits up. Kélédor, through Baron Roger, described the scene as it related to the Muslims:

> The serious men from Futa, the marabouts in particular, and they were in great numbers, did not take any part in a type of frivolous entertainment they would have refused at home and that in their deplorable position they viewed with much indignation. But [the sailors] resolved to make even the most reluctant dance without considering that their repugnance had its origin in education and religion. After roughing them up, and maltreating them, they beat them up.[107]

The filthiness of the slave holds can be imagined. Four hundred men, women, and children were aboard Kélédor's ship, and seven hundred on board Eisami's. Baquaqua remembered the "loathsomeness and filth of that horrible place," and that they were allowed to wash only twice, the second time right before going into port. Ali Eisami and his companions remained confined in the hold for three months, and another Muslim stressed that only the women were allowed on deck. All emphasized the scarcity of food and water, the punishments, and the daily deaths.

Mahommah Gardo Baquaqua may have summed up the frame of mind of many Africans when they disembarked in America: "When I reached the shore, I felt thankful to Providence that I was once more permitted to breathe pure air, the thought of which almost absorbed every other. I cared but little then that I was a slave, having escaped the ship was all I thought about."[108]

The end of the trip for Baquaqua was Brazil; for Abu Bakr, Jamaica. Ali Eisami's ship was captured at sea, and its passengers settled in Sierra Leone. John Mohammed Bath was sold in Trinidad, Omar ibn Said in Charleston, Salih Bilali in the Bahamas, and Tamerlan in Saint-Domingue. Others, including numerous Muslims, were unloaded at Buenos Aires and walked hundreds of miles across the pampas and over passes through the Andes to reach the mines of Chile and Peru. Slave caravans consisting of hundreds of barefoot and barely clad, if not naked, men, women, and children endured a haunting trip in the cold of South America's mountains and the heat of its plains, after having walked hundreds of miles to the coast in Africa and suffered weeks of dreadful confinement in the slave ship.

Data on Muslims in the Americas

Muslims were scattered all over North and South America and the Caribbean Islands, but exactly how many crossed the ocean and how many actually landed in the Americas is unknown. Actually, the total number of Africans who were shipped is a matter of controversy. Philip Curtin's figure of 9.5 million deportees (plus or minus 20 percent) has been widely rebuked as being too low. His estimates for the sixteenth and seventeenth centuries in general, and for West Africa at all times—the area the Muslims came from—have been particularly criticized, as has been his low reckoning of the smuggling that took place into the United States after 1807. A middle estimate of 11 million, plus or minus 20 percent, has been proposed, and a higher one of 15.4 million is defended by historian Joseph Inikori, who, along with Stanley Engerman concludes that as the revision process gets underway and new documentation is reviewed, the ultimate number of Africans taken out of the continent to the Americas is "unlikely to be less than 12 million or more than 20 million captives."[109]

Research regarding the enslaved Muslims in general is little more than embryonic. Allan Austin, who has produced a very informative source-book on the Muslim slaves in antebellum America, cautiously presents a total of 29,695 for the United States, based on an estimate of 10 percent of all West Africans introduced between 1711 and 1808. Michael Gomez, a professor of history, does not venture beyond "thousands if not tens of thousands"[110] for the United States.

Finding the approximate number of Muslims who landed in the Americas may prove an extremely difficult task. No precision regarding the religion of their human cargo appears in the documents produced by the slave dealers and the trade companies. One way to arrive at an esti-mate would be to study the number of Africans who were shipped from areas where Islam was present during the slave trade, such as Senegal, Gambia, Guinea, Sierra Leone, Mali, Benin, Ghana, and Nigeria. How-ever, the actual number of Muslims in West Africa at any given time up to the twentieth century is unknown, and varies considerably according to area and era. The analysis would then have to be refined to include only the populations known to be either partially or totally Muslim: Wolof, Tukulor, Fulani, Vai, Mandingo, Hausa, Nago, Nupe, Soninke, and others. But again, the actual percentage of Muslims in these popula-tions up to the twentieth century is difficult to assess. Then, of course, there might have been a small percentage of Muslims in a given popula-tion, but a large proportion among them might have been sold overseas after civil or religious disorders. Systematic comparisons between specific historical events in Africa and slavers' logs of the same period would yield valuable information. Such research would have to cover a dozen African countries and more than half a dozen European countries, with documents scattered in Africa, Europe, and the Americas. Paul Lovejoy, who studies slaves from the central Sudan and has produced a sample of 108 individuals whose backgrounds he uncovered, stresses that his ma-terial is scattered over thirty different countries.[111]

Research on the origins of Africans in the Americas is characterized by the same difficulties. Data exist on the number and percentages of differ-ent ethnic groups who landed in each region of the New World, but they do not give more clues about religious background than do the African data. Moreover, research is even more complicated because the importers used their own nomenclature to describe the origin of their slaves. For ex-ample, when they called some of them "Senegal," they were not referring to just any person born in Senegal; nor were they referring to an ethnic group of that name, which has never existed. Senegal meant somebody coming from the Senegal River area or sold at Senegal, which in those days was the city Saint-Louis du Sénégal. In Saint-Domingue, the Senegal were Tukulor and Sarakhole; in Louisiana, they were said to be Wolof. Confusion of one type or another exists for many other populations.

Suggesting figures for the Muslim presence in the Americas is, under these conditions, highly problematic and risky. Future detailed research will provide some answers, but in the meantime, a few hypotheses can be suggested.

Starting with Africa and using Philip Curtin's compilations for the period 1701–1810, we find for West Africa a total figure of 3,233,800 persons shipped by the British, French, and Portuguese, or 58.9 percent of the total number of deported Africans. For the periods before and after those dates, Joseph Inikori has shown convincingly that Curtin's figures are unreliable, but they have the merit of being published while a more precise count is not available yet.

Specifically, the Wolof, Tukulor, and Mandingo living in Mexico in 1549 made up 29 percent of the African population in that region.[112] Between 1560 and 1650, according to notarial records, the Wolof, Mandingo, Fulani, and Susu of Peru represented 15 percent of the Africans there, and many, if not most, would have been Muslims.[113] Mandingo, Fulani, Hausa, Nago, Mina, and Susu accounted for 15 to 19 percent of the Africans in Saint-Domingue between 1760 and 1800.[114]

In the United States, South Carolina planters had a predilection toward Senegambians because of their skills in rice and indigo cultivation, and they formed 19.5 percent of the slaves imported between 1733 and 1807, along with 6.8 percent from Sierra Leone and 3.7 percent from the Benin-Nigeria area. The total percentage for South Carolina of slaves from Muslim areas was thus about 30 percent. In Virginia for the period 1710–1769, the figure for importations from West Africa is 58 percent.[115] Georgia and North Carolina slaves were usually bought in South Carolina and their ethnic composition was comparable to that state's, with, as Curtin puts it, "a heavy but non-quantifiable bias toward Senegambia and Sierra Leone."[116] Curtin's total figures for North America are 13.3 percent from Senegambia, 5.5 percent from Sierra Leone, 4.3 percent from the Bight of Benin and 23.3 percent from the Bight of Biafra—a total of 46.3 percent for regions with significant numbers of Muslims.

The French imports into Martinique for the period 1748–1792 show

74 percent Senegambians and Guineans; the figures are 56.4 percent for Guadeloupe and 74 percent for French Guiana.[117] Between 1817 and 1843, 44 percent of the Cuban slaves came from Senegambia, Sierra Leone, and the Bights of Benin and Biafra.[118] For Jamaica from 1655 to 1807, Curtin proposes 423,900 Africans from the selected areas, representing 56.8 percent of the arrivals.[119] The estimated numbers for Brazil in the period 1701–1810 are 605,500, or 32 percent.[120]

If we take 15 million individuals as a basis and assign a percentage of 50 to West Africa we get a total of 7.5 million people. Based on the different percentages of potential Muslims among West African populations, we may assign a percentage of 30 to 40 to the Muslims, though in some areas it was much more.[121] We may then propose an estimate of 15 to 20 percent, or between 2.25 and 3 million Muslims over both American continents and the Caribbean Islands. As females were about 30 percent of the total number of people shipped from West Africa—35 percent from Africa as a whole—but the percentage of Muslim women was certainly lower (for the reasons proposed above), we may suggest that they made up about 15 to 20 percent of the total Muslim slave population.

Once again, it must be stressed that these figures are hypothetical, and that a very substantial amount of additional research is needed to arrive at a fair evaluation. The estimate, however, shows that even though the populations in question may not have been singularly present in large numbers, the total Muslim population was very significant. Whatever their region of origin and their ethnic heritage, the Muslims shared a set of values, a common language, a similar education, and a lifestyle that, without erasing certain differences, made them part of a global community. Therefore, if counted as a whole, on a religious basis rather than on an ethnic one the Muslims were probably more numerous in the Americas than any other group among the arriving Africans. Nevertheless, they were definitely a minority compared to followers of traditional religions as a whole, for two reasons: they were a minority in Africa to begin with, and Islam protected them. The West Indian scholar, Christian missionary, and advocate of colonization Edward Blyden summed up the situation quite aptly: "The introduction of Islam into Central and West Africa has been the most important if not the sole preservative against the desolations of the slave-trade. Mohammedanism furnished a protection to the tribes who embraced it by effectually binding them together in one strong religious fraternity, and enabling them by their united effort to battle the attempts of powerful 'pagan' slave hunters."[122]

2

Upholding the Five Pillars of Islam in a Hostile World

Scattered across every region of the Americas, the Muslims entered a hostile world—a world that enslaved free Muslim men and women; a white Christian world determined to wipe out any trace of "paganism" or "Muhammadanism" in the newly arrived Africans.

It was essential that the new land become Christian as quickly as possible, because evangelization was a large part of the justification for the enslavement of the Africans. Moreover, as stated earlier, the fight against the possible spread of Islam had been an intense preoccupation in the Spanish colonies since the beginning of the sixteenth century. All the conditions were thus present for a rapid disappearance of Islam in America, or even for its nonemergence. A religion that requires as its five fundamental principles not only the profession of faith but prayers five times a day, almsgiving, a month-long fast, and a pilgrimage to Arabia would seem to have had little chance of being followed by tightly controlled slaves. Nevertheless, the information gathered from all over the Americas demonstrates that African Muslims, wherever they lived, did not easily renounce their religion and its practice, if at all. On the contrary, they made tremendous efforts to continue observing its most important principles: the Five Pillars of Islam.

The First Pillar, the profession of faith, or *shahada*, is expressed by the formula *La-ilaha ill'l-Lah Muhammadan rasul-ul-lah*—"There is no God but God and Muhammad is the Prophet of God." According to Islam, when uttered with sincerity, the *shahada* makes anyone a Muslim. In America the *shahada* manifested itself in three ways: affirmation of the Africans' faith in Allah and his prophet, Muhammad; rejection of conversion to Catholicism or Protestantism; and, when necessary, pseudo-conversion.

"Allah. Muhammad." It was with these words that a slave found wandering in Kent County, Pennsylvania, introduced himself to the men who interrogated him one day in June 1731. He was a fugitive and could not speak English. He could not say where he came from or to whom he belonged. As a slave he was called Simon; later he was known as Job ben Solomon. But as Ayuba Suleyman Diallo he had placed his faith in Allah. When confronted with an unknown, potentially dangerous situation over which he had no control, he simply affirmed his Islamic faith. He made the *shahada* the definition of his own existence, of his person. He did so rightly, because in the end, his Islamic faith and education saved him, freeing him from bondage.

Islam appears to have been a central force in other enslaved Africans' lives as well. Omar ibn Said, from Senegal and North Carolina, has left testimonies of his faith in numerous manuscripts in Arabic. Most start with an invocation to Allah and Muhammad. His last known manuscript is a copy of *surah* 110—*An-Nasr*, or "Help"—which refers to the conversion to Islam.[1] Another testimony of the resilience of the Muslim faith appears in Ben-Ali, or Bilali Mohamed, a Guinean Pulo who became something of a celebrity in the Sea Islands of Georgia. He remained a devout Muslim all his life and died uttering the *shahada*.[2]

Clearly, some Muslims continued strongly affirming their religious convictions. They had come from areas where Christianity had not—and still has not—been accepted or from areas where it was the religion of a few traders, mostly mulattos. What the Africans knew about Christianity they had learned in the Koran or the New Testament, not through any contact with the Europeans. They were not aware of the antipathy that their religion inspired on the other side of the ocean; furthermore, they were strong believers. So they presented themselves as Muslims with self-confidence and defined themselves according to their religious creed.

To affirm one's faith is also to refuse to change it. As far as religion and the Africans were concerned, there were two schools of thought in the New World. The Catholic school extolled conversion because it morally justified slavery. The Protestant school opposed it, because Protestants feared that once converted, the slaves should be freed.

In Catholic lands, slaves were excluded and segregated on a secular, social basis but were included in the spiritual community. Baptism thus became a moral obligation of the masters toward their slaves, as was codified both in the French *Code noir* (Black Code) of 1685—a collection of all the laws and rulings dealing with the administration of the slaves—and in the Spanish regulations of the sixteenth century. As a consequence, the newly arrived Africans were converted on a large scale. The Jesuit

Pedro Claver, who officiated in Cartagena, Colombia, in the first half of the seventeenth century, reportedly baptized more than three hundred thousand Africans and was canonized for this good work.

The Catholic French West Indies offers a valuable insight into the relations between Christians and Muslims in the early stages of the colonization process. A majority of their slaves came from Senegal, western Mali, and Guinea, the very areas where Islam had spread most successfully. Most of what we know about Christian-Muslim relations in the West Indies was written by Catholic priests in charge of ensuring the spiritual salvation of the Africans. As they endeavored to turn them into good Catholics, the missionaries, who were slaveholders themselves, came into close contact with the Muslims and, according to their observations, found them uncooperative. Father Chevillard, a Jesuit stationed in Guadeloupe in 1658, had the following opinion about the Senegalese Muslims:

> We see that the blacks of the Cap-Verde have a tint of the Mahometan, but they have rarely heard the marabou being of such a stupid, materialistic, and gross mind that it is an unbearable pain to instruct them. . . . But the nations of Gorée and Angole have a more subtle mind, easy to learn the language [sic], to understand when taught and good Christians when they embrace the religion with affection.[3]

If we believe Father Chevillard, the Muslims from the Senegalese coast were too stupid to understand the Christian religion, in contrast to the non-Muslims from Central Africa. In actuality, the Muslims, who had studied in the numerous Koranic schools that dotted West Africa, were used to being taught religion. Among them were many *marabout*s, teachers, *imam*s, and scholars. All of them—whatever their level of instruction but precisely because they were Muslims and had read the Koran—knew about Adam and Eve, Moses, Abraham, David and Solomon, John the Baptist, Jesus and Mary, the Jews, and the Christians. In contrast, for the Africans from Angola (there were a few Christians among them) and elsewhere, this complex story that took place over thousands of years was totally new and, most probably, more difficult to grasp—as was, for some, the idea of a unique God. What the Jesuit saw as stupidity was instead a manifest refusal of Christianity and of conversion on the part of Muslims, who were sure of their faith and intended to keep it.

Ten years later, however, the Reverend Jean-Baptiste Dutertre was happy to note the conversion of fifteen thousand slaves in the French

West Indies, "who would never have known the real God in their country, and who would have died miserably in the impiety and errors of Mahomet, of which those who are brought from Africa are infected."[4] As Dutertre confirmed the prevalence of the Muslims among the Africans, he also pointed at the implementation of the massive conversion policy that was turning many of them into instant Catholics. But Dutertre may have been too optimistic, for years later the Reverend Father Jean-Baptiste Labat, who was posted in the French West Indies from 1693 to 1705, denounced the "Mahometans" in these terms: "Almost all Negroes are idolaters. Only those of the Cap-Verde, some of which are Muslims. When they are brought in the islands, it is better not to take them, for they never embrace the Christian religion."[5] Labat does not say if the Muslims simply refused to do so or if, even when converted, they never genuinely embraced Christianity.

Half a century later the problem still does not seem to have found a solution, as suggested by Father Vidaud, vicar general of the Dominican mission in the French Islands. He defended his meager record in the matter of conversion of the Africans in Martinique: "If they have had superstitions in paganism, isn't it necessary that they renounce them before they can be baptized, especially those from Mahometan countries? For those have a sort of religion, and more difficulty to renounce to Mohammed."[6]

The testimonies of Dutertre, Labat, and Vidaud give an idea of the dynamics at work between Catholics and Muslims in the early stages of their interaction. Two currents ran among the priests. One, probably the strongest, preached for forced conversion, as prescribed by the Black Code. Other priests, like Father Vidaud, tried to do their work with conscience, stating that baptism could be administered only if the conversion was sincere. The latter attitude contrasted greatly with that of the priests stationed in Africa, who sprinkled the human cargo on the beach en masse with holy water, in a travesty of baptism, to save the souls of those who would perish during the Middle Passage. It also contrasted with what was transpiring on the plantations, because for the most part the Africans were simply coerced into converting from whatever religion they had to Catholicism.

On the Africans' part, it is worth noting that, as was—and still is—the case in Africa, the peoples who followed traditional religions were more willing than the Muslims to convert. This does not mean that they renounced their previous faith; rather, they incorporated whatever seemed useful in the new religion into their original beliefs, as chapter 6 assesses. For that reason, they did not exhibit the defiance of the Muslims, whose creed could not accommodate Christianity.

The act of open rebellion on the part of those Muslims who rejected conversion should hardly have been surprising. Many had been deported to America because they had been fighting for or defending Islam in Africa. Warriors of the faith were certainly not ready to reject a religion for which they had risked their lives and freedom. Because of their origins and the circumstances in which most were captured, the Muslims were particularly unfit potential recruits for priests who were trying to make America a Christian land.

Though many resisted conversion, not all Muslims can be portrayed as rebels. Where the missionaries wanted convinced converts, the Muslims could reject conversion under the pretext, for instance, that they did not believe in the Trinity. Yet where pressure was strong, they had to compromise. Mahommah Gardo Baquaqua has left a vivid description of the practice of imposing Christianity on the slaves. He explains how, as soon as he arrived on his master's plantation in Pernambuco, Brazil, he had to conform to rites that were void of any meaning to him or to the other slaves:

> We all had to kneel before them [images made of clay]; the family in front, and the slaves behind. We were taught to chant some words which we did not know the meaning of. We also had to make the sign of the cross several times. Whilst worshipping, my master held a whip in his hand, and those who showed signs of inattention or drowsiness, were immediately brought to consciousness by a smart application of the whip. This mostly fell to the lot of the female slave who would often fall asleep in spite of the images, crossings, and other pieces of amusement.[7]

Conversions—at least superficial ones—were thus achieved through harsh punishment. The insistence on forced conversion accelerated in Brazil when it gained its independence in 1824. Catholicism became the state religion, the only one whose followers were authorized to hold public services and have official places of worship. The non-Catholic Europeans were allowed to continue their rites in the privacy of their homes, but the slaves' religions became illegal. After the Muslim revolt of 1835, the Brazilian masters had six months to baptize their slaves and give them some religious education, after which they were liable to a fine for each non-Christian slave they owned. Notwithstanding their large numbers and amazing degree of organization, the Muslims of Brazil, who formed the largest Islamic community in America, could not openly oppose forced Christianization because of the repression it entailed.

In the British, Danish, Swedish, and Dutch West Indies, the situation was quite different. The Protestants were opposed to conversion because they feared that enslavement was no longer justified if the "heathen" became Christian. The *Royal Gazette* explained in 1808 that

> it is dangerous to make slaves Christians, without giving them their liberty. He that chooses to make slaves Christians, let him give them their liberty. What will be the consequence, when to that class of men is given the title of "beloved brethren" as is actually done? Will not the negro conceive that by baptism, being made a Christian, he is as credible as his Christian white brethren?[8]

Actually, Protestantism, which emphasizes personal choice, free will, and freedom, was not compatible—in theory—with slavery. Thus in the Protestant colonies, forced conversion was not the policy. On the contrary, slaves who tried to become Christians were punished. Only at the beginning of the nineteenth century did the slaveholders' attitude start to change. The British abolitionists began forcefully denouncing the fact that the slaves were maintained in paganism, and the Protestant masters, as their Catholic counterparts had done earlier, responded by imposing conversion on their property.

Hostility toward conversion of the slaves existed in the United States until the Great Awakening at the end of the eighteenth century, when classical Protestantism gave way to fundamentalism in the slaveholding regions of the South. With its sudden spiritual conversion, its accent on orality rather than on the written word, and its emphasis on obedience, piety, and reward in the hereafter, fundamentalism did not threaten the status quo. On the contrary, it reinforced the master's authority over his slaves and, like Catholicism, became a means of social control.

Numerous Muslims responded to the forced-conversion policy by a pseudoconversion. They adopted the outward signs of the religion that had been imposed on them but secretly retained their own beliefs. As Count de Gobineau, the French minister to Brazil, wrote in mid nineteenth century:

> Most of the Minas, if not all, are outwardly Christians, but they are actually Muslims, but as this religion would not be tolerated in Brazil, they hide this fact, and most are baptized, with names borrowed from the calendar.

> Notwithstanding outward appearances, I have been able to ascertain that
> they faithfully cherish the beliefs they bring with them from Africa and
> zealously hand them on, since they study Arabic thoroughly enough to un-
> derstand the Koran, at least roughly.[9]

The Reverends James Fletcher and D. P. Kidder, two American Protestants who visited Brazil in the 1860s, concurred, noting that the Muslims
did not renounce their faith even after they had been baptized.[10]

As the forced-conversion policy spread to the Protestant colonies,
pseudoconversions followed. In Kingston, Jamaica, Magistrate Richard
Robert Madden, who met many Muslims, noted that "very few"
Africans who had received a Muslim education renounced their religion.
"But this," he wrote in a letter in 1834, "they do not acknowledge, because they are afraid to do so."[11] Just as was the case in the Catholic
colonies, the slaves risked punishment if they openly defied their masters.

The pseudoconverts had to maintain a credible facade while they
strove to remain faithful to their religion. The story of one Jamaican
Muslim illustrates the kind of "duplicity" they exhibited. Mohamed
Caba (Kaba) was a Malinke from Bouna in present-day Guinea. Kidnapped in 1778 at the age of twenty, he had been deported to Jamaica,
where he spent fifty-six years as a slave. After his coreligionist Abu Bakr
al Siddiq (a.k.a. Edward Donlan) was released from apprenticeship or
virtual slavery in 1834, Mohamed Kaba (a.k.a. Robert Tuffit) sent Abu
Bakr a letter of congratulation in Arabic. He gave it to an intermediary,
the esquire B. Angell, stressing that the letter was intended to push Abu
Bakr to abjure "mahometanism" and to embrace the "true religion." In
a cover letter, Angell mentioned that Robert Tuffit had converted twenty
years before and did not regret his captivity because it had given him the
opportunity to know Jesus. But Kaba's letter did not actually refer to
conversion. Its integral text reads thus:

> In the name of God, Merciful omnificint [*sic*], the blessing of God, the
> peace of his prophet Mahomet. This is from the hand of Mahomed Caba,
> unto Bekir Sadiki Scheriffe. If this comes into your hands sooner or later,
> send me a satisfactory answer for yourself this time by your real name,
> don't you see I give you my name, Robert Tuffit, and the property is named
> Spice Grove. I am glad to hear you are the master of yourself, it is a heart-
> felt joy to me, for Many told me about your character. I thank you to give
> me a good answer, "Salaam aleikoum." Edward Donlan, I hear of your
> name in the paper: the reader told me how so much you write.[12]

As Madden remarked ironically, "So much for the old African's renunciation to Islamism."[13] Not only had Kaba not renounced his original faith, but he was using his particular writing ability to deceive those who were assisting him.

Abu Bakr, who owed his freedom to Madden's intervention, had become a master in the art of manipulating the Christians' goodwill without, however, renouncing his faith. He wrote to two priests:

> Reverend Gentlemen,—I beg leave to inform you that I am rejoiced and well pleased in my heart for the great boon I have received in the Testament, both of the old and new law of our lord and Saviour, in the Arabic language. I am now very anxious to get a prayer-book, the psalms, and an Arabic grammar—*also a copy of the Alcoran.*[14]

This request of a Koran, casually dropped at the end of the letter, as if added after reflection, is both touching and revealing. The emphasis is Madden's, who noted that this was the wish of somebody who had not given up his religion.

Nor had another group of Muslims with whom Madden was in contact. One day, as they were visiting him, he took up a book and

> commenced repeating the well-known Mussulman Salaam to the Prophet Allah Illah, Mahommed rasur allah! In an instant I had a Mussulman trio, long and loud: my negro Neophytes were chanting their namez [prayer] with impressible fervour; and Mr. Benjamin Cockrane, I thought would have inflicted the whole of "the perspicuous book" of Islam on me, if I had not taken advantage of the opportunity for giving him and his companions a reproof for pretending to be that which they were not.[15]

Madden presented himself as "a friend of the Blacks" and proved indeed to be so, in Jamaica, Cuba, and the United States.[16] Nevertheless, the "Mandingo trio" was on its guard, another indication that being overtly a Muslim was problematic during slavery.

The study of other individual cases sheds light on the workings of the pseudoconversion. The example of Omar ibn Said of North Carolina is revealing. He was first presented as a practicing Muslim, who "deemed a copy of the Koran . . . his richest treasure."[17] Some later statements on the Senegalese slave and scholar mention that he converted to Christianity around 1819. Yet his autobiography, written in 1831, opens with these words: "In the name of God, the merciful, the gracious—God grant his blessing upon our prophet Mohammed."[18] The first words introduce 113 *surahs* among the 114 of the Koran. Then follow about sixty lines drawn from the Koran—all this ten years after Omar had been baptized. His conversion was questionable, to say the least, but once in the good grace of his master, he saw his work considerably lightened.

An unusual illustration of pseudoconversion appears in the case of an old slave, "Old Lizzy Gray," who died in South Carolina in 1860. Born a Muslim, she was considered a Methodist, but that did not prevent her from saying that "Christ built the first church in Mecca and he grave was da."[19] After years of Christianity, acquired under unknown circumstances and pressures, the old lady found a way to affirm her original faith by substituting the name of the prophet Jesus for that of the prophet Muhammad.

Other Muslims are known to have done the same. A priest who wrote on the "moral and religious condition of the Negroes in the United States" emphasized that "the Mohammedan Africans remaining of the old stock of importations, although accustomed to hear the Gospel preached, have been known to accommodate Christianity to Mohammedanism. 'God,' say they, 'is *Allah*, and Jesus Christ is *Mohammed*—the religion is the *same*, but different countries have different *names*.'"[20] Christian missionaries perceived a similar attitude among Muslims in Jamaica: "The educated Mohammedan negros . . . are less frequently converted to christianity; and in cases where they have become nominal believers, they have been found to blend it, with the superstitions of their forefathers."[21] It is unlikely, though, that the Muslims—especially the educated ones—would have blended Christianity and Islam. What the missionaries took for syncretism may rather have been an attempt on the part of the Africans to evidence parallels between the two religions. It may have been a way not only of affirming their faith but also of positioning it at the same level as Christianity.

Another example of questionable conversion is Angelo Solimann's. Born in 1721 as Mmadi-Make (or, most probably, Mamadi), he was the son of a Muslim leader. According to his biographer, the French revolutionary Abbé Grégoire, he was captured during a war when he was seven years old and became the slave of a marchioness in Messina, Italy. Only after many refusals did he accept conversion, and he took the name Solimann (Solomon) or Suleyman in Arabic, a sign that he had not severed all links to his religion. Years later, as a slave of Prince Wenceslas of Liechtenstein, Angelo became the friend of Emperor Joseph II. At the end of his life, after the death of his European wife, the old man led an austere life that resembled very closely that of a practicing Muslim: "He no longer invited friends to dine with him. He never drank anything except water."[22] Angelo Solimann, his youth notwithstanding, had rebelled against conversion but then likely found it easier to accept with seeming sincerity, out of commodity or gratitude. Nevertheless, he seems to have gone back to his original faith in his old age.

A direct result of pseudoconversion was reconversion or a return to the first religion in the instances when Muslims were able to return to Africa. Such a reconversion occurred in the case of Ibrahima Abd al Rahman, the son of the *almami* Ibrahima Sori. Abd al Rahman's protectors stated that the Pulo prince had expressed a willingness to convert out of gratitude to the Christians who had helped him. He even went to church. Nevertheless, he came back to Africa a Muslim. Ibrahima had been a slave for almost forty years, appreciated by his master, and well liked by the white population of Natchez. During his years of servitude he had remained faithful to Islam, but when he was lured with bright prospects of going home, he seemed ready to do what was expected of him: to become an instrument of the propagation of "civilization" and Christianity in Africa. But at the first opportunity, when he was safely home, he returned to his original faith.

Baron Roger, the governor of Senegal and novelist, recorded two cases of group reconversion. He noted that in 1819 and 1822, Senegalese freedmen and women boarded boats from Havana, Cuba, to Tenerife in the Canary Islands, where they took French vessels to go back to their country. Converted to Christianity while they were slaves, they became Muslim again on arrival. The baron emphasized:

> Those facts are historical and I guarantee them to be true. They are of such an extraordinary nature, that many people will refuse to believe them. I myself would doubt if I had not seen it. This is history, as much for the truth, as for the interest, and the consequences. It has to be explained that almost all of the black population of Saint-Louis profess Islamism.[23]

The Africans' faith was strong and apparently did not need to be galvanized; but it was—at least it had once been—from Africa. In 1831, a *wathiqa*, or pastoral letter, circulated in Jamaica before ending up in the hands of Mohamed Kaba. The document had been brought from Kingston by a boy. This letter, according to the esquire Angell, had been written in Africa "in the forty-third year [1786] of the age of the King, Allaman Talco, who was thirty-five years old when he (R.P.) [Mohamed Kaba] left the country [1778]. The paper exhorted all the followers of

Mahomet to be true and faithful, if they wished to go to Heaven, &c."[24] Historian Ivor Wilks has stated that the dating is wrong and should read as forty-three years after the year 1200 of the hegira—the first year of the Muslim calendar—or 1827/28, which is only three to four years before the document appeared in Manchester Parish, Jamaica.[25] Whatever the case, the fact that this letter came up at all is of immense interest. If it really circulated during forty-five years—between 1786 and 1831—it may have gone from one colony to another before reaching Jamaica. That would suppose the existence of Islamic networks—a hypothesis that will be explored in other chapters. If, however, it took only three years for the letter to reach Mohamed Kaba, this relative speed would show the importance that the Muslims who transported it from the interior of Guinea to the coast and across the Atlantic gave to the maintenance of the faith in the lands of servitude. Unfortunately, the document no longer exists: Mohamed Kaba's wife destroyed it during the slave rebellion of 1831 because she feared it was too compromising.

The African Muslims clearly remained attached to their faith, and their enslavement was itself a good reason to be even more devout. Faith meant hope, moral comfort, and mental escape. It was also a link to the past, to a time when they were free, respected, and, for many, engaged in intellectual pursuits, not menial labor. Kélédor expresses well the emotional support that religion could give to the slave:

> I had resolved to be faithful to the religion in which I had been carefully raised. I was attached to it by conviction; I was attached to it so much more that it was the only thing left to me from my family and my country; so much more that I attached to it the memories of the causes of my captivity, and the hope of release which was promised to me.[26]

This faith, preserved openly or secretly, manifested itself in the various acts that mark the life of a Muslim believer throughout the year. First was *salat*, prayer, the Second Pillar of Islam. Constraining so as to promote self-discipline, it is done five times a day, at precise times, and is preceded by ablutions (the washing of the feet, forearms, hands, and face). It also requires a mat, prayer beads, and a veil for women. In a situation of servitude in a non-Muslim environment, the discipline of *salat* seems a particularly difficult endeavor. Though it considers prayer a pillar, the Koran is flexible, and a believer is allowed to abstain from praying if circumstances are not favorable. Understandably, then, the Muslims who prayed did so by choice, not by obligation.

Some, such as Job ben Solomon, prayed secretly. The erudite Job had been sent to the tobacco fields, but after he got sick, his master, seeing his lack of physical resistance, made him tend his cattle. Unbeknownst to the slaveholder, this was probably a real pleasure—within the limits of slavery—for the young man, because stockbreeding is the traditional occupation of the Fulani. Job had more freedom than in the fields, for he was far from the overseer's eyes, so he regularly left his cattle and hid in the woods to pray. But a young white boy had been watching him and amused himself by throwing dirt in his face. This experience, coupled with other problems, prompted Solomon to flee. He was soon captured, however, and taken into custody until his owner reclaimed him. While in jail, the young Senegalese man acquired some notoriety because he could write Arabic and was thought to be of high lineage. This new fame may have contributed to his owner's good disposition, for he gave him a place to pray and lightened his workload.[27] This major accommodation to a non-Christian slave's spiritual welfare was far from being the norm, but it was not completely exceptional, as other examples of slaveholders who tolerated their Muslim slaves' habits attest.

In the absence of a vast corpus of references to Muslim prayer in the Americas, and because of the policy of forced conversion, it seems natural to assume that secret prayer was the most common. Yet a few cases of public prayers have been recorded. Yarrow [Yoro] Mamout, for instance, used to pray publicly. He had been deported to Maryland at the beginning of the eighteenth century and lived there for the rest of his long life. When his story was reported, he was more than 110 years old according to his former owner and more than 130 according to himself. The painter Charles Wilson Peale, who made his portrait, wrote in 1819, "he professes to be a Mahometan, and is often seen & heard in the streets singing Praises to God—and conversing with him."[28] Peale described Mamout as an honest, courageous, serious man, well liked by everyone. His age, his Islamic dress, and his economic success for a former slave had made him a celebrity. In Maryland—the very Catholic land of Mary—he had been able to retain his Muslim African name and to have others respect his faith and his right to express it publicly. That was no small feat. Yarrow Mamout must have possessed a strong determination and a very deep faith.

"An old native African named Philip, who was a very intelligent man, . . . not a pagan but a Mohammedan," used to pray in public too. Scientific writer Joseph Le Conte mentioned in his autobiography that "he greatly interested us by going through all the prayers and prostrations of his native country."[29] Another example of public prayer has been preserved through the literary genre so particular to the United States: the slave narrative. Charles Ball, a non-Muslim native-born slave who published his autobiography in 1837, related in great detail the story of a Muslim enslaved in South Carolina. He noted his peculiar habits: "In the evening, as we returned home, we were joined by the man who prayed five times a day; and at the going down of the sun, he stopped and prayed aloud in our hearing, in a language I did not understand."[30] Though the slaves' schedules were extremely rigorous, the man still managed to do his five daily prayers. Just as he would have done in any Muslim country, he did not hesitate to pray publicly, wherever he was.

These individual accounts find an echo in the practices of the only U.S. Muslim community whose traditions have been recorded. The Sea Islands of Georgia and South Carolina were home to a large enslaved community made up disproportionately of first-generation Africans, even after their introduction had become illegal in 1808. This community, regularly renewed by clandestine arrivals, kept alive the memory of many Muslims. Just before World War II their descendants, as well as other former slaves, were interviewed by the Work Progress Administration (WPA). The WPA's interviews—notwithstanding the restraints that poor blacks interviewed by Southern whites would have imposed on their discourse—provide a very direct and personal portrait of this Muslim community and of its religious habits.

Ed Thorpe, an eighty-three-year-old former slave, recalled his grandmother Patience Spalding, who came from Africa, in these terms: "Wen muh gran pray, she knell down on duh flo. She bow uh head down tree time an she say 'Ameen, Ameen, Ameen.'"[31] *Ameen* is the Muslim equivalent to *amen*. Sophie Davis, another former slave, who was eight at the beginning of the Civil War, saw old people on Saint Catherine's who prayed at the rising and at the setting of the sun and concluded their prayers with the words "meena, Mina, Mo."[32] Rachel Anderson, seventy-three years old, remembered her great-grandmother: "Muh great gran—she name Peggy—I membuh she pray ebry day, at sunrise, at noon, an at sunset. She kneel down wen she pray an at duh en she bow low tree times, facin duh sun."[33] Rosa Grant, sixty-five, had more detailed memories: "Muh gran come frum Africa too. Huh name wuz Ryna. I membuh wen I wuz a chile seein muh gran Ryna pray. Ebry mawnin at sunup she kneel on duh flo in uh ruhm an bow obuh an tech uh head tuh duh flo tree time. Den she say a prayuh. I dohn membuh jis wut she say, but one wud she say use tuh make us chillun laugh. I membuh it wuz 'asham-negad'. Wen she finish prayin she say 'Ameen, ameen, ameen'."[34] *Ashamnegad* could have been *Ashhadu anna*, which would be followed by the formula *Muhammadan rasul-ul-lah*. The complete sentence means "I bear witness that Muhammad is the Messenger of God." *Ashamnegad* could also have been *Ashhadu alla*, which would be followed by *allah ilaha ill-Allah*, meaning "I bear witness that there is no God but God." Both formulas express the Muslim's profession of faith, the *shahada*.

The Sea Islands Muslims did not hide to pray; they did so very publicly in front of the other slaves, and some prayed in front of their masters. Thomas Spalding's grandson, for example, mentioned that his grandfather had slaves, "devout Mussulmans, who prayed to Allah . . . morning, noon and evening,"[35] and that Bilali faced east to "call upon Allah."

In addition to both secret and public prayers, some Muslims managed to hold prayers in groups, in specially designated areas. On Fridays, the Muslim Sabbath, Brazilian Muslims in the eighteenth, nineteenth, and early twentieth centuries prayed in a group as recommended by the Koran, because the *jama'ah*, or prayer in congregation, is thought to be more effective. After completing their ablutions, they put on white garments, covered their heads, each took a rosary made of one hundred big beads, and prayed on a skin mat, men in the front and women in the back.[36] In Brazil, enslaved and emancipated Africans had succeeded in secretly maintaining a Muslim community large enough and sufficiently organized that the common prayer could be held in a consecrated place. The house of a free Muslim, a hut that the Africans had been allowed to build on their master's property, a room that others rented with their pooled resources—all these makeshift mosques enabled the Muslims to accomplish their devotions together, in the best way they could afford. African religions were forbidden at the time, and these slave meetings could not have gone unnoticed—even in Bahia, where city life was more flexible than anywhere else in the slave colonies. As is discussed in chapter 5, the Africans were watched. They probably knew it but were willing to take risks to maintain the rites of their religion.

All the references to prayers in the Sea Islands mention three daily prayers, and there are examples of Africans saying two daily prayers in Bahia. As Islam requires five, the incidences of fewer prayers indicate that the Muslims had to adapt to the limits imposed on their time. "Old Ben" explained these circumstances to his grandson, Charles Ball. The old man "prayed every night, though he said he ought to pray oftener; but that his God would excuse him for the non-performance of his duty in consideration of his being a slave, and compelled to devote his whole time to the service of his master."[37]

The Muslims prayed and had what was required to do so properly, as was evident in the case of Bilali Mohamed from Timbo, Guinea, who lived with his family on Sapelo Island, Georgia. His wife, Fatima or Phoebe, and their seven daughters Margaret, Hester, Charlotte, Fatima, Yaruba, Medina, and Bintou were also practicing Muslims. In the 1930s, Katie Brown, Mret's granddaughter, remembered her grandmother i and his wife "hab lill mat tuh kneel on." The mat ry of prayer. After having accomplished his or her cleanliness, a person engaged in prayer must not forehead on the ground. Israel, also of Sapelo Island lill mat an he say he prayuhs on it. Dey ain none on a mat. He hab he own mat."[38] Prayer rugs are th shoes and should not serve any purpose other ot surprising that the old man was so particular his. In addition, he may not have wanted any non-Muslim to touch it. These mats or rugs were likely pieces of cloth, quilt, or skin—the Brazilian Muslims used animal skins, as is done in West Africa—something personal, at any rate, acquired and kept with care by men and women who had very few possessions.

Besides the rug, an indispensable item of the Islamic prayer is the chaplet. Resembling a Catholic rosary, it is made of round beads and has an elongated bead in lieu of a cross. Katie Brown remembered that her great-grandfather had one: "Duh beads is on a long string. Bilali he pull bead an he say, 'Belambi, Hakabara, Mahamadu'."[39] Shadrach Hall, Hester's grandson, mentioned that "Hestuh an all ub um sho pray on duh bead. Dey weah duh string uh beads on duh wais. Sometime duh string on duh neck."[40] Calina and Hannah, an African couple living on the same plantation, were described by former slave Nero Jones: "Day talk lot uh funny talk tuh each udduh an dey is mighty puhticuluh bout prayin. Deye pray on duh bead. Duh ole man he say 'Ameela' and An Hannah she say 'Hakabara'."[41]

There is no information concerning the provenance of the prayer beads, at least in the United States. The Muslims may have made them themselves, with beads found locally. The prayer beads also may have come from afar. The Brazilian Muslims imported theirs, called *tecebas,* from the coast of West Africa even into the twentieth century.[42]

Both the Brazilian and the Georgian communities used the long rosary made of one hundred beads, as opposed to the regular one that has thirty-three beads. Anybody can use the long rosary, but men and women who belong to a Sufi order and do *dhikr* (incantatory formulas that may consist of the repetition of certain names of God or Koranic excerpts) use it systematically. These rosaries are more convenient for them because a bead is pushed back each time the formula is pronounced; and as the *dhikr* can be repeated hundreds or thousands of times, the more beads on the chaplet, the easier the count. The presence of these rosaries in the Americas is an indication that the Muslims who used them were no "ordinary" believers but men and women deeply involved in the religion, in its most constraining and most mystic aspects. They had sought a particular type of knowledge, dispensed only to those who are deemed worthy of receiving it. *Dhikr* are passed down from *shaykh* to disciple. Without a direct transmission from a master, incantations are considered invalid and even dangerous. The passing on of *dhikr* among some enslaved Muslims took place in Africa, but there is little doubt that for others the event took place in America. Enough learned men were around for this transmission to occur.

The Third Pillar of Islam is the *zakah,* or legal alms, an annual tax, paid according to the believer's revenues and assets, that is given to the poor and needy, the slaves who want to buy their freedom, and the debtors. It is intended to instill in the believers a sense of collective identity as well as responsibility, by making it a duty to participate actively in the welfare of the community. The *zakah* is mandatory when conditions are favorable, whereas charity is not but is strongly recommended. For slaves to pay a tax or even give alms seems incongruous; nevertheless, Islamic almsgiving did take place between slaves, as has been recorded in Brazil, the West Indies, and the United States.

In Brazil, Ramadan, a month-long fast, ended with a feast during which Muslims exchanged gifts called *saka*[43]—at least, that is what their observers understood. In actuality, the Brazilian Muslims were involved in two kinds of almsgiving. One was the *zakatul-Fitr,* a special charity that must be paid during Ramadan. It consists of whatever is necessary for an adult person to eat for one day. In addition, the faithful are required to pay the *zakah* on their property, between 2 and 3 percent of their earnings or possessions, and they often chose to do so during this particular month. Even enslaved or nominally free, Muslims who were devoid of even the bare minimum found ways to be charitable in order to respect a fundamental tenet of their religion.

Other Muslim communities in other parts of the Americas were also faithful to the commandment. Among the Sea Islands Muslims, Katie Brown on Sapelo Island remembered that her grandmother Margaret— one of Bilali's daughters—used to make funny cakes she called *saraka*. She made them on the same day every year, and it was an important day. Hester, another daughter of Bilali, made these cakes every month. On Saint Simons Island it was Bilali, Salih Bilali's son, who made the *saraka*. According to Shadwick Rudolph of Saint Marys, his grandmother Sally made the best.[44] In some parts of Trinidad the offering of food to the ancestors is called *sakara*; in Grenada and Carriacou, *saraka*.[45] Popular memory has associated the word *saraka* to rice cakes in the Sea Islands and *sakara* and *saraka* to ritual offerings in the West Indies, but there is little doubt that these words are slight corruption of the Arabic word *sadakha* (see chapter 6). *Sadakha* are voluntary alms that the believer offers to acquire merit with Allah. Freewill offerings are given during the holy days, on Fridays, during funerals or baptisms, or whenever the believer wants to do good.

The Sea Islands *saraka* and the Brazilian *saka* are the exact transposition to America of an African Muslim custom. The rice ball is the traditional charity given by West African women on Fridays. The testimonies from the Sea Islands refer to one distribution a month or a year, which indicates a lack of means in no way surprising. The Muslim women of Georgia had to accumulate, day after day, small quantities of rice and sugar—taken from their rations, gathered in the rice paddies, or bought with their limited savings. The cake is still made in West Africa in the same way that Bilali's daughter made hers, as described by her granddaughter: "She wash rice, an po off all duh watuh. She let wet rice sit all night, an in mawnin rice is all swell. She tak dat rice an put it in wooden mawtuh, an beat it tuh paste wid wooden pestle. She add honey, sometime shuguh, an make it in flat cake wid uh hans."[46] As is the case in Africa, the cakes in Georgia were given to the children, and being religious in nature, the distribution was accompanied by the traditional *ameen*. "Duh cake made, she call us all in an deah she hab great big fannuh full an she gib us each cake," recalled Shadrach Hall, "Den we all stands roun table, and she says 'Ameen, Ameen, Ameen', an we all eats cake."[47] The *saraka* of the Georgian women perfectly filled its charitable function. It is easy to imagine how young slaves, whose diet was poor and monotonous, could appreciate the sugary cakes. The *saraka* were so important to the children that a special song about them could still be heard in the Sea Islands well into the twentieth century. The confection of the rice cakes represents the only recorded example of Islamic behavior specifically expressed by slave women. As slaves, as women, as Africans, and as Muslims, Muslim women did not receive much attention during and after slavery, and very little has been reported about them.

Muslim men and women further succeeded in respecting one of the most constraining Koranic commandments: the fast, or *sawm*. The Fourth Pillar of Islam is meant to remind the believer of the poor's hard lot and of the compassion of God, who gives people their sustenance, as well as to enhance self-discipline. The Muslim fast lasts twenty-nine or thirty days, during which one may not eat or drink between sunup and sundown. It is a very demanding fast that provokes headaches and general fatigue and results in weight loss. To better appreciate the effort Ramadan could represent for a slave, it is necessary to remember that if the slave trade lasted so long and took away so many people, it was in part because the slaves' mortality rate was very high. The average life of a slave was fifteen years, no more than six in harsh climates. Planters worked their slaves to death because it made better sense financially, they reasoned, to buy full-grown men and women to replace deceased slaves than to have to care for them, even in a limited way, for the rest of their lives. The French writer Médéric Louis Elie Moreau de Saint Mery, who visited the United States at the end of the eighteenth century, informed his readers that a slave brought about $257 a year to his owner, whereas his upkeep was only $13.[48]

The slaves were, as a rule, underfed and overworked. Yet these extremely brutal conditions notwithstanding, Muslims fasted. Salih Bilali of Saint Simons was one of them. James Hamilton Couper, his owner, described him as "a strict Mahometan; [he] abstains from spirituous liquors, and keeps the various fasts, particularly that of the Rhamadan."[49] If Salih Bilali fasted outside the period of Ramadan, he may have been just a regular believer who wanted to purify himself to strengthen a request, or he may have been a *marabout* going into retreat. Other famous Muslims who fasted included Bilali Mohamed of Sapelo Island and his large family. Job ben Solomon's "religious abstinence" was noted by his friend and biographer, Thomas Bluett. Omar ibn Said was described as a "staunch

Mohammedan, and the first year at least kept the fast of Rhamadan with great strictness."[50] In Bahia, Ramadan was strictly observed by the large Muslim community, who had two periods of fasting: one of twenty-nine or thirty days for the ordinary believers and an additional one of the same length for the *marabouts*.[51] Shortly before the Muslims' uprising of 1835 in Bahia, the guards of the prison where the *imam* Licutan was held heard his visitors tell him that they would come to deliver him as soon as the fast was over.[52] In the aftermath of this revolt, as the police were searching a Koranic school, they found a calendar indicating the days of the Ramadan.[53] Afro-Brazilian physician and historian Manoel Querino, who studied the Muslims of Rio at the beginning of the twentieth century, relates that Ramadan started the week during which the Catholics celebrated the Holy Spirit. It is not clear in Querino's text if this was the case only in a particular year or if it happened regularly. Since Islam follows a lunar calendar, the date of Ramadan changes every year, going backward. If it is held in February one year, for example, it will be in January the following year. Because it is linked to the phases of the moon, its disappearance and reappearance, it is very doubtful that Ramadan was a fixed event in Bahia, and Querino most probably was referring only to a specific year. He observed further that during Ramadan, every morning at four and again at eight in the evening the Muslims ate a dish made of cornmeal, milk, and honey. In the meantime, he noted, they did not drink or eat, nor did they swallow their saliva.[54]

African Muslims enslaved in the Americas were not obligated to fast; they chose to do so. The Koran is not strict on the matter and allows a believer to abstain from fasting if he or she is far from home or is involved in strenuous work, which was the Africans' case. The decision to fast indicates that they were well aware that their stay in America was definitive and that no circumstance, as bad as it might be, could justify, in their eyes, derogation to the demands of their religion.

The Fifth Pillar of Islam, the *hajj*, or pilgrimage to Mecca, which develops the believers' sense of brotherhood and unity, was fundamentally out of the question. It is clear that some Muslims enslaved in America and the Caribbean had made the pilgrimage before their capture; West Africans, including teenage boys, had routinely accomplished it since the twelfth century. They walked to Arabia, crossing the African continent from west to east, on a journey that took some of them several years as they settled along the way, opening up schools and proselytizing. Some enslaved Muslims made references to their family and friends going on the pilgrimage. Mohammed Ali ben Said of Detroit mentioned that both his brothers had been to Mecca. Abu Bakr stated that his grandfather had made the pilgrimage when Abu Bakr's mother was a baby. Omar ibn Said had made the pilgrimage himself, as had Mohammad Abdullah from Kano and Bahia.

In addition to such references to the pilgrimage as having been accomplished by the Muslims themselves or their relatives in Africa, one clear instance linking Mecca to the American slaves has been documented. Before the abolition of slavery, Brazilian scholar Raymundo Nina Rodrigues, who was visiting a house used as a mosque, saw pictures on the walls depicting the "temple of Mecca," with Arabic inscriptions.[55] The presence of these images reinforces the "Islamic networks" hypothesis. It also shows that the African Muslims had not renounced the pilgrimage, even if they were to make it only in their imagination.

Another American reference to the pilgrimage may lie in one of the religious traditions of the American South, Trinidad, and Jamaica: the shout or ring shout, during which men and women turn in a circle while clapping their hands and shuffling their feet. The common explanation of the shout is that it was originally an African dance. But there is another, very intriguing explanation.

In her book *Slave Songs of the Georgia Sea Islands*, published in 1942, Lydia Parrish was the first to report a linguistic scoop, given to her by Dr. Lorenzo Dow Turner. The black linguist had been studying Africanisms in the language and culture of the Gullahs of Georgia and South Carolina and had come up with an interesting hypothesis concerning the origin of the shout, which he communicated to her:

> There appears to be a difference of opinion regarding the use of the word "shout" in designating a religious ring-dance, which was enjoyed during plantation days after prayer meeting and church service. Formerly writers thought that the Negro used the word because dancing was so sinful that it was wise to avoid even the name. But Dr. L. D. Turner has discovered that the Arabic word Saut (pronounced like our word "shout"), in use among the Mohammedans of West Africa, meant to run and walk around the Kaaba. I believe he has provided the right explanation for the difference in the meaning of the word, as used by the whites and the blacks, for I have seen Negroes do the holy dance around the pulpit in their churches in such a manner.[56]

In a linguistic book published in 1949, Turner explains, "Shout = a religious ring dance in which the participants continue to perform until they are exhausted." The word would come from the Arabic *shaut*, which means, according to Turner, "to move around the Kaaba . . . until exhausted. Sauwata = to run until exhausted."[57] Turner's first interpretation, however, seems to be the best. Actually, the circumambulation of the Kaaba is called *tawaf* and is made up of seven tours. To accomplish one tour is called *sha'wt*; it is pronounced in Arabic as *shout* is in English. Neither the *sha'wt* nor the *tawaf* imply exhaustion.

The linguistic hypothesis seems reinforced by the observation of the "dance" itself. Just as the pilgrims do in Mecca, the shouters turn counterclockwise. As in Mecca, they do so around a sacred object, such as the church itself (in the Sea Islands) or a second altar built especially in the middle of the church (in Jamaica and Trinidad). One can wonder if Muslims who knew that they would never go to Mecca re-created in a certain way the major event of the most important pilgrimage a Muslim can make. This hypothesis is fascinating and, if ever verified, would show an extremely puzzling phenomenon of retention and re-creation. However, in the absence of other, more revealing clues, one can only conjecture.

Affirmation of the faith, prayers, alms, fasting, and dreams of Mecca: Islam did survive on the American continent. It adapted itself to the local realities when necessary, while retaining its force and specificity. It is not surprising that the enslaved Africans did not waver in their faith in God. A certain amount of fatalism, expressed in the word *mektoub*—"it is written"—is an integral part of Islam. Besides, it is in the most difficult situations that faith of whatever sort prospers best. In fact, far from making the Africans' religious fervor disappear, slavery deepened it. This was true for both Muslims and non-Muslims. That African Muslims kept their faith is not exceptional. What is, is that they had the will to follow rites that were difficult to live by, and that they retained them in the most orthodox manner.

The bulk of the testimonies show that the Muslims did not content themselves with living their faith in silence, as recommended by the Koran when one is confined to a hostile environment. Fear of ridicule, the suspicion and incomprehension of others, not to mention the constraining aspect of some practices did not discourage them. The Muslims actively preserved their religion. They took difficult and sometimes astonishing steps to ensure its continuity in the New World. They were willing and able to organize themselves in a most efficient way with religious networks reaching into Africa and Europe, as is discussed in the following chapters. They showed realism; under certain conditions, they opted for a surface assimilation that guaranteed them physical survival and, beyond this, the survival of their creed. They were able to manipulate or gain the goodwill of some individuals or groups—not only abolitionists but slaveholders as well.

The African Muslims of America demonstrate that, contrary to what is sometimes asserted, Islam was not superficially implanted in West Africa. It was deeply rooted and for that reason could withstand deportation. During slavery, on both sides of the Atlantic, Africans were devout Muslims, sincere believers, strict practitioners, and active agents in the development and shaping of their religious and cultural world.

3

The Muslim Community

Muslims in America during slavery strove hard to keep their religion alive, in both the enslaved community and the larger Christian society. But to be a Muslim was more than just respecting the Five Pillars of Islam. It implied a distinctive lifestyle. Especially for West Africans, with their community-based traditions, Islam is a highly communal, public, and visible religion. It dictates and regulates the daily life, material culture, and demeanor of the faithful. To be a Muslim entails following strict dietary rules, behaving in a certain way, dressing in a particular fashion, and interacting with coreligionists and non-Muslims in the manner deemed appropriate. The Africans enslaved in the Americas were no exception; they formed close-knit communities and distinguished themselves in numerous ways, as they had in their homeland.

As a minority scattered all across North and South America and the Caribbean, and with an ethnically mixed population on any given plantation, the possibility of the Muslims forming coherent communities may seem to have been remote. Much has been said about the cultural disruption that the mixing of people from different areas induced. Recent research has shown, however, that the magnitude of this fragmentation has been overstated. For some new crops, such as rice and indigo, slaveholders relied on the expertise of Africans who were already involved in or familiar with such cultivation in their homelands. Large groups of Africans from the same area were thus transplanted as specialized units.[1] In the United States, for example, South Carolina, Virginia, Georgia, and Louisiana slaveholders had a predilection toward Senegambians, who knew how to work the rice paddies and indigo plantations, and slaves from this area represented between 20 and 40 percent of the workers. Furthermore, pseudoanthropology was rampant during slavery and assigned particular qualities and defects to specific African peoples, so planters often chose their laborers from among a precise ethnic group and bought them in quantities.

As the slave owners' choices were based on ethnicity, even a thorough mixing did not mean that individual Muslims were inevitably isolated. Ethnic groups who belonged to different geographic areas can be classified as one group if religion is used as the criterion. There may have been as many as twelve nations on a single plantation, but if the Muslims were counted together, they sometimes represented the largest single group. The case of a plantation in Saint-Domingue can serve as an illustration. It employed seventy-nine slaves: among them were eleven Nago, five Fulani, three Senegal, and four Hausa, or twenty-three potential Muslims. The other largest single group was made up of seventeen Congo.[2] The study of the Islamic vocabulary of the Gullah language reveals that the Muslims who introduced it were Wolof, Pulaar, Mandingo, Vai, and Hausa speakers.[3] Though they came from different countries, these Muslims all shared a religion, a language, a writing system, a set of values, and habits that transcended the traditional categories of identification and belonging, such as the ethnic group, the caste, or the region.

European and American observers noted this Muslim communality and cohesiveness. One of the first to mention it was Father Sandoval, who wrote in 1620 that the Wolof, Mandingo, Berbesie (Mandingo from Sine), and Fulani of Cartagena, Colombia, had different languages and were of different "races" but communicated well with one another because they all belonged to the "cursed sect of Mahomet."[4] A traveler to Brazil in the mid-1800s observed the same phenomenon and stressed that the Muslims were "more united among themselves than the other nations."[5] The Muslims certainly sought out one another, though they still regrouped along ethnic lines—there were Hausa and Mandingo subcommunities, for example. But whatever their origin, they all shared a number of characteristics that made them stand out.

The Muslim Dress Code in the Midst of Slavery

The most visible distinction was the way in which they dressed. Slaves were poorly outfitted with British-made "Negro cloth"; "osnaburg," another coarse fabric, manufactured in Germany; or, in the nineteenth-century United States, homespun fabric. Whatever their country of servitude, they usually received, at the most, two changes of clothes a year or enough fabric that they could make their own garments. Provision of clothes or fabric was not an obligation, however, and numerous planters did not do so. The slaves were thus compelled to work overtime, rent themselves out in their free time, or sell the products of their hunting or gardening to get money to clothe themselves and their children.

Native-born slave Charles Ball has left a vivid description of how his companions looked:

> He [an old man] had no clothes on him except the remains of an old shirt, which hung in tatters from his neck and arms; the two young girls had nothing on them but petticoats made of coarse tow clothes, and the woman who was the mother of the children, wore the remains of a tow linen shirt, the front part of which was entirely gone, but a piece of old cotton bagging tied round her loins served the purposes of an apron. The younger of the 2 boys was entirely naked.[6]

Many runaway notices mention that the fugitive had no clothes on but a rag around the waist. Such runaways were generally Africans who had just arrived and still wore the piece of cloth handed down to them when they disembarked. The lack of clothing could be even worse, as attested—among other such notices—by a plantation owner who reported, in the *South Carolina Gazette* of September 12, 1770, that his slaves Pompey and Sambo of the "Guiney country" had run away "entirely naked." In their memoirs and narratives, many travelers to slave areas expressed shock at seeing half- or totally naked slaves.

Slaveholders made various justifications for not clothing their slaves adequately or at all. One planter in Saint-Domingue, when confronted by his French nieces, replied, "And why not ask us to dress our cows, our donkeys, and our dogs too?"[7] The assertion made by scholars that "African slaves were quickly clothed in European garb and made to conform to European concepts of decency"[8] is a sweeping generalization. It does not take into account the numerous examples of slaves who were not given clothes; nor does it account for the very different standards of decency used by the slaveholders concerning their chattel.

Africans certainly disliked the ugly, uncomfortable clothes they had to wear, but contrary to common belief, there is no indication that they chose to go naked, as they were alleged to have been doing in Africa. Western and Central Africans experienced the state of public nudity at the hands of the Europeans; indeed, the first violation imposed on the captives was to strip them when they boarded the slave ships. Far from being an expression of African "primitiveness," the public nudity of grown men and women in the Americas was rather evidence of the depravity, utter racism, and vice of the slaveholders.

The slaves' clothing displayed an intrinsic ugliness that had its roots in contempt, greed, and the will to humiliate and dehumanize. The dress codes for slaves, wherever they were located, were very rigid. Laws were passed that forbade the enslaved men and women from wearing their owners' cast-off clothes, because the types of fabrics, colors, and shapes were reserved for whites. The humiliation did not stop upon gaining one's freedom; free blacks were subjected to the same laws as the slaves. In Guadeloupe and Martinique, for example, a decree of 1720 stipulated that freed people could be fined and reenslaved if they did not conform to the dress code. Some legislation went to extremes in the degradation process of the slaves. A proclamation issued in Surinam in 1830 warned that "no negress is permitted to wear clothes above the waist, the breasts are to be exposed, and a petticoat from the waist to the knee is the only covering allowed."[9] These codes were designed not only to stress social stratification but mainly to debase and to deny its humanity to the black population.

The scarcity of clothes was, without a doubt, distressing to the Africans in general, but for the Muslims it was even more disheartening and humiliating. Traditionally, Muslims have kept themselves very covered: long and large pants for men are worn with a long-sleeved shirt and are completed by a *boubou*, a large tunic that falls to the ankles. A head-cover, which can be a turban, skullcap, or fez, is de rigueur for older men and religious leaders. Women wear a wraparound skirt down to the ankles and the same *boubou* as the men wear—with a different collar—and wrap their heads in a piece of cloth and, when praying, wear a veil covering part of their hair but leaving their face completely visible. Whether the clothing is for men or for women, therefore, large quantities of cotton fabric have always been used among Muslims in Africa, as emphasized by historian Charles Monteil: "Islam and cotton are always side by side because Islamic morals contain an exterior decency."[10] The particular garments also serve the function of distinguishing the Muslims from the non-Muslims. Very aware of the visual impact that the modestly draped Muslims had on the rest of the population, the Hausa ruler Nafata, who felt threatened by Muslim influence, forbade the Muslims to wear turbans and veils in 1794.

As their physical appearance was part of their religious distinctiveness, the Muslims did not seek out Western clothes. Europeans who traveled through West Africa mentioned how the natives mocked them because of their attire. Nineteenth-century French explorer Gaspard Mollien noted that his "tight pants" provoked laughter throughout Senegal and Guinea. The affirmation that "the elite of African society also adopted some European . . . styles"[11] does not apply to African Muslims. In America it was precisely these European clothes, once derided as ridiculous and indecent, that the Africans had to wear. Like their companions, the Muslims had to comply with slaveholders' dress codes and accept whatever clothing was handed out; but examples gathered throughout the Americas show a sustained effort on their part to retain as much as possible of their traditional dress.

On Sapelo Island, among the Georgia Sea Islands, Margaret—one of Bilali's daughters—had a particular way of wearing her headdress: "She ain tie uh head up lak I does," remembered her granddaughter Katie Brown, "but she weah a loose wite clawt da she trow obuh uh head lak veil an it hang loose on uh shoulduh. I ain know wy she weah it dataway, but I tink she ain lak a tight ting roun uh head."[12] What Katie Brown described is the veil that Muslim women must wear when praying and may wear in any other circumstances. On neighboring Saint Simons Island, Ben Sullivan—a grandson of Salih Bilali—recalled a woman who, in slavery times, "weah loose wite veil on he head."[13] She, too, was a Muslim, as attested by her way of praying, and as such, she followed the Islamic dress code.

Men were similarly preoccupied with preserving their distinctive Muslim appearance. Bilali, the patriarch of Sapelo, "always wore a cap that resembled a Turkish fez,"[14] noted a white woman who met him and his family in the late 1850s. The Turkish fez is still worn by some West African Muslims, but one can wonder how and where Bilali got his. He had been deported as a young man and could not have worn anything of the sort in Africa because it is the attire of men only of a certain age. Nevertheless Bilali, who spent all his adult life in America, was so attached to the Islamic dress that he managed to find or create its accessories on an isolated Georgia island.

Drawings of slaves realized in nineteenth-century Brazil depict an amazing display of Islamic headgear: women wearing veils, men sporting skullcaps or turbans, and others draped in fabric covering their head and shoulders in a fashion typical of the Muslims.[15] These examples of Islamic headdress are portrayed side by side with the completely different fashion of wearing European-style hats.

One very typical Islamic headdress was worn by "ole man Israel," as recalled by Muslim descendant Ben Sullivan: "He alluz tie he head up in a wite clawt an seem he keep a lot uh clawt on han, fuh I membuh, yuh could see em hangin roun duh stable dryin."[16] The old man clearly wore a white turban, as did Ben Sullivan's maternal grandfather, the African-born Alex Boyd, who was remembered by his grandson as always having "he head up in a clawt."[17] Omar ibn Said, when he was not wearing a skullcap, wore a white turban.[18] This symbol of the Islamic faith can still be seen in the Dominican Republic, where the leader of the religious community called the Morenos wears a distinctive white turban and, though a Catholic, holds the same functions as a *marabout*.[19]

According to Islam, the archangel Djibril (Gabriel) is turbaned, and at the battle of Badr (624 C.E.), which opposed Muslims and infidels, five thousand angels were said to be wearing turbans, as were the warriors of the faith. Muhammad himself turbaned one of his generals to protect him from evil and the fire of hell. Thus the Muslim headgear, and the turban in particular, has a protective as well as a distinctive character. Specific colors also have particular meanings. The *sharufa*, the descendants of Muhammad, wear a white and green turban. A student who has reached the educational level of the exegesis of the Koran is presented with a white turban, as an insignia of his rank and office, by the clerics who have tested his knowledge for a week. The Africans who wore white turbans were not following a fashion of their country; they had earned the right to don them, through study and hard work. The turbans around their heads meant, for the majority, that before being sold to the Europeans and Americans, they had been clerics, *marabouts*, men well versed in the religious disciplines. Further, it is not unlikely that some had acquired the distinction in the New World, after having been schooled and tested by deported *ulama*. In any event, the white turban not only signals that the Muslims were attached to the symbolism of their religion but demonstrates that those who wore it, though enslaved, continued to consider themselves, and were considered by others, as clerics and spiritual leaders. Working long hours as slaves on the plantations clearly did not prevent the Muslim clerics from fulfilling their duties as spiritual guides of their communities. (It is also worth considering that the insistence of the Muslim men on having their heads covered by a turban or skullcap may have contributed to the widespread habit among American black males of wearing a cloth around their head, in the form of handkerchiefs, rags, and bandannas.)

In addition to distinctive headgear, some Africans managed to retain their complete traditional dress, with its numerous yards of cotton and flowing pattern. In Liechtenstein, Angelo Solimann, the Muslim slave who became the teacher of Prince Francis's—a nephew and successor of Wenceslas—son, "always wore the costume of his country. This was a kind of very simple garment in Turkish fashion almost always of dazzling whiteness."[20] Solimann was living at the court, and it was *de bon ton* in Europe at the time to have "exotic" Africans in full regalia attending the nobility, so his attire may have been a product of European caprice. But since he kept that costume to the end, even when he was living on his own, it was likely his own choice. Angelo Solimann had been forcibly baptized as a Catholic, and by keeping his religion's distinctive garment, he may have attempted to negate the conversion.

Far from European courts, a complete Muslim garment can be seen in the drawing of an *alufa* realized in 1930 Rio de Janeiro. The illustration shows a man wearing a long white robe with large sleeves and a pointed collar, over large black pants, and a cap whose point falls on his left shoulder.[21] Another cleric, the *imam* John Mohammed Bath, chief of the Free Mandingo of Trinidad, "always appeared in public in the dress of a Moslem priest."[22] The British administrator who mentioned this did not say what Bath's attire looked like, but the description of another religious leader, the *emir* Samba Makumba, a companion of Bath, reveals that Makumba wore "a flowing white tunic."[23] As senior "priests" Bath and Makumba were entitled to the white garment, since, according to a British lawyer who visited the island in 1840, the "Mandingo priests or African negro Mohammedans" walked about town "in large sleeved white surplices, made very nearly like ours, broad-brimmed straw hats, bare legs, and coolie sandals. The lower class Mandingo priests usually wear the common robe of light blue."[24]

Job ben Solomon's portrait, realized in London in 1733, shows a quintessential Pulo with long hair and wearing a white turban, a white *boubou*, and an Islamic gris-gris pouch. What he was really wearing when he sat down for the painter is not known, but he had insisted on being represented "in his own country dress."[25] He had to describe it minutely, as the artist stated that he could not draw something he had not seen. Job displayed some Islamic humor by retorting, "If you can't draw a dress you never saw, why do some of you painters presume to draw God, whom no one ever saw?"[26] His insistence at being immortalized in the dress of his country and religion indicates the utmost importance he gave to the retention of his cultural integrity.

The display of Islamic garb could take place under the most improbable circumstances. During the celebration of the Epiphany in Cuba, blacks used to parade in their nations' clothes. The Arara, for example, wore necklaces of shells, teeth, and beads and raffia hoops around their waists. The Mandingo who marched during this Catholic celebration wore their Islamic wide pants and turbans.[27]

These wide pants, very typical of Muslims, also appear in an intriguing description of a "hoodoo man" given by Southern blacks in the 1920s. They stressed that he "usually wears a turban on his head, wears a Turkish dress with bloomer pants."[28] According to author Newbell Puckett, the informants may have seen a show with a Hindu and made the confusion between hoodoo and Hindu. This may have been so, but it may also have been that the hoodoo man who made gris-gris dressed differently, like a Turk or a Muslim. As is explained in the next chapter, the Muslims were major providers of amulets to the slaves, so to find them associated through their clothes with the occult is quite logical.

The Muslims who could not wear the *boubou* found ways to retain the spirit of their former attire. Yarrow Mahmout, the centenarian from Maryland whose portrait was painted by Charles Peale in 1819, is immortalized wearing a hat typical of the African Muslims. He is also very much covered with a shirt and coat. This old man, who prayed in public and sang praises to Allah in the street, retained not only his religion and his name but also the dress that signaled him as a Muslim. Similarly, Omar ibn Said's picture shows him wearing a skullcap and an austere, black, buttoned-up coat. His appearance seems to echo the description of Mandingo men made by a Trinidadian woman as late as the 1940s: she stated that they "wear pretty little caps, an' their blouse button up like a priest's."[29] Evidently, non-Muslims recognized that the Muslims dressed differently, and their dress was unique enough to be noticed and remembered. To the Trinidadian woman, as in other instances, what distinguished them was their forbidding appearance, their physical austerity, and their insistence at being thoroughly covered "like priests."

Next to nothing has been recorded concerning the clothes Muslim women wore. But a white woman who traveled through Brazil in 1865 has left a description and two drawings of Muslim women. They used to wear "a high muslin turban, and a long, bright-colored shawl, either crossed on the breast and thrown carelessly over the shoulder, or if the day be chilly, drawn closely around them, their arms hidden in its folds."[30] This attire made an impact on the black population in general, as Gilberto Freyre remarked in the 1930s: "In Bahia, in Rio, in Recife, in

Minas, African garb, showing the Mohammedan influence, was for a long time worn by the blacks. Especially by the black women who sold sweets and by the vendors of *alua*."[31] The women's many-layered skirts, their shawls, and their headcovers were all elements of the Islamic tradition of covering up the body.

The extreme importance that the Muslims gave to their particular dress became very obvious on January 25, 1835, in Bahia. Luis Tavares Macedo, a member of the National Guard, described what he discovered from his window when the Muslim uprising broke out: noises, shots, and screams, and then he saw "a group of black Africans wearing white skull-caps and large smocks over their pants."[32] The insurgents' clothes also struck another witness, who testified "They were armed with swords and wearing white tunics."[33] The Muslims of Bahia who revolted could have been mistaken for the troops of the *almami* of Futa Toro on their way to war a few years earlier: "All the men of Futa Toro wear for war a costume similar to the mamelouks'. All those white turbans and those gowns of the same color."[34] For the insurgents to don these clothes deliberately was a way of assuring and indicating the holiness and sacredness of their mission. If killed in battle, they would go to heaven, whose symbolic color is white. They were also displaying their pride in their Islamic and African culture and their rejection of the Christian whites' impositions on their persons and bodies.

The white clothes were so closely associated with the Bahia revolt that the Brazilian authorities immediately, and very rightly, called them war clothes and proceeded to arrest anybody found with them. Aprigio, a free Nago, had been observed by a lieutenant who testified that he had seen him sewing "huge shirts and skullcaps, which the insurgent donned as uniforms."[35] A Koranic teacher, Aprigio was condemned to death on April 29, 1835; his sentence was later commuted to forced labor. At the house of Belchior da Silva Cunha, another free Nago, the police found papers written in Arabic and white tunics. He, too, was condemned to death but ultimately received six hundred lashes instead. Luis Vieira, a fifty-year-old Nago tailor, was condemned to five hundred lashes because he had made tunics similar to those worn by the insurgents. Joao, another Nago slave, was found in possession of weapons, Arabic papers, and seven white tunics and was thrown in jail. In a house shared by fifteen Africans—among them a couple and their four children—the police found Arabic papers, a quill, four writing slates, several rings, and a Muslim garment. Ajadi Luis Dople, a free man and the father of the children, admitted that the frock was his but claimed that he used it as a nightshirt.[36] He was condemned to death, while his pregnant wife was condemned to five years in jail. Ajadi appealed, and his sentence was commuted to eight years of hard labor.

In addition to the white garments, the police noticed the presence of suspicious metal rings. African Muslims routinely wear silver rings and bracelets as protection. Some of these items have a special cavity, in which the *marabout* puts a gris-gris before sealing it. One type of ring has hieroglyphs on the top, said to be similar to the ones inscribed on Prophet Suleyman's (Solomon's) ring with which he controlled the jinn (evil spirits). In Bahia, as numerous rings were found along with the Arabic papers and the white clothes, it became evident to the police that they were linked to Islam and, by extension, to the uprising. It was a correct assumption: the rings, like the Arabic papers, were protections against anything that could go wrong during the revolt. Because she had been handing out such rings, Emereciana, the companion of the *alufa* Dandara—a former Koranic teacher in Nigeria—was condemned to receive four hundred lashes.

Thousands of miles from Bahia, people in Mississippi had protective rings too. An observer noted in 1926 that a "silver ring is also efficient [as a protection] as is also a ring made of a horseshoe nail or a ring with Chinese writing on it, all of which I have seen worn by Mississippi Negroes for that purpose."[37] The silver ring as a protection could be the continuation into the twentieth century of a Muslim tradition. Two hypotheses can be offered for the presence of "Chinese writing." If the Mississippians were indeed wearing Chinese rings, it may have been because, with their strange writing, they looked like Suleyman's ring. Their owners, the children and grandchildren of Muslims, could therefore have attributed the same virtues to them. The observer may have been wrong, however, and may have taken imprecise hieroglyphs for Chinese writing. There is no reason that the Muslim rings of the Suleyman type could not have been reproduced in America. Through the years the writing would have become approximate, but the purpose of the object would have been remembered. It is also worth noting that even though the Africans were transported naked to the Americas, they retained their rings, earrings, arm rings, and gris-gris. Some of these rings may have been passed on from one generation to another.

In addition to their clothes and protections, the Muslims also distinguished themselves by a physical trait that Ben Sullivan of Saint Simons

Island revealed: "Now ole man Israel he hab shahp feechuch an a long pointed beahd."[38] Like Israel, the *emir* Samba Makumba from Trinidad wore his white hair and beard long. As a former *marabout* enslaved in Bahia said derisively, "Many Hausa negroes attach goat beards to their chins to give themselves the appearance of men."[39] The pointed beards of the Brazilian Muslims in twentieth-century Rio are also mentioned by Manoel Querino[40] and can be seen in the drawing of an *alufa* illustrating Arthur Ramos's 1934 book *O negro brasileiro*. This trait was a particularity that differentiated Israel, Makumba, and their coreligionists from the "heathens." The beard was—and still is, for certain groups of Muslims—as important a distinctive feature as specific clothes.

Clothing and the lack of it played an important role in slave cultures because they were linked to rewards, punishments, a sense of dignity, pride, and individuality; further, clothing constituted the only affordable luxury. There is ample evidence that African and American-born slaves had their own aesthetic and reinterpreted European-style clothes to fit it.[41] They used European concepts in clothes and imprinted their mark on them by clashing colors, mixing styles, and contrasting patterns, all aesthetic principles that came from Africa. The Muslims, in contrast, sought to re-create the exact clothes and accessories they wore before their deportation. Those garments did not borrow anything from the European fashion. Since no other enslaved population throughout the Americas and the Caribbean Islands made such an effort to preserve its distinctive attire and accessories, it is clear that for the African Muslims, to wear the symbols of their faith and, for some, the emblem of their former status was of extreme importance. To short-circuit the demeaning dress code by reestablishing their own was not only an act of subversion against white domination; it was a way of reclaiming and stating their human, cultural, and social value and their fidelity to their religion. The traditional garb represented a negation of their present status and a refusal of the abjection of the slaves' material life. It was furthermore a rejection of acculturation, an affirmation of their dignity as Africans, and, for the clerics, an assertion of their religious accomplishments. The retention of their particular dress also served as a sign of recognition among them; it distinguished the Muslims and made them visible to each other. The Muslim community was composed of Fulani, Hausa, Wolof, Vai, Mandingo, and Yoruba, who had had little or no contact in Africa and could not rely on familiar physical features to recognize one another. The retention of the African

Muslim garb therefore served as an essential first element in the building up of a community.

Names and Identity among African Muslims

Just as they were handed down strange, ill-fitting clothes, the newly arrived Africans were given strange names by their owners, in a move whose intention was not only for the convenience of slaveholders but also an attempt to annihilate their past, sense of self, culture, kinship, ethnic origin, and religion. The dehumanizing naming practice that was present throughout the Americas was essentially a problem for the Africans. American-born slaves were usually given a name by their parents—among whom were first-generation Africans—though in some circumstances the owner had a final say. A minority of slaveholders accepted African names without attempting to substitute others, but the vast majority chose to erase them.

Though openly they had to conform, Africans tried in different ways to keep their names. One technique was to answer to two names, as is often mentioned in the advertisements for runaways. A Georgian notice for a runaway Muslim slave, for instance, mentioned that a "new Negro Fellow, called Jeffray, sometimes, BRAM, or IBRAHIM,"[42] had escaped. A more secretive and common technique was for slaves to retain their real names within their community while using the name imposed by their owner when dealing with the outside world. During their trial, some Bahian Muslims acknowledged that they knew their fellow conspirators only by their African names.

The Africans who could choose their new names sometimes did so in a way that let them keep a link with their past. Job ben Solomon is one of these interesting examples of African retention in the naming practice. He was called Simon by his master but was also known as Job ben Solomon, which was the English translation of his Senegalese Muslim name, Ayuba (Job) Suleyman (Solomon). In a similar way, a Muslim enslaved with Ibrahima abd al Rahman gave the name Sulimina (Suleyman) to his sons, but the boys were called Solomon. It is very likely that many named Moses or Moïse (in French), Solomon or Salomon, Abraham, Jacob, Adam, and David were formerly Musa, Suleyman, Ibrahima, Ayuba, Adama, and Dawda. Omar ibn Said retained the memory of his name in yet another manner: he was called Moro or Moreau, a corruption of his real name, Umaru or Omar.

Muslims used all the retention techniques available to them and did so with a certain amount of success. Islamic names can be found, along with other African names, in the records of plantation owners, runaway notices, censuses, probate records, will books, deed registers, tribunal records, payrolls of free soldiers, as well as in the memories of former slaves and their descendants. Muslim names are, in fact, Arabic names that predate the religion but were spread around the world by Islam. They are easy to identify because they are the names or Africanized versions of the names of Muhammad's family members or relate to the ninety-nine attributes of Allah. In the latter case, they begin with *abd*, which means "servant," and continue with one of the names and attributes of Allah, such as *Rahman*, "the most Merciful"; *Aziz*, "the Beloved"; and *Rahim*, "the most Compassionate." Abd Allah (Abdulaye in West Africa) is the "servant of Allah."

Muslim names can be found all over the Americas and the Caribbean. The records concerning the maroons of Saint-Domingue, for example, show the names Ayouba, Belaly, Tamerlan, Halaou, Aly, Soliman, Lamine, Hayda, Fatima, and Yaya.[43] Mohammad, Sule, Aluna, Sanim, Bilal, Musa, Ali, Usman, and Abdullah are names that have been recorded in Brazil.[44] Mohamed, Abouberika, Hammadi, Malick, Mohammado, Abdoulie, Salhim, Mohammed, Mohammedu, and Mohammedou were some of the Muslim names surviving in Trinidad.[45] Jamaica had Abu Bakr, Harouna, Mohammed, and Mousa.[46] In French Louisiana, court records list Amadit, Almansor, Fatima, Yacine, Moussa, Souman, Baraca, Mamary, Mamaroux, Marieta, Bakary, and Barra.[47] Selim, Musa, Alik, Abdalli, Fatima, Bilali, and Ismael appeared in Georgia.[48] A list compiled by Newbell Puckett from records from all over the United States contains about 150 names of Arabic origin amid 1,200 African names.[49] Among them are Akbar, Bilah, Hamet, Fatima, Amina, Alli, Kaleb, Fato, Balla, Bamba, and Araam. Moustapha was "fairly popular" in the Carolinas.[50]

Not surprisingly, the Sea Islands were a significant reservoir of African Muslim names. Linguist Lorenzo Dow Turner recorded many, along with other African names, in the 1930s. From the list he compiled for his book *Africanisms in the Gullah Dialect* (1949) it is possible to extract about one hundred Muslim names concentrated in that small area. Some are the names of Muhammad's family members or companions: Fatima, Kadi, Kadijata, Ayisata, Binta, Ali, Aminata, Safiyata, Hasana, Fatuma, Fatu, Famata, Marieta, Malik, and Belali. Others are the Arabic names of the prophets, such as Birahima, Iba, Ibrahima, Biram (Abraham), Isa (Jesus), Mamadi, Mamadu (Muhammad), Musa (Moses), and Salama (Solomon). Other biblical and Koranic names include Yaya (John the Baptist), Gibril (Gabriel), Ayuba (Job), Mariama (Mary), Hawa (Eve), and Adamu (Adam). Sea Islands Muslims also used names based on the Arabic name for the day on which a baby was born. The practice has now fallen into disuse in Africa but was widespread at the time of the slave trade. Female day names remembered in Georgia sixty years ago were Altine (Monday/*Ithnain*); Talata (Tuesday/*Thalatha*); Araba (Wednesday/*Al Arbia*); Alkamisa and Aramisa (Thursday/*Al Khamis*); Arajuma and Jumare (Friday/*Al Djouma*); Sabala (Saturday/*Assabt*); and Aladi (Sunday/*Ahad*). Other Islamic names included titles such as Wali (protector or saintly man), Lamami (*almami*), Mori, Moriba (*marabout* in Mandingo), Kalifa (caliph), and Karamo (teacher and leader in Mandingo). Names relating to prayer included Sala (*salat*), Salifano (second prayer of the day in Pulaar), Alansaro (third prayer in Mandingo), Safo (fifth prayer in Mandingo), and Sago (sheepskin mat in Pulaar). Parents also gave names such as Sadaka (alms), Madina (Medina), and Male and Imale (Muslim). These names were nicknames, also called pet names or "basket names." Though they were second names, Turner stressed that "so general is [their] use that many of the Gullahs have difficulty in recalling their English given-name."[51]

Islamic names by no means indicate the exact measure of the Muslim community. In addition to those who had imposed Christian names, Muslims who could retain their names also used names particular to their ethnic group. Coumba, Samba, Sambo, and Demba are names borne by Muslims and non-Muslims alike, so when one encounters them in historical records, one cannot be sure that the bearer was a Muslim, but the possibility cannot be excluded either.

It is difficult to assess why some Muslims who were openly faithful to their religion and whose owners allowed them to practice it had to answer to a Christian name. Salih Bilali, the devout slave driver of Hopeton Plantation on Saint Simons Island, was called Tom and registered as such on the plantation records of 1827. However, other Muslims who appear in the same document retained their proper names, such as the six Fatimas, two Mahomets, and one Maryam who were Salih Bilali's coreligionists.[52] Notwithstanding his demeaning nickname, among his descendants and slave acquaintances he was called—and is recalled as—Bilali.

Ibrahima abd al Rahman was nicknamed "Prince" in reference to his high status in Futa Jallon, but Samba (a common Pulo name), a man who had been captured and sold with him and was living on the same plantation, kept his name. It is obvious that Samba is easier for an American to pronounce than Ibrahima. But the different treatment of their names could mean that their owner, Thomas Foster, wanted to break the morale of a slave who had come to him as an equal, asking to be released and presenting his family as willing to pay a lot of money for him. To call him "Prince" was derisive, given his present status, and a way of reminding Ibrahima that, whoever he had been, he was now just another slave. In such a case, the imposition of a European name or nickname would have filled its proper function: to negate and annihilate the human being inside the slave.

Whether or not they had been able to retain their own names, the first-generation Africans faced a dilemma concerning the names they would give their children. The well-known North American Muslims who had families responded in diverse ways. Ibrahima, though he remained a Muslim, married a native-born Christian woman. Their children's names were Simon, Susan, Prince, and Lee. Interestingly, Ibrahima passed his own slave nickname to one of his sons. Was it a way of appropriating the ridiculous name and giving it its true meaning?

In contrast, Ibrahima's countryman, Samba, gave Muslim names to his sons. His wife's name was Celia, and she may or may not have been a Muslim. Samba's sons were called Sulimina (Suleyman)—which became Solomon, following the pattern seen above—and Samba. Just as he had kept his name, Samba passed on Muslim names to his sons, indicating his strong will in the maintenance of a cultural—perhaps also familial—and religious continuity.

Salih Bilali gave an Islamic name to at least one of his sons, calling him Bilali. As West African parents usually give the name of a particular person—relative, friend, or religious leader—to a newborn, as opposed to a choice based on personal taste or general fashion, it is not unlikely that young Bilali was named after Bilali Mohamed of Sapelo, who was his father's friend. The young Bilali, who retained Islamic customs such as the making of the rice cakes and married the daughter of an African Muslim, apparently gave Christian names to his children. One of them was Ben Sullivan, who was interviewed by the WPA in the 1930s and has left vivid descriptions of the Sea Islands Muslims. Ben Sullivan probably had a basket name, which may have been Islamic.

The naming of Bilali Mohamed's children presents some interesting points. Bilali had arrived on Sapelo Island around 1802, having been purchased with his family in the Bahamas. It is said that he had seven daughters and twelve sons. Though his daughters have been very well remembered, nothing is known about his sons. It is possible, if they ever existed, that they were sold in the Bahamas before the rest of the family departed for Georgia. One of Bilali's great-grandsons remembered that his "gran," Hester, used to talk about Africa, but she was most likely talking about the Bahamas or another island—probably French-speaking—where the family may have lived.[53] Bilali's wife is sometimes called Phoebe, sometimes Fatima, the latter also being the name of one of Muhammad's daughters. Phoebe and Fatima may have been the same person bearing an African name, Fatima, and an official name, Phoebe; or, as a Muslim, Bilali may have had two wives, as hinted by his great-granddaughter Katie Brown: "Maybe he hab mone one wife. I spects das bery possible."[54] Bilali's wife or wives were practicing Muslims as he was, and so were their daughters Margaret, Hester, Charlotte, Fatima, Nyrrabuh or Yarrabuh, Medina, and Bintou. The first three names are clearly Christian whereas the other four are Islamic. The first girls may have been born in a Catholic colony where they were forcibly baptized—the fact that they spoke French or Creole reinforces this theory—whereas the other four may have been born in the Bahamas, a Protestant colony with less emphasis on conversion. In any event, the presence of Christian names within a practicing Muslim family reinforces the argument that the prevalence of Islamic names does not, by itself, give a fair measure of the size of the Muslim communities. It also shows that Muslim slaves were pragmatists, and though they strove for orthodoxy, they adapted to their local conditions when necessary. Bilali, who wore a fez, had a Koran, prayed, fasted, and wrote a document in Arabic, made a very concerted effort to ensure that his family would follow his religion. As he kept his own name, Bilali Mohamed, he passed on Islamic names to part of his progeny. At least one, Hester, gave a Muslim name to one of her children. She named him Bilali.

In a situation of servitude such as that prevailing in America and the Caribbean, where absolute conformity and obedience were required, to keep one's name was a defiant act. It was a refusal to surrender one's identity—a personal as well as familial, ethnic, and religious identity. Islamic names, by their very origin, have no ethnic markers, or very few; a Fatimata may be from Senegal, Mali, or Nigeria. They identify not an ethnic group but a religious one. In America these were the only names—besides the imposed Christian names—that transcended geography, culture, and ethnicity. They clearly indicated to those familiar with Islam which persons on a plantation were Muslims and could facilitate the identification of coreligionists. They also defined the Muslims as a particular group, along lines that were not ethnically exclusive but religiously inclusive.

Observing Dietary Rules under Slavery

Another distinctive trait of the enslaved Muslims was their diet. In addition to Ramadan, Muslims must follow particular dietary rules on a daily basis. The Koran is quite specific about what a follower of Islam may and may not eat and drink: "Forbidden to you are: dead meat (carrion), blood, the flesh of swine" (5:3). Concerning wine it says, "In [it] is great sin, and some profit, for men; but the sin is greater than the profit" (2:219). Some Africans managed to follow Koranic rules and prohibitions in the New World. As James Hamilton Couper noted, his slave Salih Bilali did not drink alcohol.[55] Respecting the same rules, Job ben Solomon, as he was taken out of his cell in Maryland to be interrogated, refused the wine offered him.[56] Yarrow Mamout used to say, "It is not good to eat Hog—& drink whiskey is very bad."[57] Ibrahima abd al Rahman made "no use of ardent spirits,"[58] and John Mahomed Bath, "Chief of the Free Negroes of the Mohammedan religion" in Trinidad, emphasized to the king of England that "while slaves we did not spend our money in liquor as other slaves did and always will do."[59] Bath made a stern moral judgment about the non-Muslim slaves. Alcohol certainly represented escapism to slaves and access to something pleasant; but to the Muslims among them it was a sign of weakness and, as stated in the Koran (5:90), "an abomination" that "excite[s] enmity and hatred."

That alcohol was widely available near the plantations has been documented in various regions and countries: "Immense quantities of ardent spirits are sold in the Southern States to the Negroes, by *retailing shops*, established for the express purpose of *Negro-trading*,"[60] lamented a missionary in 1847. Moreover, in the French West Indies slaves were forced to drink alcohol, as part of a diet designed to make them work harder.

Mornings and evenings the planters held a distribution of spirit for their workers, and they provided additional alcohol to those employed in the most strenuous jobs: they received one pint of brandy a week. Abuses were so widespread that the French Black Code of 1685 stressed that it was forbidden to give alcohol to the slaves in lieu of food. So when Muslims such as Yarrow Mahmout or John Mohamed Bath denounced the use of alcohol by their companions, they may have been basing their condemnation not only on the Koran but also on their observations of the reality of slavery.

Concerning the consumption of meat and their diet in general, enslaved men and women had no control whatsoever on the quantity, quality, and type of food they received. Because pork was cheap and easy to keep, it was by far the planters' favorite meat for their laborers. A Muslim originally from Mali, enslaved in Mississippi, spoke for many others when he lamented to a merchant "in terms of bitter regret, that his situation as a slave in America, prevents him from obeying the dictates of his religion. He is under the necessity of eating pork, but denies ever tasting any kind of spirits."[61]

The consequences such insubordination could bring notwithstanding, some Muslims refused to eat pork. In the French West Indies, the rejection of pork by the enslaved population reached disturbing proportions for the administration. On November 20, 1672, Mr. de Baas, governor of the islands, wrote to his minister, "This people cannot see any longer how to feed the slaves for bacon is their aversion and they eat it only through force."[62] No reason other than the religious taboo dictated why the Africans refused to eat pork and had to be forced to do so, for this meat is widely consumed in Africa by Christians and non-Muslims.

Though no reference to their diets has been found, one can speculate that Ibrahima abd al Rahman, Salih Bilali, Omar ibn Said, and Bilali, among others whose other religious habits were tolerated, ate beef or fish instead of pork. Nero, a Muslim from Cooper River in South Carolina, obtained that right. The plantation books of his owner, William Ball, show that he drew his ration in beef instead of pork.[63] Job ben Solomon followed the Koranic dietary rules; he "has no scruple about fish; but won't touch a bit of pork, it being expressly forbidden by their law,"[64] mentioned his biographer.

Besides these examples, it can be assumed that a number of Muslims were able to keep their Islamic diet. As a general rule, enslaved men and women were ordered to fish, hunt, and cultivate a small garden, enabling the owner to forgo his or her obligations while further burdening the slaves, who in addition to their free work had to feed themselves by working on their only day off. As exploitative as it was, the custom was also a source of income for the slaves; they sold their surplus, an activity that helped them buy clothes and sometimes their freedom. For the Muslims the arrangement must have proved very advantageous, as they could remain faithful to their religious principles by escaping the imposed diet.

Not only are certain meats forbidden to the Muslim, but the way in which an animal has died is also of the utmost importance. One may not consume the flesh of an animal "killed by strangling, or by a violent blow, or by a headlong fall, or by being gored to death; that which has been (partly) eaten by a wild animal" (5:3). In addition, the animal has to be slaughtered solemnly by a Muslim who, as he cuts the animal's carotid, says, "Bismillahi" (in the name of Allah). If the proper procedure has not been followed or is in doubt, a Muslim should not eat the meat. For a slave who had no control over how the animal was butchered and who wanted to remain faithful to the Koranic precepts, the only alternative was to abstain from eating meat altogether. There is some indication that enslaved Muslims followed that rule. One Muslim who refused to eat non-*halal* (lawful) meat was the very orthodox Job ben Solomon. Thomas Bluett, who traveled with Job from Maryland to London in March 1733, related that on the ship they "permitted him to kill our fresh stock, that he might eat of it himself; for he eats no flesh, unless he has killed the animal with his own hands, or knows that it has been killed by some Mussulman."[65]

On Salih Bilali's plantation, which counted a number of Muslims, most of the slaves did not touch meat the year round, as reported by their owner, James Hamilton Couper.[66] The slaveholder had instituted the policy as a way of ensuring peace, since he was convinced that meat could induce excitement. His Muslim slaves may have found the idea to their liking. This hypothesis is indirectly confirmed by a descendant of Bilali of Sapelo Island, who stressed that he and his family did not eat wild animals or fresh meat.[67] The Koran states that one may not eat the product of a hunt while on pilgrimage, but it is lawful in other circumstances. It is therefore not clear why Bilali insisted on that prohibition. Concerning fresh meat, however, his reluctance likely had its origin in the non-*halal* manner in which the animals had been killed. Rather than go contrary to their religious principles, Bilali and his family abstained from meat, as Salih Bilali and his coreligionists were also doing on the Hopeton Plantation, through the will of their owner and probably according to their own.

When the Muslims could rely on an organized community, they took the opportunity to follow closely the dietary restrictions of Islam, as exemplified in Brazil. In Bahia, enslaved and freed Muslims used to gather to eat. These numerous dinners were mentioned by witnesses interrogated during the trial of the insurgents in the 1835 rebellion. The Muslims killed the animals—often rams—themselves, so that they could eat *halal*.[68] These communal suppers may have represented the only times the Africans ate meat.

In the matter of diet, again the African Muslims showed orthodoxy, though they were under no religious obligation to do so. Actually, the Koran tolerates the consumption of any type of meat ordinarily forbidden, including the non-*halal* meat, in cases of famine: "But if any is forced by hunger, with no inclination to transgression, Allah is indeed Oft-forgiving, Most Merciful" (5:3). The slaves' situation was very close to starvation, and there is little doubt that some Muslims interpreted it that way. Nevertheless, others chose to deprive themselves of the bare minimum provided to them. Though they were living precarious, deprived lives in the slaveholders' world, they chose to live austere lives, full of extra privations in their own sphere. By persisting in their religious dietary habits, the Muslims were not only remaining faithful to their religion but they were also retaking control of themselves. They—not their owner—decided what they could eat or drink, and when.

Other Manifestations of Cultural Continuity and Community

The Africans retained other Islamic customs. Circumcision, for example, was practiced by the Brazilian Muslims on boys ten years old.[69] The practice in Africa is not restricted to the Muslims, but there is no indication that non-Muslims maintained the custom in America.

Polygamy was another practice transported to America. It was widespread in Africa long before Islam, which limits the number of wives one man may have to four. Not much attention was given to the marriages of slaves—when they were allowed—and data on their matrimonial habits are lacking. If a slave seemed to have more than one woman, the frame of reference used to describe his behavior was Western, that is, he had a wife and lovers. This was a constant complaint of the priests, who deplored what they perceived as the slaves' immorality. Africans, for their part, probably saw these unions as very legitimate marriages, since their religious leaders must have sanctified them. This view is confirmed by Manoel Querino's observations: Brazilian Muslims practiced polygamy, he stressed, as a "hygienic measure" and regarded marriage as "a real cult, observed with rigor, in the same way as a fraternal friendship."[70] But polygamy, though it definitely existed in the Americas, was certainly not widespread. For the Africans to find even one mate presented real difficulty because there were about seven African men for every three African women. This huge sexual imbalance meant that many Africans could not form families, a phenomenon that had a decisive impact on the survival of Islam. (See chapter 6.)

As they tried to maintain a religious and cultural continuity, individual Muslims and Muslim communities had to interact with the larger world of their fellow slaves and their enslavers, all of whom were non-Muslims. Information about the relationship between Muslim and non-Muslim slaves shows what has sometimes been described as a divide between the two groups. Closer observation and knowledge of the interactions between Muslims and non-Muslims in Africa are essential if one is better to appraise what their relationship may have been in America.

There is hardly any mention of Muslims on the part of the non-Muslim former slaves who, during and after slavery, described their communities. Still, a few African and American-borns expressed strong opinions about what they perceived as the Muslims' disdain. Some Bahian slaves and free men, for instance, complained about the Muslims' arrogance and standoffishness. "The Nago who can read," commented a slave, "and took part in the insurrection, would not shake hands with nor respect outsiders. They even called them *gavere* [*kafir*]."[71] These comments were made in the aftermath of the failed Bahia rebellion of 1835 and therefore must be taken with caution, because it was in the interest of the suspects to appear as detached as possible from the Muslims.

In Cuba, former slave and maroon Esteban Montejo remembered that the Mandingo "kept apart from the rest."[72] A few expressions of disdain emanating from the Muslims have been recorded. Marcelina, a slave in Bahia, was told that "she was going to Mass to worship a piece of wood on the altar, because images are not saints"[73]—a typical Muslim remark, since figurative representations of religious figures are *haram* (forbidden). Charles Ball recalled in his autobiography how his grandfather—who was a Muslim, unbeknownst to the grandson—expressed "great contempt for his fellow slaves, they being, as he said, a mean and vulgar race, quite beneath his rank, and the dignity of his former station."[74] In the same manner, the *imam* of the Mandingo of Trinidad emphasized to the king of England that the other slaves did not get out of bondage because they spent their money on liquor instead of buying their freedom. But Bilali provides the most dramatic illustration of this attitude: during the Anglo-American War of 1812, he reportedly told his owner that he would not defect to the British—who had promised freedom to the slaves if they joined their ranks—and could "answer for every Negro of the true faith, but not for the *Christian dogs* you own."[75] Evidently, the 450 men and women living on the plantation were divided in his view along religious lines. The eighty or so Muslims and the rest of the slaves did not form, in his opinion, a homogeneous community of fellow sufferers.

Bilali's words are particularly harsh and reflect a strong contempt of the other slaves. They also show an amazing degree of self-confidence on the part of the slave. As he was extolling his own religion and disparaging his Christian companions, he was addressing his Christian owner, letting him know in no uncertain terms what he thought of his master's religion. He seems to have held onto his opinion and maintained his distance until the end. A woman who met him and his family emphasized that "these Negroes held themselves aloof from the others as if they were conscious of their own superiority."[76] Bilali's behavior, however, may also have had something to do with his status as a slave driver, a professional who was indeed "above" the rest of the field hands. In any event, it is very likely that the family felt morally superior not only to the non-Muslim slaves but to the slaveholders as well.

There were certainly aloof Muslims, but the fact should not be overstated, as has been done by scholars such as Roger Bastide, who saw in their pseudosnobbishness one of the reasons why Islam disappeared. The emphasis on the Muslims' standoffishness is, at best, anecdotal; there is no mention in slave narratives or other sources, except for the trial transcripts in Bahia, of tensions between Muslims, Christians, and animists. The WPA interviewees, who described at great length a mixed Muslim and non-Muslim community in the Georgia Sea Islands, did not make any reference to aloofness on the part of the Muslims, nor did they mention particular problems relating to them. In addition, the presence in America of syncretic cults with Islamic components proves that a close interaction took place on a social and even on a religious level between Muslims and non-Muslims. (See chapter 6.) Comments made by a descendant of Bilali concerning the relations between Muslims and non-Muslims on Sapelo Island are revealing. Cornelia Bailey (an Anglicization of Bilali) stated that Bilali kept to himself because he "did not like mixing"; she further emphasized that Muslims and non-Muslims tended to "keep to themselves," although they generally "got along" and could work with others for specific purposes or special occasions.[77]

The tendency for each group to remain separate from others under certain circumstances, but maintaining cordial relationships nevertheless, is consistent with African customs. Before they were deported to the New World, African Muslims had been in contact with *kafir*. Some were, without a doubt, former *kafir* who had converted. The pattern of Islamic expansion in West Africa, through the clerics and traders who established themselves in non-Muslim villages, is evidence that close contacts existed between the communities although they often lived in distinct neighborhoods. Non-Muslim rulers routinely employed Muslim scribes and *marabouts*. That non-Muslims sent their children to Koranic schools and bought amulets from the *marabouts* are other proofs of this interaction. As a rule, African Muslims participate in events that bring communities together, whether the other components of the population are Christian or animist. Relations in earlier times, as today, were usually cordial on an individual and communal level. Wars did not arise from strained interaction on a small scale. As summed up by historian Lamin Sanneh, in Africa, "the controversial dimension of interreligious encounter has very shallow local roots. It was an importation constructed on the notion of exclusiveness."[78]

African Muslims and non-Muslims coming from the same cultural areas of West Africa were used to one another; but this was not the case with populations from different geographic areas. An animist from the Congo was foreign to a Muslim Mandingo but he was also foreign to a non-Muslim Bambara, who came from the same area as the Mandingo and spoke the same language. The cultural differences that existed among the men and women from western and central Africa added a layer of separation between the slaves that had little to do with Islam and a lot to do with differences in civilization. In other words, Muslims may have remained on their own not only because of their particular religion but also because the African and American-born populations they were living with were from different cultural worlds.

Slave and Slaveholder Perceptions of Each Other

Besides their fellow slaves, the Muslims had to interact with the Christian slaveholders. Starting in Africa, they had regarded the Europeans with a certain amount of disdain. As Mungo Park realized, his coreligionists were not held in high esteem by the Muslims, who thought the Europeans were "ignorant heathens."[79] The religion itself hardly impressed the Africans, lamented slave dealer Nicholas Owen: "As to our religion it has made no impression in the least otherwise than a matter of ridicule or laughter in so many years as they have had us among them, notwithstanding there has been some trials to convert them to a notion of a better state."[80] The Muslims were firm believers, and they defined themselves and the rest of the world according to religion. Quite consistently, the Muslims who spoke or wrote about their capture and enslavement stressed that they had been captured by "infidels" and sold to Christians. It is clear that, in their opinion, the main difference between them and their captors was not ethnic but religious. In the same manner, the main difference between them and the Europeans was not skin color but religion. When they got to America, they entered the Christian world.

It goes without saying that their new environment must have seemed repulsive and brought them near despair, but the culture of their enslavers may not have looked more appealing. A unique analysis of the Africans' psyche in that regard has been offered by Charles Ball, who observed that

> the native Africans are revengeful, and unforgiving in their tempers, easily provoked, and cruel in their designs. They generally place little, or even no value, upon the fine houses and superb furniture of their masters; and discover no beauty in the fair complexions, and delicate forms of their mistresses. They feel indignant at the servitude that is imposed upon them and only want power to inflict the most cruel retribution upon their oppressors, but they desire only the means of subsistence, and temporary gratification in this country, during their abode here.[81]

Ball thought that this disposition came from the Africans' religion, which told them that in death they would go back to their country, where they would be provided with plenty of food and beautiful women. This depiction resembles heaven as described in the Koran: a place where the true believer is fed the best fruit and is accompanied by pure women in a landscape of flowing rivers and beautiful gardens. Though Ball's description of the Africans' disposition may be general, it applies to the letter to the Muslims. They were unquestionably indignant at being made the slaves of Christians, and they were indeed sober and austere as far as their earthly needs were concerned. Feelings of contempt and a lack of envy for what they would have perceived as the degenerate, heathen way of life of the Christian masters are wholly consistent with the Muslims' mentality.

The coldness of the Muslims to the whites was noted by a white woman from the United States, who observed them in Rio: "They do not seem to me so affable and responsive as the Congo negroes," she stated, "but are on the contrary, rather haughty. One morning I came upon a cluster of them in the market breakfasting after their work was done, and I stopped to talk with them, asking what they had for breakfast, and trying various subjects on which to open an acquaintance. But they looked at me coldly and suspiciously, barely answering my questions, and were evidently relieved when I walked away."[82]

Some Muslims looked down on the whites as Christians. Their line of thought and attitude are exemplified in an anecdote relayed by the French count Francis de Castelnau, who was stationed in Bahia in the middle of the nineteenth century. He had employed an old man, Mohammad-Abdullah, a Pulo from Nigeria who had liberated himself and become a carpenter. The man, who had been a *marabout* and gone to Mecca, was, according to the consul, "very intolerant, very fanatical, he tries by every means to convert me; and though I received him as well as possible and gave him money, etc., he refuses to come back, and told another Negro that he does not want to go to a Christian dog's house."[83] This sort of expression of contempt had come a long way, both in time and in space. A lieutenant in the English navy had recounted in a letter in 1788 how the Mandingo of Sierra Leone "vilify those Europeans who reside among them, and whom they frequently see drinking and rioting with the appellation of dog" which is an impure animal in Islam.[84]

Ibrahima abd al Rahman, who was a deeply religious man but also a pragmatist and a moderate, held similar, if not quite as strongly worded, views of the Christians: "I tell you, the [New] Testament very good law; you [Christians] no follow it; you no pray often enough; you greedy after money. . . . [If] you good man, you join the religion. [But] you want more land, more neegurs; you make neegur work hard, make more cotton. Where do you find dat in your law?"[85]

Other Muslims shared the same opinion and let it be known. the Senegalese *emir* Samba Makumba of Trinidad remarked that

> it was safe to judge people by their actions, and when he saw the Christians holding those of their own faith in slavery, engaging in wars with members of their own church, and addicted to habits of intemperance, all of which the Koran forbids, he thought it was sufficient evidence that the religion of Mahomet was superior to the religion of *Anna Bissa* (Jesus Christ).[86]

Four Mandingo, who sent a long letter to Magistrate Richard Madden in Kingston, Jamaica, on October 2, 1834, pronounced the same condemnation on the Christians for their cruelty and hypocrisy. They expressed their view about the different religions—or rather, about those who professed them—and made clear that their "nation of Mandingo" did not condemn any "book towards the Almighty," as did all the other nations, but they did "not agree with the readers of them."[87] They went on to explain that those who oppressed the poor would go through a long and severe punishment after death, a direct reference to the fate awaiting the Christian slaveholders. The writers of this letter were William Rainsford, Benjamin Cockrane (Anna Moosa, a practicing doctor in Kingston, who asked in vain to be admitted to the college of medicine), Benjamin Larten (who wrote his own copy of the Koran), and Edward Donlan (Abu Bakr al Siddiq).

These Muslims were expressing views deeply rooted in their religion. Actually, Islam holds the Bible, the Torah, Judaism, and Christianity in high esteem but affirms that the Jews and the Christians do not follow their holy books. The Koran says, "If only the People of the Book had believed and been righteous. . . . If only they had stood fast by the Torah and the Gospel, and all the revelation that was sent to them from their Lord, they would have eaten both from above them and from below their feet" (5:65–66).

Besides what their religion had taught them about the Christians, the Muslims could pass their own judgments based on personal observations. Ibrahima, for instance, pointed out "very forcibly the incongruities in the conduct of those who profess to be the disciples of the immaculate Son of God."[88] The Africans had experienced or witnessed forced conversion as a justification for slavery, whereas in their religion, conversion was a means of emancipation. They were in daily contact with religious men and women who were nevertheless sadistically brutal. The debauchery of Christian men who sexually exploited powerless women could not have escaped them. As slaves, they had experienced the Christians at their utter worst. Because they did not have a race or class consciousness, they saw the Americans primarily not as whites or as slaveholders but rather as Christians.

Ironically, these same Christians often expressed a certain consideration for the African Muslims, claiming they were "superior" to the non-Muslim slaves. As late as 1953, William Caruthers' biographer Curtis Carroll Davis said that the Muslims "were generally of far superior intelligence to the ordinary darkey, by whom they were held in much awe and over whom, accordingly, they were often placed as drivers."[89] The myth of the Muslims' superiority had started to develop almost two centuries earlier and had taken many forms over the years. Sir Charles Lyell, for instance, who traveled through the United States in the mid-1800s, emphasized the parallel he saw between intelligence and "white looks" as sported by the Muslims. On Saint Simons Island, he had met Salih Bilali and his children and mentioned that they were of superior intelligence and had "countenances of a more European cast than those of ordinary negroes."[90] Bilali, or Tom, had, according to the Englishman, a "higher cast of feature."

A British planter who, as a medical doctor in 1811, wrote a manual on the slaves' health for the planters of the sugar colonies made a foray into this pseudo–religious anthropology. He emphasized that among the slaves he was familiar with, "the negroes from Senegal are a handsome race of people, in features resembling the whites, and with bodies tall and well limbed. Many of them converse in the Arabic language, and some are sufficiently instructed even to write it."[91] In the same vein, Richard Madden stressed that "the Mandingos are said to be superior in intelligence to the other classes. Many of them read and write Arabic."[92] According to both authors, these particular Africans were physically and intellectually superior to the others, as was confirmed by their ability to speak and write Arabic. The colonists unmistakably made a correlation between the degree of intelligence of the Africans and their knowledge of Arabic.

British naturalist George Gardner, who traveled in Brazil from 1836 to 1841, gave another illustration of this bias. His opinion was that the enslaved men and women

> from the Northern parts of Africa are by far the finest races. . . . Both the men and women are not only taller and more handsomely formed than those from Mozambique, Benguela and the other parts of Africa but have

a much greater share of mental energy, arising perhaps from their near relationship to the Moor and the Arab. Among them there are many who both read and write Arabic.[93]

The view here is slightly different. Whereas in the medical doctor's and Madden's minds, the superior Africans were those capable of reading and writing Arabic, for Gardner the same Africans owed their greater mental capacities to the Arabs' influence.

Another step was taken by some whites who transformed the African Muslims into Moors or Arabs. Ibrahima abd al Rahman, for example, because of his regal behavior, honesty, dignity, and intellectual skills (he could speak five languages and write in Arabic), was said to be a Moor. In a series titled "Prince, the Moor," southern journalist Cyrus Griffin, extolling the virtues and accomplishments of the Pulo "Prince," made an amazingly strenuous effort to assure his readers that the noble man was not an African:

> Prince is a Moor. Of this, however, his present appearance suggests a doubt. The objection is that "*he is too dark for a Moor and his hair is short and curly.*" It is true such is his present appearance; but it was materially different on his arrival in this country. His hair was at that time soft and very long, to a degree that precludes the possibility of his being a negro. His complexion, too, has undergone a change. Although modern physiology does not allow color to be a necessary effect of climate, still one fact is certain that a constant exposure to a verticle sun for many years, together with the privations incident to the lower order of community, and an inattention to cleanliness, will produce a very material change in the complexion. It is true his lips are thicker than are usually, those of the Moor; but the animal frame is not that of the negro; his eyes, and, in fact, his entire physiognomy is unlike that of any negro we have ever seen. And if the facial angle be an infallible criterion the point is established, his being equal and perhaps greater, than most of the whites.[94]

The demonstration is more than forced. Clearly, it was of great importance to deny any trace of Africanness to the "outstanding" slaves. In a similar manner, Omar ibn Said became an Arab: "He is an Arab by birth," wrote a journalist for the *Providence Journal* in 1846, "of royal blood."[95] In the *Wilmington Chronicle* of January 22, 1847, he is rightly presented as a Pulo but, according to the writer, "the Foulahs, or Falatas, are known as descendants of the Arabian Mahomedans who migrated to Western Africa in the seventh century. They carried with them the literature of Arabia, as well as the religion of their great Prophet, and have ever retained both. The Foulahs stand in the scale of civilization at the head of all the African tribes."[96]

Bilali of Sapelo was also reputed to be an Arab. Joel Chandler Harris, using what he had understood of Bilali's story, transformed him into "an Arab—man of the desert—slave hunter" in his novel *The Story of Aaron (So Named) the Son of Ben Ali*. Such confusions could reach ridiculous proportions: the members of a Muslim family who had lived in Sumter County, South Carolina, since the Revolutionary War were alternately reputed to be "Turks," "Free Moors," "nobles of the Delhi Court," and "subjects of the Emperor of Morocco." Then, in a complete turnabout, they were labeled "free blacks" in 1830; but another shift in perception enabled them to serve in white regiments during the Civil War.[97]

Muslims who distinguished themselves and were literate were thus presented as superior to the rest of the slaves on the basis their racial origin was different. It was more acceptable to deny any Africanness to the distinguished Muslims than to recognize that a "true" African could be intelligent and cultured but enslaved nevertheless. So, gradually, the African Muslims were seen as owing their perceived superiority not to their own "genes," not even to their culture or proximity to the Arab world, but to foreign "blood." Because he was not a true African, the Muslim could be trusted and put in charge of controlling the bondmen. As an almost-white, as an Arab, he was supposed to feel contemptuous of the blacks and be loyal to the whites.

The story of S'Quash is a perfect example of this mode of reasoning. This African man was shipped to Charleston, South Carolina, at the close of the North American trans-Atlantic slave trade, which took place officially on January 1, 1808. Though he was "extremely dark," he was said to be "obviously" not a Negro. He could read and write Arabic and Greek and had been to Cairo. The narrator of his story insisted that S'Quash was an Arab slave trader caught up in the last-minute scramble for slaves. Once in America, he immediately chose sides and "threw his lot with the ruling class."[98] The other slaves showed great respect for him, but he refused to live with them. As he was so different from and, racially and culturally, "superior" to the slave populace, he became the overseer of the plantation. S'Quash had refused to mate with the local women but asked to marry a "Dinka" whom, according to the writer, in his "subtle Arabic caste system," he deemed worthy of his favors. These assertions do not make sense. For one thing, the Dinka, from southern

Sudan, were not represented in the Atlantic slave trade. In addition, they were animists and constituted a traditional reservoir of slaves for the Arabs. In all probability S'Quash asked to marry a particular Mandinka (Mandingo in Mande) woman because, like him, she was a Muslim. His staying on his own was likely due to his being among non-Muslims or people from different cultural areas. What the whites chose to see, however, through their own ethnocentrist and racist lenses, was that he felt uncomfortable being surrounded by "inferior blacks."

Because the American system of racial classification did not recognize intermediate strata—the mulattos, for example—as the Latin system did, there could only be inferior blacks and superior whites. Within these limits, a particularly "intelligent black" had to stop being black and become an ersatz white. He could be one solely by becoming an African white, that is, an Arab. The only Africans who could qualify for this co-optation were the Muslims, as their religion and their literacy in Arabic could be touted as tangible proofs of their Arab origin. With the whitening of the "elite" slaves, the basis on which slavery rested was not threatened. Blacks were still subhumans and thus fit to be enslaved, whereas the Moorish princes, warriors, and fellow slave traders could elevate themselves to the highest positions within the boundaries of the rigid slave society.

Few negative comments on the Muslims have been recorded, and those that exist almost exclusively deal with their rebelliousness rather than with any supposed inferiority. The exceptions come from two renowned French scholars. In an amazing display of gross ignorance, Roger Bastide, the internationally recognized expert on African American religions, stated in 1961, that the Brazilian Muslims were "'passive' Moslems, i.e. Islamized blacks, converts, not pure Semites"[99]—as if the Semites were genetically Muslims and had never converted. Another scholar, Father Etienne Ignace, a professor at the Seminary of Bahia, had a low opinion of the Muslims he met at the turn of the century: "With their thick intellect full of nonsense, the Malês are swollen with a stupid pride. They are full of hate for the Whites and the Christians. Their ignorance is 'crass and supine,' they cling with fanaticism to bland and exterior practices."[100]

Overall, however, few discordant voices emerge concerning the Muslims, and the racist view according to which they were superior to the other Africans has had a long life span. Writing in 1933, Gilberto Freyre, the renowned Brazilian scholar, repeated the same racial fantasies. Fulani, Hausa, and Mandingo had, he maintained, Hamitic, Arabic, Tuareg, or Berber "blood," a widely held view at the time. He went on to draw a comparison between blacks in the United States and in Brazil, stating that the former were of a lesser stock because there had not been as many Muslims enslaved in North America as in Brazil. The African Muslims were superior not only to Southern blacks but also to almost anybody else: "The Mohammedan Negroes brought to Brazil from that African area which had been most deeply penetrated by Islamism were culturally superior not only to the natives, but to the great majority of the white colonists—Portuguese and the sons of Portuguese, with almost no education, some of them illiterate, most of them semi-literate."[101] Though he stressed culture, Freyre nevertheless attributed the superiority he detected in the Muslims to their mixed origin.

The most unexpected positive comments about the Muslims come from Joseph Arthur de Gobineau, the French writer and diplomat, who was stationed in Rio in 1869–1870. Count de Gobineau, a staunch anti-Semite and "scientific" racist, is the author of the infamous *On the Inequality of the Human Races* (1855), in which he theorized on the inferiority of the Latin races and the superiority of the Nordics. Gobineau's racial discourse gave rise to the concept of Aryan superiority in 1894. Adolf Hitler and his cohorts used his theories—they founded the Gobineau *Vereinigung,* or Gobineau Association—to ground theirs scientifically.

About the blacks he saw in Brazil, the count had, understandably, nothing good to say. Their "naive depravation" was total and, further, influenced their masters, to the degree that slavery was "more harmful to the slaveholders than to the slaves themselves."[102] But there was one notable exception, he stressed in a dispatch to the minister of foreign affairs in Paris: "There is nevertheless a certain category of blacks mostly settled in Bahia and its surroundings that stand out in a remarkable way from the rest of the individuals of the same race." These men and women were, according to the count, taller, more robust, and more intelligent than the other Africans. They were also considered obstinate, disobedient, and capable of resistance. After a whole page devoted to the Muslims' solidarity, frugality, devotion to their religion, and striving for literacy, Gobineau concluded by stressing that "the existence of a Muslim colony in America has never been noticed, as far as I know and though it is not necessary to mention it in this dispatch, I hope that your Excellency will forgive me this digression because of the singularity it reveals. In fact, it explains the particularly energetic attitude of the Mina negroes."[103] Gobineau was certainly impressed and, in contrast to other pseudoethnologists or pseudoanthropologists, did not attribute what he thought was a superior trait to "mixed blood" or Arabic culture. In his view of the world as being divided between superior and inferior races, Gobineau probably envisioned the Muslims as being the Aryans of Africa.

Rising in the Ranks of the Wider Slave Community

The reasoning behind the commentators' conclusions about the Muslims was definitely flawed, but their opinions may have had some connections to reality. Muslims seem to have distinguished themselves among the rest of the slave population more frequently than their numbers alone could have warranted. There is some indication that the Muslims succeeded in the slave structure, that they were promoted and trusted in a particular way. Both Bilali and Salih Bilali, for example, were slave drivers. As such, their tasks were to carry out the overseer's instructions to the slaves, organize the work gangs, and act as intermediaries between whites and blacks. The position was the highest a slave could reach. That the two men did very well in their capacity and were highly trusted by their owners and respected by their companions is attested by visitors to the plantations where they worked.

Other Muslims also did well. Captain Conneau described Cuban slaves in authority in these terms: "A Black postillon in his red jacket and silver spurs alights from a prancing horse and in the language of their mothers bids [the arriving slaves] welcome and in the name of Allah blesses their safe arrival."[104] There was an Ismael who became the driver of the East Hermitage Plantation on Argyle Island, Georgia.[105] Another Ismael was "the best driver I ever knew," acknowledged his Louisiana owner, Thomas Butler.[106] Bob, called "the Mahometan," was promoted to driver of the Brothers Plantation in Demerara, Guyana.[107] S'Quash was an overseer and Samba Makumba the superintendent of his master's plantation in Trinidad. All these men were Africans and worked in positions that were usually held by native-borns, who were more cognizant of the slave system, the rules and regulations of the plantation world, and the language. To get these jobs, the African Muslims certainly showed particular qualities that enabled them to climb quickly up the social ladder of the plantations.

There are records of other trusted Muslims. Among them were Abu

Bakr al Siddiq, who kept his owner's books in Arabic; Ibrahima abd al Rahman; and Omar ibn Said, the latter two also highly regarded by their owners. For the first two men, the trusted position they held proved to be a disadvantage when they sought to obtain their freedom. Because they were extremely valuable, their owners for a long time refused to sell them.

Depending on the individual, various reasons may have pushed some Muslims to look for better positions within the slave structure. As intellectuals not used to hard, manual work, some may have sought to escape the intensive and brutal labor of the fields. Some had been leaders, rulers, or they came from aristocratic families. They were militaristic to begin with and had spent their earlier lives at the heads of armies, organizing men, and giving orders. Many had had slaves themselves and were used to directing them. Those who formerly had been teachers and spiritual leaders had also been in charge of free and enslaved men, in schools and on the battlefields. As discussed in chapter 1, Muslims came from advanced, highly organized, stratified, and diversified societies. Many were thoroughly urban and had traveled in their subregion and beyond as traders, Koranic students, teachers, or pilgrims. They were adaptable, cosmopolitan, well-traveled men. They were used to dealing with diverse peoples and different cultures, and they belonged to populations fluent in at least two or three languages. All these skills must have proved valuable in the plantation world, where men and women had to interact with peoples from different origins and backgrounds.

Besides, the Islamic education had molded the Africans. They were frugal, ascetic people. Their discreet and devout lifestyle may have indicated to their companions that life under a Muslim driver would be less brutal than life under somebody else. This, in turn, may have prompted the other slaves to cooperate more readily with their supervisors. Slave owners, for their part, may have utilized the men's known frugality, seriousness, and honesty for their own benefit.

There is ample evidence that the Muslims actively used their cultural and social background and the formation they had received in Africa as tools to improve their condition in the Americas. It is one more example of the direct impact that the personal stories of the Africans had on the development of a particular African American identity and culture.

Muslim Associations and Attainment of Freedom

There is no question that the bulk of the African Muslims remained enslaved. Even some famous ones, such as Bilali, Salih Bilali, and Omar ibn Said, spent their entire lives in servitude. But other renowned Muslims gained their freedom, such as Job ben Solomon, Yarrow Mahmout, Ibrahima abd al Rahman, Abu Bakr al Siddiq, Lamine Kebe, John Mohamed Bath, Samba Makumba, Mohamed Ali ben Said, Mohamad-Abdullah, and Mahomma Gardo Baquaqua. Just as there seems to have been an unusual proportion of professionals among the Muslims, there are indications that they were often quite successful in gaining their freedom.

Decades before Emancipation, Trinidad had a free Muslim community, mostly made up of Mandingo, who stressed in various documents that no more Mandingo slaves were present in Trinidad. The early arrivals, such as the Senegalese Samba Makumba, had managed to buy their freedom by using their particular skills and their frugality to earn and save money. They then founded an association whose objective was "to maintain their religious profession, Samba acting as their priest."[108] Their next step was to buy land, build houses, and make a living through agriculture and petty trading. Once their means of subsistence had been secured, they raised funds to redeem the Mandingo who were still enslaved. According to Makumba, association members would be the first on board when a slaver landed and would redeem the Mandingo. In turn, the newly freed men had to work and pay their dues to the group in order for another Mandingo to be released from bondage. Samba Makumba stated that the society redeemed five hundred Mandingo in Trinidad and extended its operations to other islands.[109] There is no corroboration of this amazing revelation, but if Makumba's claim is legitimate—and there is no reason to doubt him—it reveals an extraordinary degree of organization on the part of the Muslims and provides another illustration of the efficiency of the Islamic networks.

A strong solidarity existed among the free Muslims—who, in Port of Spain had formed their own neighborhood—based not only on a common ethnic origin but also, and maybe foremost, on a shared religion. The importance of Islam as a bond was noted by Sir Andrew Halliday, who pointed out in 1837 that "they all succeeded in procuring their freedom long before the abolition of slavery, and formed a distinct society of themselves, strictly bound together by their Mahometan faith."[110]

This solidarity was exemplified in Brazil by the Mina, who pooled their resources to buy the freedom of "any one of their number who was the most respected,"[111] as recorded in the 1850s. Later, in 1869, Gobineau noted that the Mina still used the same method, not only to buy their freedom but to secure passage back to Africa as well: "Every year, they buy, in the name and with the resources I just wrote about, a certain number of their compatriots. Often they send them back to Africa."[112] Other Muslims, as well as non-Muslims, were involved in similar associations. In the aftermath of the 1835 Bahian rebellion, it was discovered that Sanim, a Nupe slave who was a religious leader, had organized what West Africans in general call a *tontine* and the Yoruba *esusu* (which became *susu*, a word still used today throughout the West Indies). A *tontine* or a *susu* is a communal fund to which each participant contributes the same sum on a weekly or monthly basis. In Sanim's fund, the fixed amount was 320 reis, which represented a slave's daily pay. The common money was used to buy Muslim garments, to pay part of the money the slaves owed their masters, and to help pay for the freedom of the members.[113] Sanim's was only one of several such associations. At the time of the rebellion, Licutan, an enslaved Nago who was also a religious leader, was in jail awaiting auction, "and it was known . . . that the others had the money ready to buy his freedom when he went on the auction block,"[114] as was mentioned by the head jailer. Twice already the Muslims had offered to pay his owner for the freedom of the old Nigerian sultan who had become a tobacco roller, but both times their offer had been rejected.

The longing for freedom was unquestionably in the heart of every slave, but Muslims may have had additional religious and cultural reasons to want their independence and to seek it actively. One may have been their abhorrence at being made the slaves of Christians, and another their desire to pursue their religion and its teachings freely. The enslaved Africans may have managed to enact their dietary rules, prayers, particular dress codes, observation of the holy days, and religious writings and readings, but it goes without saying that these were much easier to comply with when one was free.

If religion was an added incentive for enslaved men and women to get their freedom, Islam, by its very nature, could only help the believer in his or her task. The Muslims did not spend money on superfluous items such as alcohol. Due to the austerity of the Islamic appearance, they did not spend money on clothes either, except for the Islamic garb produced by their own tailors. They could count on their coreligionists' financial help when needed. Their being part of a community that emphasized frugality, stressed dedication to religion, devoted much of its free time to praying and studying, and watched its members closely represented a powerful tool in their successful pursuit of freedom or at least some degree of independence. As the sub-Saharan Africans in general and the members of the Sufi orders in particular practiced a highly communal Islam that forged close bonds among the faithful, the religion became, in the Americas, a force that enabled its followers to rely on the strength of a community to improve their individual and at times, communal lot.

The Muslims' deliberate maintenance of their cultural and religious distinctiveness, as opposed to adaptation, demonstrates that they did not stop considering themselves Africans and Muslims. They chose to keep their previous frames of reference and values, and in so doing, they made it evident that neither the white Christian world nor a creolized identity and culture appealed to them. Clearly, they were convinced that what they had left behind was not only superior but could, with strong will and organization, be replicated, within certain limits, in the Americas.

4

Literacy

A Distinction and a Danger

A large proportion of the Muslims arrived in the New World already literate, reading and writing Arabic and their own languages transcribed in the Arabic alphabet. As other Africans came from exclusively oral cultures, and as learning to read and write was either illegal or actively discouraged for all slaves in the Americas, literacy became one of the most distinguishing marks of the Muslims.

The Muslims' literacy clearly set them apart from the rest of the slaves and became as distinctive as a physical trait. A slaveholder was so impressed with his literate slave, for example, that he mentioned only this characteristic when he put a notice in the *Charleston Courier* of February 7, 1805, to advertise him as a fugitive. Thirty-year-old Sambo was a "new negro" who had absconded with another African and a native-born woman. He was, reported the owner, a man "of grave countenance who writes the Arabic language."[1] It would be interesting to know how the slaveholder came to learn about his new slave's literacy, as well as what, and under which circumstances, Sambo—a common name among Hausa—had been writing.

Illiteracy among men and women was not restricted to the slave quarters. Many male colonists and most women could neither read nor write, because literacy in European cultures was reserved for the wealthy males. The furthest some societies went was to allow the poor and women to read for religious reasons—so that the Bible could be accessible—but not to write. As a result, a large number of American colonists who came from what were considered the lower European classes were illiterate or barely literate. In the colonies themselves, education was reserved for the privileged few; the movement toward mass literacy started only in the nineteenth century. Prior to that, in Brazil for instance, "the simplest rudiments were so little diffused that not infrequently wealthy ranchers of the interior would charge their friends of the seaboard to secure for them a son-in-law who, in place of any other dower, should be able to read and write."[2]

Because the literacy rate was high in Muslim Africa, and because of a concentration of learned Muslims in America, as discussed in chapter 1, the literacy rate among Muslim slaves was in all probability higher than it was among slaveholders. As Gilberto Freyre, the Brazilian scholar, remarked, "in the slaves' sheds of Bahia in 1835, there were perhaps more persons who knew how to read and write than up above, in the Big Houses."[3]

This situation was sometimes used to the advantage of the owners, who relied on their slaves' skills. Such was the case with Abu Bakr al Siddiq's owner in Jamaica, who had him keep his property's records in Arabic. But the disparity in education of master and slave also created animosity. To some illiterate or barely literate masters, having slaves who could read and write was vexing. In that regard, Theodore Dwight, the secretary of the American Ethnological Society, observed that

> several other Africans have been known at different periods, in different parts of America, somewhat resembling Job-ben-Solomon in acquirements [e.g., of literacy and education]; but, unfortunately, no full account of any of them has ever been published. The writer has made many efforts to remedy this defect, and has obtained some information from a few individuals. But there are insuperable difficulties in the way in slave countries, arising from the jealousy of masters, and other causes.[4]

Further, Dwight mentioned that writer and ethnologist William Hodgson, who had resided in North Africa, tried to make inquiries about the literate Muslims in the American South but had to abandon the undertaking "in despair," due to the hostility of their masters.

The hostility toward the literate Africans that many slaveholders expressed did not arise from the fear that their property would somehow trick them by forging passes or getting access to useful news. Even though Brazilian slaveholders discovered that the Africans' literacy in Arabic could indeed be hazardous to their safety, the animosity described by Dwight had another origin. In the eyes of the slaveholders, the Muslims' literacy was dangerous because it represented a threat to the whites' intellectual domination and a refutation of the widely held belief that Africans were inherently inferior and incapable of intellectual pursuits. The Africans' skills constituted a proof of humanity and civilization that did not owe anything to the Christians' supposed civilizing influence. If these men and women could read and write, if they were not the blank slates or the primitive savages they had been portrayed to be in order to justify their enslavement, then the very foundation of the system had to be questioned. This issue was so potent that, as discussed in the previous chapter, North Americans felt compelled to deny the Africanness of the "outstanding" Muslims and to portray them as Arabs.

Preserving Literacy in Servitude

The Muslims had arrived in America and the Caribbean with the knowledge they had patiently acquired when, sitting cross-legged around a bonfire, their wooden tablets on their knees, they traced day after day the letters and the words that form the Koran. Children fresh from their first year in school, teachers, *ulama*, cultured *marabouts*—the slave trade did not spare anyone. Some Muslims could write perfect Arabic as well as Hausa, Wolof, or Mandingo. Others had been stopped in their tracks and possessed only a few rudiments of the written word and a clumsy calligraphy. There were many degrees of knowledge among the Africans brought to the New World, and since no universal definition of literacy exists, the one used throughout this study is the basic knowledge of reading and writing. Whatever the level of their reading and writing skills, the Africans had to face the problem of how to preserve them. Without books, schools, teachers, paper, pens, and ink, it is particularly difficult to keep one's ability to read and write.

George Renouard, the priest who translated the autobiography of Abu Bakr al Siddiq, noted how much their new environment was detrimental to the preservation of the Muslims' knowledge. He understood how difficult it was for them to acquire the tools they needed to retain their literacy. Abu Bakr, he stated,

> could scarcely have completed his fifteenth year when taken away from Africa; was two years in the West Indies before he could obtain the use of pen, ink and paper; and with the exception of two or three negroes—one fortunately on board the slaver which carried him off,—had no means of reviving his remembrance of what he had learned, till a very late period.[5]

Nevertheless, Abu Bakr preserved his literacy and used it to improve his situation. Magistrate Richard Madden, who helped him gain his freedom, remarked that he had an excellent reputation, thanks to his exemplary conduct and "attainments as a scholar, which few of his country-men have ever gained, or at least preserved in slavery."[6] Madden knew that many Muslims had come literate to the New World and that the conservation of their knowledge was a difficult endeavor. The obstacles notwithstanding, he stressed, some succeeded in doing so.

For others, in contrast, the loss must have been heavy. During the trial of the Bahian Muslims in 1835, Pompeu, an emancipated African, de-clared that he had learned Arabic as a small child but that he remembered almost nothing.[7] One has to look at this testimony with some caution, for Pompeu had good reasons to distance himself from the revolt, in which writing had played a major part. But there can be no doubt that he was describing reality—perhaps not his own experience but certainly the reality of many others, the youngest in particular. If a child was kid-napped at age ten, after three years of schooling, chances are he or she would not have retained much literacy afterward. Besides those who could not preserve their literacy at all were some who managed to keep part of their skills: they could read but could no longer write. Salih Bilali, the driver of the Couper Plantation on Saint Simons Island, "reads Ara-bic, and has a Koran (which however, I have not seen) in that language but does not write it," noted his owner.[8] Salih Bilali had been kidnapped as an adolescent, and he was seventy-three when these observations were published. Young men or women who had had from five to seven years of schooling may have retained enough to be able to read, but some would have had difficulty writing.

The long years of bondage took their toll even on some Muslims who seem to have kept their knowledge intact. Omar ibn Said was very con-scious of the weakening of his abilities after twenty-four years of servi-tude. He acknowledged in his autobiography, written in Arabic in 1831, "I cannot write my life because I have forgotten much of my own lan-guage, as well as of the Arabic. . . . Neither can I write very grammati-cally or according to the true idiom."[9] He nevertheless went on to write a fifteen-page document. Omar's written production was impressive and his calligraphy excellent. Deported at age thirty-seven, he had had time to sharpen and deepen his knowledge in Senegal. Yet, as he deplored, a large part of what he had known had been lost.

It is impossible to assess the degree of success the Muslim men and women had in preserving their literacy, and it is likely that the youngest and the most isolated were those who endured the heaviest losses. When even a small group of Muslims came together they could help one another, refresh one another's memories by passing along a Koran or a Bible in Arabic when they were available. The isolated Muslim, in contrast, could count only on himself or herself, his or her own memories, and if the education had not been very good to begin with, the loss must have been irremediable.

The methods the Africans used to retain their knowledge were varied. Ibrahima abd al Rahman in Mississippi followed the traditional African technique: he traced the letters on the sand of his master's cotton plantation when the field hands were given a break.[10] One can suppose that this method was the most widely used because it did not require any particular tool. The non-Muslim slaves who were learning how to read and write European languages in secret also utilized the technique.[11] They may actually have borrowed the method from the Muslims. This process represented the first level in the preservation of one's literacy. In Africa, children were taught to trace their letters on the sand in the absence of paper or slates, but adults usually used paper. It was thus a singular regression for a man such as Ibrahima, the son of a religious and political ruler and a learned man himself. It must have been a frustrating exercise for him and for the other adults who had to content themselves with the sand of the plantations.

For Ibrahima, however, the dedication worked. After thirty-two years of servitude he could still write, and when shown some Arabic writings, he copied them "in a very neat and handsome style, producing a facsimile; he also rendered it in English."[12] Ibrahima had been deported at twenty-six, an age when he had already been able to master Arabic quite well.

Sand writing was in all likelihood the most widespread technique used to preserve one's literacy, but there were other, more elaborate methods. Muslims from Bornu who had been deported to the Artibonite region in Saint-Domingue made their own writing implements, as they had done in Africa. A French contemporary described them using sticks of mimosa boiled in lemon juice, "bamboo feathers," wood tablets, and parts of palm trees.[13]

Much further up the scale, the Muslims who had succeeded in gaining the sympathy of the whites could see a whole world of opportunity opening up to them for the preservation of their knowledge. References exist in nineteenth-century documents to Bibles in Arabic that the Christians gave to the Muslims, and some have been preserved. The Christians were certainly motivated by the urge to make the zealots of the "false prophet" discover the beauty of the Holy Book and of Christianity, but for the Muslims, any book was probably heaven-sent. Contrary to appearances, the fact that Muslims read the Bible was not usually an indication that they were on their way to conversion. Ibrahima, Abu Bakr, and Omar ibn Said, for example, had Bibles in Arabic, but none of these men converted truthfully; all, however, benefited from their apparent willingness to conform to their owners' religion, and they were treated with leniency.

Reading the Bible could also present a real intellectual and religious interest to the Muslims and be a true comfort, for it enabled them to go back to a spiritual world they had devoted many years of their free lives to study. They all knew the characters and stories of the Holy Book, since the Koran speaks abundantly of the Old and New Testaments. In addition, some had already read and studied Christian texts in Africa, as confirmed by Mungo Park for Senegambia, where he had seen manuscripts of "an Arabic version of the Pentateuch of Moses, which they call *Taureta la Moosa*. This is so highly esteemed, that it is often sold for the value of one prime slave. They have likewise a version of the Psalms of David (*Zabora Dawidi*); and lastly, the book of Isaiah, which they call *Lingeeli la Isa* [it is, rather, the "New Testament of Jesus"], and it is in very high esteem."[14] Ibrahima abd al Rahman had read some of these very books prior to his deportation from Guinea, as he confided to his friend Andrew Marshalk, who asked Secretary of State Henry Clay to procure a New Testament in Arabic for the prince.[15]

Besides the intellectual interest, the Muslims may have had another reason to be eager to receive Bibles in Arabic: to have them was the most efficient way—when Korans were not available—of preserving their literacy. The Muslims were looking for an opportunity to maintain important skills, not to exchange their religion for another. The three reasons— owners' indulgence, spiritual interest, maintenance of literacy—that could induce Muslims to read the Bible in Arabic were probably intimately linked, but one cannot exclude the possibility that for some, the preservation of their ability to read was the main objective.

Islamic Books and Koranic Schools in Christian Lands

If the Muslims actively sought Bibles in Arabic, one can assume that Korans were much more prized. As mentioned in chapter 1, the Koran is essential to the Muslim, who cannot turn to a member of clergy or to saints for comfort, inspiration, and assistance and who has to live, pray, eat, wash, and generally function according to rules enunciated in the book. The Koran is truly indispensable to the Muslim, and therefore, one can expect that the Africans attempted to get hold of the Holy Book even in slavery. The recorded presence of Korans in Arabic in the hands of slaves on the plantations of Georgia, Trinidad, Brazil, and Jamaica might seem the result of extraordinary chance, but in reality, it was the product of thorough planning. Korans were likely available elsewhere too, and documentation confirming their presence may still be found in other parts of the Americas. Wherever these books eventually found their way, the question of their origin is an intriguing one.

A decisive answer can be provided in few cases. Only two sources have been identified, and these because they were mentioned in the writings of contemporary European Americans. The first recorded source of Korans, as surprising as it may seem, was sympathetic Christians. Just as some gave Bibles in Arabic to the Muslims, others offered them Korans. Omar ibn Said's pastor, who mentioned that "through the kindness of some friends, an English translation of the Koran was procured for him, and read to him,"[16] confirmed this interesting fact. Omar seems to have had two Korans; the secretary of the American Colonization Society reported in 1837 that the old Senegalese had "retained a devoted attachment to the faith of his fathers and deemed a copy of the Koran in Arabic (which language he reads and writes with facility) his richest treasure."[17] It is likely that the same people procured both copies to him.

In the same manner, Abu Bakr al Siddiq asked missionaries who had already procured him a Bible to send him a Koran.[18] The readiness on the part of some Christians to help slaves sustain their own religion is an indication of the high esteem in which they regarded the Muslims. As was discussed in chapter 3, this regard most likely stemmed from their perception of the "Mohammedans" as Arabs instead of Africans. Whatever the case may have been, it had a positive outcome for the Muslims who benefited from their goodwill.

On a much larger scale, Muslims were able to obtain Korans through their own resourcefulness. How they achieved this feat has been explained by Count de Gobineau. He observed that the Koran was

> sold in Rio by the French booksellers Fauchon and Dupont, who import copies from Europe, and sell them 15 to 25 millereis, or 36 to 40 francs. Slaves who are evidently very poor are willing to make the greatest sacrifices to acquire this volume. They go into debt to do so and sometimes take

a year to pay off the bookseller. About a hundred copies of the Koran are sold every year.[19]

It is very doubtful that French booksellers in Brazil routinely had Korans in Arabic in their inventories. The Muslims must have informed them of the demand. Gobineau's information gives an idea of the degree of devotion of the slaves, who possessed nothing but devoted their meager savings to the acquisition of the Koran and their free time to its reading. It also gives an idea of the degree of their erudition, since only those Muslims with good knowledge of the written language could read the book. If one hundred slaves every year could buy themselves a Koran after much sacrifice, it is very likely that hundreds of others succeeded only after many more years, and that even greater numbers never did. There were probably thousands of highly literate, devout, practicing Muslims in the city.

For other communities, the chain of events that led to the presence of Korans on the plantations is not documented. Korans were available in Trinidad, but their origin is unknown. There a Protestant missionary reported that a Mandingo "priest" gave away to North American blacks scraps of prayers he had copied from the Koran. The recipients of these copies were former slaves who had fought in the Corps of Colonial Marines against the Americans in the War of 1812 and who had been settled by the British on the island after their defeat. According to the missionary, they had "relapsed into Mohammedanism." These free blacks, close to five hundred, lived "in forests hitherto untrodden by civilized men,"[20] yet a *marabout* among them had a Koran in Arabic. No mention was made of its provenance, as if the fact did not deserve an explanation.

On the same island, the attorney general accepted affidavits from Muslims who had sworn their oaths on the Koran.[21] It was a recognized practice, and again, apparently, no question was raised as to the origin of the books. The same lack of curiosity can be observed in the writings of James Hamilton Couper, Salih Bilali's owner, who mentioned that the elderly Malian had a Koran without expressing any surprise or saying anything concerning its origin. He was not the source of this gift, however, since he also noted that he never saw it.[22] Years later, former slave Ben Sullivan remembered having seen a Muslim, "ole man Israel," praying with a book "wut he hide."[23] Salih Bilali's friend Bilali, of Sapelo Island, was buried with his copy of the Koran, but his descendants and his owner have given no indication of where it came from.[24]

It thus appears that Korans in Arabic were taken for granted, by both blacks and whites, on the remote islands off the Georgia coast, in Trinidad, and in Brazil. If the presence of these books was not surprising then, it certainly is now. In the absence of recorded evidence about how these Korans came into the Muslim slaves' hands, a hypothesis can be proposed.

Slaves and freedmen may have organized themselves to acquire Korans not only from Europe, as they did in Brazil, but from Africa as well. During the nineteenth century, Bahia had developed an important trans-Atlantic commerce with West Africa; in addition to the Portuguese and Brazilian (white and mulatto) traders living on the African coast who dealt in slaves and agricultural products to be sent to the Americas, native African traders exported their goods to Brazil. Concerning the Muslims specifically, Sir Harry Johnston, who got information from the British consuls in West Africa, reported that Mandingo and Fulani who had returned to Africa after having bought their freedom traded with Brazil.[25] After the abolition of slavery in 1888, these traders traveled back and forth on Brazilian ships. The ex-slaves' exports included many types of goods. Some, such as African soap, kola nuts, shea butter, palm oil, cowries, and fabrics, were used by the Africans in general; but only the Muslims bought the Islamic chaplets and the ink made in Africa. The *aliwa*, or wooden tablets, used in the Brazilian Koranic schools likely came from the African coast as well. These Mandingo and Fulani may well have supplied their coreligionists with Korans. An interesting clue could confirm this hypothesis. The last orthodox Muslim of Bahia, Djibirilu, whose father was a Yoruba *marabout*, had a Koran in Arabic imported from Nigeria, which is kept at the University of Bahia.[26]

The type of trade that existed between Bahia and the Gulf of Benin has not been recorded for other regions in the Americas, but documents and other items made their way from Africa to various parts of the New World. At least one letter in Arabic traveled from Africa to Jamaica. (See chapter 2.) "Inflammatory pamphlets" were brought from Sierra Leone to Charleston, South Carolina, in the years before the 1822 uprising led by African-born Denmark Vesey, as reported by the magistrates who prosecuted the insurgents.[27] A "remarkable scrap of paper from Africa concerning the return of a woman slave, *signed in Arabic*,"[28] was discovered by the historian Peter Wood in papers held at the South Carolina Library at the University of South Carolina, Columbia. Also in the United States, it has been established that the paper which Bilali of Sapelo

Island, Georgia, used to write a manuscript in Arabic, was produced in Italy for the African Islamic market.[29] This paper traveled all the way from Africa to a remote American island. As it has been ascertained that the Africans arrived in the New World empty-handed, it is clear that whatever they got from Africa came after they had settled in the Americas and the Caribbean. There may have been a good reason for U.S. slaves to import paper from Africa secretly: it was illegal in some states for them to write, and to buy paper could only have led to suspicion. Smuggled paper, in contrast, would have gone unnoticed.

There is ample evidence that Africans enslaved in the Americas and those free in Africa maintained a certain degree of contact. Newly arrived Africans kept their companions abreast of events and shared local and familial news; enslaved and freed people sent news to their loved ones through the returnees; returnees, in turn, maintained contact with those they had left behind. The Africans in the Americas and in Africa were truly part of the Atlantic world.

Besides these direct connections, black sailors linked Africans on both sides of the Atlantic. Enslaved and free black men were routinely employed on ships throughout the Americas and the Caribbean, including on slave ships. Roughly 9 percent of skilled slaves in South Carolina were sailors, as were tens of thousands of West Indian men.[30] A large proportion of these sailors were born in Africa. The mariners sailed from island to island, from the islands to the mainland, from the North of the United States to the South, and across the Atlantic to Europe and Africa. In addition to the slaves and free men employed on the ships in various capacities, free African sailors went back and forth between their homeland and the Americas as members of the crews of slavers and cargo ships. These black men—free, freed, and enslaved—crisscrossed the Atlantic bringing news, information, and ideas of a larger world. They harbored and transported fugitives and smuggled goods. They also carried dangerous mail, as the cook William did when he agreed to remit a letter addressed by Denmark Vesey to the president of Haiti, asking the president's assistance for Vesey's planned rebellion.[31]

Some books, Korans, and other religious items found in different areas of the Americas were certainly transported and passed along by the black mariners who traveled to Africa and were in close contact in the Americas with a black population of stevedores, porters, boat builders, skippers, fishermen, mule drivers, blacksmiths, rope makers, carters, food vendors, mechanics, rowmen, tavern keepers and servants, coachmen, domestics, and other sailors bound for yet another destination—all of whom could distribute the goods brought from overseas, both in the city and further away in the plantation areas. This link was vital to the Muslims in Brazil and probably in the other colonies as well. It enabled them to pursue their religious life in the best way they could and helped them maintain their literacy, which was essential not only to their religion but also to more worldly causes.

Besides Africa and Europe, the Americas had a potentially large source of supply for Korans: the Muslims themselves. Benjamin Larten, a Mandingo enslaved in Jamaica, had written his own copy and showed it to Richard Madden.[32] At the end of a basic Koranic education, a student must be able to recite the Koran by rote, and the best can also write it. Larten's work, produced in the most difficult circumstances, is an extraordinary testimony of piety, an indication of the degree of education reached by the scribe, and, as if such were needed, another example of the immense waste caused by the slave trade. To accomplish such an endeavor Larten needed patience, time, and will and, more prosaically, ink and paper, which were expensive items. That he was willing and able to get these materials in such quantity points to an achievement that meant months or maybe years of savings. Benjamin Larten personified the dedicated Muslim at his best, sure of his faith and willing to go to great lengths to preserve it. Yet he, too, had to repudiate Islam publicly and state in front of Madden that he had written his Koran before he became a Christian. The Muslims' fake professions of faith must have broken their hearts.

It is likely that other Muslims did as Larten and drew on their memories to fill the void left by their removal from their traditional sources of continuing education. During his stay in England, Job ben Solomon, to the general astonishment, wrote three identical copies of the Koran, each time without ever looking at the preceding version.[33] Job was in a much better position than Larten: he was given time, paper, and ink. But his accomplishment shows that Larten's feat was not an isolated case, the work of an exceptional man. Not all Muslims were capable of producing their own Koran, but as is the case today in West Africa, many could if they had the required raw materials.

Lastly, some Korans arrived in the West Indies in the hands of free Africans after the abolition of slavery by Great Britain and France. Between 1840 and 1867, thirty-six thousand African indentured laborers were recruited by Great Britain to work on plantations that the free men and women had deserted to cultivate their own plots. Some West Africans left voluntarily, but others were recaptives, just off the slave ship, who were shipped by force from Sierra Leone. The Africans were dispatched to Grenada, Saint Lucia, Trinidad, Montserrat, Guyana, Saint Vincent, and Jamaica; others, "recruited" by the French, were sent to Guiana, Martinique, and Guadeloupe. Among these laborers were Muslim Wolof, Mandingo, Hausa, and Fulani. Their traveling conditions were hardly better than on a slave ship, but they were allowed to carry a few items with them. Religious books—including Protestant literature distributed by the missionaries—made up part of their baggage, and though few have been recovered, an old Koran brought by a grandfather was among the belongings of a Trinidadian interviewed recently.[34]

The ways in which the American and Caribbean Muslims obtained their Korans reveal not only an extremely strong attachment to their religion and willingness to preserve their intellectual skills but also an extraordinary spirit of abnegation, enterprise, and organization, in the worst possible circumstances. Their tenacity and ultimate success in their endeavor also demonstrate a large degree of autonomy, a fact that has not received enough attention from scholars of slavery. Evidence shows that despite the limits that slaveholders imposed, slaves were able, through their own resourcefulness and strong will, to develop autonomous communities. The Muslims were particularly apt at doing so. They made decisions, planned, gathered information, tried different avenues, built networks, and tested alternatives, all unbeknownst to white society; and they met with success.

In Bahia, this autonomy manifested itself in a bold way for the sustenance and sharing of Islamic education. The Africans there operated Koranic schools, as the Christians discovered after the revolt of January 1835, when the police searched their habitations. It was established that Dandara (also known as Elesbao do Carmo), an emancipated Hausa, had given classes in Arabic and conducted prayers in a tobacco shop that he owned at the Santa Barbara market. During his trial, he admitted that he was a schoolteacher in his country and that he had taught the youngsters in Bahia, "but not to do evil."[35] A native-born woman testified that Aprigio, a free African, had been writing in "strange characters" and, with others, had gathered men from their nations "to whom they taught to write with pointers dipped in ink they had in a bottle."[36] Another witness, Lieutenant Ladislau dos Santos Titara, had observed this African group, which met in Mangueira Street, and had heard that Aprigio taught others of his nation how to read. Aprigio, the freeman, was not the only teacher; slaves, too, were involved in pedagogy. Sanim, a Nupe slave whose Christian name was Luis, gave classes in the house of an emancipated Muslim, the Nago Belchior da Silva Cunha, a bricklayer. Sanim had been a teacher and a *marabout* in his country, and in addition to Nupe, he spoke Hausa and Yoruba. Carlos, a slave, testified that he did not know how to read but was learning from Dassalu, Nicobe, and Gustard, all three of whom were Nago slaves. Their real names were Mama (Mamadu?), Sule (Suleyman), and Burema (Ibrahima?). At the conclusion of his inquiry, Francisco Goncalves Martins, the police chief, stated in his report on the rebellion that many cultured men were among the rebels, some of whom gave classes.[37] These few testimonies give an idea of the significance of the Koranic schools and number of Koranic teachers who operated in Bahia at a time when the slaves' religions were illegal and people of African descent were nominally Christians.

Not only did Koranic schools exist in Bahia, but they were fully equipped. During the police searches, dozens of wooden slates were confiscated in the houses of Manuel Calafate, Dandara, Jose da Costa, Joaquim, Miguel Goncalves, and others. Besides the writing slates, the police confiscated papers written in Arabic. These have been studied and translated by different scholars,[38] but the first to decipher them was an enslaved Hausa *marabout* named Albino. He was requested to do so by the police, who thought the papers in strange characters might be subversive propaganda. Nine pieces of paper were presented to him. The fourth document, he explained, was a sort of alphabet lesson that students used to learn how to write Arabic, and the seventh was a writing lesson.[39]

Thirty of the documents seized by the police were published in Brazil in 1970.[40] They show the array of Islamic writings done by the Africans, enslaved and freed. Some were written with a perfect calligraphy and grammar and testify to the high level of knowledge attained by the Muslim intelligentsia before its deportation to Brazil. Other papers were apparently written by beginners: they copied, time and again, passages from the Koran as a way of memorizing them and exercising their writing skills.

Many documents seem poorly written, which has prompted scholars to conclude that students produced them. This interpretation may not be correct in all cases. Most *marabout*s, who have a strong grasp of Arabic, write the gris-gris, or amulets, in a deliberately unclear manner in order to preserve their secrets. When they need to write correctly and legibly, they do so. In any event, to judge the degree of erudition of somebody according to his or her handwriting is of little value.

Teachers and students of the Koranic schools had books at their disposal: "Many books were found, including works of religious instruction,"[41] stated the police chief. As mentioned earlier, it was common for West African scholars to own various manuscripts: "They have great bookes, all manuscripts of their Religion,"[42] noted a British trader traveling in the Gambia in the 1620s. Lamine Kebe, the Koranic teacher from Guinea enslaved in the American South, gave Theodore Dwight a list of thirty books, written in Sarakhole with the Arabic alphabet, that were used in the schools of his native region; and Benjamin Cockrane, a Khassonke deported to Jamaica, told Richard Robert Madden that there were plenty of books in the Mandingo country.[43] Books in Hausa, Wolof, Pulaar, Mandingo, or Vai, some of them translations from the Arabic and others original works, were available across West Africa. Even portions of the works of Plato, Aristotle, and Hippocrates could be found, as reported by West Indian missionary and scholar Edward Blyden.[44] African Muslims produced different kinds of works: genealogies, legal documents, chancery letters, miracle literature, prophecies, polemical verses, poetry, religious commentaries, mystical literature, grammar manuals, legal and theological works, legends, biographies. The array of subject matters was wide, and an African-American who resided in Sierra Leone at the turn of the century was surprised by the library of a "Black Mussulman" who had nearly 150 volumes in Arabic. Fifty of these books were "written by African (Negro) authors on law, theology, music, grammar, rhetoric and medicine."[45] So books were produced and imported and could be bought in Africa, and they made their way to Brazil, probably through the Muslim traders and sailors. Their presence in Bahia and Rio is another proof of the vitality and efficiency of the Islamic networks.

As was the case for some Korans, books were also ordered in Europe. Gobineau reported that, in Rio, the Muslims used Arabic grammars written in French, and he emphasized how he found it "singular to see an African population using a European language in order to know its sacred book."[46] For slaves to order grammar books from overseas shows a real concerted effort to maintain, deepen, and share their intellectual and religious knowledge. The Koranic teachers had adapted to their new environment with pragmatism.

The Koranic schools were not only offering classes to beginners and those with intermediate levels of education but were also forming high-level clerics. Around the beginning of the twentieth century, the novelist and scholar Joao do Rio reported that the Muslims of Rio de Janeiro sanctioned their own *alufa*. After they had successfully completed their studies—which implied that they had recited the Koran in its integrity many hundred times—the new clerics were paraded through the streets of a suburb of Rio on a horse, amid songs and dances.[47] The custom came directly and unchanged from West Africa, where, Edward Blyden recounted, "before the student is admitted to the ranks of the learned, he must pass an examination, usually lasting seven days, conducted by a Board consisting of imams and ulemas. If he is successful, he is led around the town on horseback, with instrumental music and singing."[48] More than fifty years after the legal end of the Brazilian slave trade, there was still a need for clerics who could interpret Islamic law, dispense justice according to the *sharia*, and, in their turn, form new scholars.

Koranic teaching was also alive in Lima, Peru, where "the Mandingo scholar, the traveler, the Caucasian man of Africa," observed a French traveler, revealed "forgotten and original versions of the Koran or the Bible."[49] But evidence for the existence of structured Koranic schools in other parts of the New World is lacking. Nevertheless, that literacy is essential in Islam and that there was a concentration of Muslim scholars in the Americas justifies extrapolating from the Brazilian experience and asserting that such schools were most likely operating in places where the Muslim community was large and organized enough. Some Koranic education was probably provided to neophytes or to Muslims willing to perfect their knowledge in places such as Trinidad, Saint-Domingue, and Jamaica. Where the community was not extensive, a *marabout* may have shared his knowledge with a few students in an informal setting, as is customary in Africa. In any event, the presence of Muslim schools had to be kept a secret, and only in unusual circumstances, such as the failed uprising in Bahia, would their existence have come to light.

The establishment of Koranic schools on the American continents during slavery was quite an accomplishment. On a practical level, it required the pooling of resources to buy books and other supplies. It entailed establishing networks that extended overseas into Africa and Europe. It demanded a good collaboration between slaves and freedmen, whose rooms or houses were used as classrooms. The operation of Koranic schools was a purely African phenomenon; it was the actual transposition to America of African didactic methods and supplies. But to maintain their traditions, the Africans had to create an entirely new system, defying the restrictions imposed on them by servitude in a non-Muslim environment and finding new avenues and opportunities. They had to be resourceful, strong-willed, and self-disciplined. The trade they established with the African coast for Korans, books, ink, and writing slates was a logical step in the continuity of their religious and cultural life, but the importation of Korans and grammar books from France was a highly ambitious, sophisticated, and audacious endeavor on the part of an enslaved people. The efficiency of the Islamic networks was quite remarkable. Their existence is a clear demonstration of the resilience, organizational skills, and strong will of the African Muslims who took their destiny into their own hands and exhibited a forceful determination to re-create, in the New World, the structures they had enjoyed and found useful in Africa.

Muslims were not the only enslaved men and women interested in reading and writing. Other Africans, as well as American-born men and women, tried whenever possible to acquire skills in the European languages. It is estimated that between 5 and 10 percent of the slaves in the United States were literate in English.[50] Literacy in a European language fulfilled very practical as well as psychological needs. As stated by historian of slave literacy Janet Duitsman Cornelius, "Through literacy the slave could obtain skills valuable in the white world, thereby defeating those whites who withheld the skills, and could use those skills for special privileges or to gain freedom."[51] Whether on a personal level or on a communal one, however, this type of literacy was a means of integration, even when used as a tool against the slave system. Literacy in European languages enabled the slaves to improve their situation within the context of the larger white society. What they were acquiring were tools from the white society—very often provided by slave owners—that could be used to their best advantage within that framework. Some Muslims availed themselves of these opportunities. Mohammad-Abdullah, from Kano and Bahia, for instance, could "read and write not only in his own language but also in Portuguese."[52] There were thus multilingual men in the Americas and the Caribbean who spoke African and European languages, mastered a dead language, and could read and write in two very diverse alphabets. Only a small handful of these were European American intellectuals; most were Africans, working as cotton pickers and cane cutters.

In contrast to the men and women who learned to read and write in

English, French, Spanish, or Portuguese, the Muslims who strove to maintain their literacy in Arabic did so even though it had no relation to the larger world in which they were living. A slave literate in Arabic could not forge a pass. His or her ability to read could not help access useful information. In the world of the slaveholder, the Muslims' skills seemed completely useless. In the Muslims' own world, however, they were of the utmost importance.

Upholding the Tradition of Religious Writing in the Americas

From the preserved documentation it appears that one of the main functions of writing for the Muslims was, as could be expected, the production of religious material. The Africans were involved in Koranic writings that went from simple copies of a *surah* to more elaborate manuscripts. Before he left for Africa, Ibrahima abd al Rahman—who was trying to raise funds for the purchase of his family—used to write down a few lines in Arabic as a giveaway to the curious and to benefactors. He told them it was the Lord's Prayer. It was, in reality, *Al-Fatiha*, the opening chapter of the Koran, which is recited in every prayer and on many other occasions. *Al-Fatiha* is a description of the relation of man to Allah:

> In the name of Allah, Most Gracious, Most Merciful
> Praise be to Allah The Cherisher and Sustainer of the
> Worlds: Most Gracious, Most Merciful;
>
> Master of the Day of Judgment.
> Thee do we worship, and Thine aid we seek.
> Show us the straight way,
>
> The way of those on whom thou has bestowed Thy Grace,
> Those whose (portion) is not wrath. And who go not astray.

Ibrahima was making use of his literacy in a very practical and constructive way. He was playing on the whites' fascination with a slave who could write in a foreign language in order to free his children and grandchildren. It is certainly fitting that religious writings, and *Al-Fatiha* in particular, with its verse on the seeking of God's help, enabled Ibrahima to raise some funds for the redemption of his family.

William Caruthers provided a more common illustration of the use of *Al-Fatiha* by an enslaved Muslim. In his novel *The Kentuckian in New*

York, he depicted the encounter of his principal character, Randolph, with a tall, old, bald man who, according to other blacks, knew how to write "in his own language." The man, called Charno—*marabout* in Pulaar—mentioned that he could write the last time he had tried, "which was many years previous." Randolph gave him a piece of paper and a quill, and Charno wrote *Al-Fatiha.* The author provided a translation in his book, as well as the facsimile of Charno's writing.[53] Similarly, an enslaved African originally from Timbuktu gave a written sample of Arabic to a pork trader in New Orleans in 1822. The man wrote and spoke Arabic "with apparent fluency and ease" and was asked by the trader to write the "Mahometan creed," the *shahada.*[54]

A similar scene happened some years before in Saint-Domingue. In 1791, Colonel Malenfant, a French officer who was fighting against the insurgent slaves, met an enslaved African named Tamerlan, who was bringing him a letter. He noted that the man seemed interested by the paper and asked him if he could read. The "black messenger," as the colonel called him, said he could not do so in French but could read and write in his "country's language and in that of a kind of mulattos with long hair." Tamerlan had probably described the Fulani, who in Malenfant's understanding were mulattos because many have a light complexion and straight hair. The colonel asked the man to write something down:

> He takes a feather and starts to write from right to left; his characters were very well painted and he was writing very quickly. —"What have you written? I don't know this language, I think it is Arabic; is that what you call it?—No, he said." I made him write the name of his language; I kept it for a long time; but I have forgotten it as well as the spelling. The first letter was as far as I can remember, a kind of *g* and the last one a *o.* —So, what have you written? —It's a prayer." There were more than twenty lines.[55]

Tamerlan, who had written a prayer in *ajami*—his language written with Arabic characters—was "a priest in his country . . . he wrote books . . . , the great king of Africa had chosen him to be his son's teacher." It is unfortunate that Malenfant did not remember the scribe's language and that he lost the paper altogether.

Yet another Muslim, the Hausa Arouna, wrote down "a formula" he used before eating—probably *bissimilah al rahman al rahim,* "in the name of Allah, Most Gracious, Most Merciful"—for the benefit of two British missionaries who were visiting him near Yallah's Bay, Jamaica, in

1837.[56] Other religious writings, by the Mandingo of Jamaica, were noticed by a negrophobic, proslavery British traveler: "Some of them," he wrote, "can scrawl a few rude Arabic characters, but without understanding or being able to explain much of their meaning. Probably they are scraps from the Alcoran which they have been taught by their imams, or priests."[57]

It is evident that there was much display of Arabic writing in the form of passages from the Koran on the part of the Muslims, who seem to have been eager not only to show their skills but also to take advantage of any situation that enabled them to use pen and paper. The Muslims' literacy was not a secret, and if many slaveholders disliked this fact, cultured whites seem to have taken some delight in witnessing the slaves' performance. Their patronizing attitude toward the Muslims' accomplishments was never far from the surface and it appears blatantly in a communication that William Hodgson wrote to the American Ethnological Society on October 13, 1857. The secretary presented a manuscript written by London, a Mandingo enslaved in Savannah, Georgia, "in the negro patois of English." The man had transcribed the Gospels and a book of hymns into Arabic characters. What seems to have amused Hodgson was that London did not use standard English but what is called today "Black English." The first lines have been transcribed in this manner:

> Fas chapta objon
> Inde beginnen was de wad
> ande Wad waswid Gad
> ande wad was Gad.[58]

This very original piece represents yet another effort at religious writing, although it did not relate to the Koran.

Not much writing was needed to impress outsiders, but for themselves and their companions, the Muslims—clerics in particular—were involved in much more extensive exercises. In Trinidad, one of the *marabout*s living in the North American settlement "was accustomed to communicate to his followers scraps of the Koran that he had copied."[59] These consisted of excerpts from the *surah*s and were more extensive than *Al-Fatiha*. The *marabout* had about three hundred followers to provide with his writings. In Brazil, a large number of the manuscripts seized by the police during the 1835 Bahia uprising were religious in nature. Some related directly to the Africans' situation and shed a light on their concerns right before their rebellion. One long document consists of excerpts from the Koran, from *surah*s 114, 113, 112, 111, 110, 109, 108, 107, 106, and 105, in that order.[60] These are the last ten *surah*s and deal with trust in Allah as shield and protection, with the fact that cruelty and persecution will ultimately turn against those who inflict them, with true faith and tolerance, and with the help that Allah provided to those who defended Mecca against the much more numerous and better equipped invading Abyssinians, who were Christians. All were direct references to the upcoming rebellion. In addition, *surah*s 112, 113, and 114 are frequently used in magic practices and in the making of protective amulets.

Similarly, part of what Omar ibn Said was writing in Fayetteville, North Carolina, was intimately related to his own life and fate as a Muslim and a slave. In a letter written in 1819, he stressed poignantly, "I am wanting you to know I want to be seen in a place called Africa in a place called Kaba in Bewir."[61] He also asked Allah for forgiveness in the land of the unbelievers.

Beyond the *surah*s copied from the Koran or from memory, Muslims enslaved in the Americas probably produced religious texts similar to those found in West Africa, either in Arabic or in African languages written with the Arabic alphabet. Given the quality of many of the Muslims, this would not be surprising. Surviving manuscripts of this type are rare, however. For such a document to come to light, it had to meet the interest of the whites. As can be gathered from the examples above, a simple excerpt from the Koran was usually enough to satisfy their curiosity. When a slave produced a more elaborate piece of work, to which he was attached for its significance as well as for the effort it represented, chances are he would not give it away. Like their other meager possessions, most of the Muslims' literary productions have disappeared, but some documents still exist and may yet reappear.

The well-known autobiography of Omar ibn Said has just recently been found. Omar originally sent the manuscript in 1836 to Lamine Kebe, his coreligionist, who was going back to Africa. Kebe gave it to Theodore Dwight. The document, which had been translated, commented on, and reprinted in scholarly journals, had not been seen for more than seventy years when it resurfaced in 1996 and was put up for auction. That year a document written by *Shaykh* Sanna See (Sy is a Tukulor family name), a *marabout* deported to Panama, was also recovered.

The most famous religious slave manuscript is certainly the *Ben-Ali Diary*, as it is officially recorded at the University of Georgia Library in

Atlanta. It is a thirteen-page, skin-covered manuscript in Arabic, which was given in 1931 to the now defunct Georgia State Library by the son of Francis Robert Goulding. Goulding's son stated that the Southern writer received it in 1859 from its author, Ben-Ali (most commonly called Bilali) of Sapelo Island. This date is wrong, however, since William Hodgson mentioned on October 13, 1857, that Bilali had died "recently."[62]

Joseph Greenberg, a professor at Northwestern University in 1939 who had the document deciphered, stated that Bilali had informed Goulding of the manuscript's supposed contents.[63] Goulding, in turn, communicated the slave's confidence to Joel Chandler Harris. According to this account, the piece was a record of Bilali's adventures in America. Joel Chandler Harris, who had built his fame upon his racist and paternalistic interpretation and rendition of Southern black culture, used the information in one of his novels, *The Story of Aaron (So Named), the Son of Ben-Ali*. Another source, noted Greenberg, stated that Bilali had kept the plantation records in Arabic. However, Goulding's son produced an affidavit affirming that the booklet contained Bilali's meditations. Closer to the truth, William Hodgson mentioned a few months after Bilali's death that the old man had left "various papers supposed to be rituals."[64]

As it turned out, the diary was no diary; nor was it a plantation record or a meditation pamphlet. One wonders if Bilali really told Goulding that he had written about his adventures. At the time slave narratives were flourishing, and most were adventure pieces.[65] They related the stories of slaves who had escaped from bondage. Bilali had nothing of the sort to write about, but he may have heard from Goulding that this was the norm for slaves' writings. By presenting his own manuscript as an adventure book, he may have attempted to—and succeeded in—getting the writer's attention. Whatever he told Goulding, and it is only of peripheral interest, Bilali clearly wanted his manuscript to be safely preserved, and he may have thought that by giving it to a writer he had better chances of having it saved than by passing it on to his own family.

After Goulding's son gave the manuscript to the Georgia State Library, copies were dispatched for translation to different institutions in the United States, then to England, South Africa, and finally al-Azhar University in Cairo. No translation could be made. The turning point came in 1937, when the enlightened amateur folklorist Lydia Parrish sent a copy of the manuscript to anthropologist Melville Herskovits, who forwarded it to the Department of Anthropology at Northwestern University in Illinois. Joseph Greenberg, who finally received the booklet, showed it to Hausa Muslims during a field trip in Kano, Nigeria, in 1939–1940. At the end of his stay, he stated that the enigma had been deciphered: the major portion of the document could be identified as excerpts from a "message," or *Risala*, including the title page and parts of the introduction and of chapters dealing with ablutions and the call to prayer. The said *Risala* is an Islamic legal work that was written by Ibn Abu Zayd al Qairawani in Kairouan, Tunisia, in the tenth century. It is part of the curriculum of higher Koranic studies in West Africa, which consists of courses in theology, Muhammad's sayings (the *Hadith*), law (*sharia*), philology (*lughah*), grammar (*nawh*), and jurisprudence (*fiqh*). One of the two main treaties of jurisprudence used is the *Risala* of Ibn Abu Zayd al Qairawani.

The *Ben-Ali Diary* has recently received much attention, but new readings of the manuscript have helped decipher neither its contents nor its meaning. Parts are not legible because the ink has seeped through the paper on both sides, and others are difficult to make sense of because the author apparently used a mixture of classical Arabic and Pulaar written with Arabic characters. The latest attempt at explaining the manuscript, a book so heavy on deconstructionist jargon that it is hardly intelligible, theorizes that the document was written by two persons.[66]

That the paper used by Bilali was manufactured in Italy for the Muslim market of North Africa, as noted earlier, is not the least of this work's mysteries. Bilali's manuscript remains enigmatic and opaque. But maybe more interesting than what he wrote is why he did it, and what he saw in his work that was so essential that he had to give it away to ensure its preservation. Unfortunately, those are questions that no major effort at deciphering the text will answer.

Occult Protection and Rebellion Planning

Religious writings were only one part of the Muslims' literary production. Another, very substantial element was the making of gris-gris. One early description of the object and its function was made by Richard Jobson, the British trader who traveled in the Gambia in 1623:

> The Gregories bee things of great esteeme amongst them, for the most part they are made of leather of severall fashions, wounderous neatly, they are

hollow, and within them is placed, and sowed up close, certaine writings, or spels which they receive from their Mary-buckes, whereof they conceive such a religious respect, that they do confidently beleeve no hurt can betide them, whilst these Gregories are about them.[67]

Though seen by some commentators as *kufr* (an act of unbelieving), the making of amulets is common practice in popular Islam and has been defended by such major scholars as Ibn Abu Zayd al Qairawani. It is part of the occult sciences, which include astrology, divination, geomancy, oneiromancy, theurgy, and other categories of magic. Gris-gris are based on the relationships that exist between Koranic texts, letters, stars, and numbers; therefore, the *marabout* who produces them must have a knowledge not only of the texts but also of numerology, astrology, mathematics, and astronomy. Most Islamic gris-gris consist of a folded, written piece of paper sewn in leather for preservation. The paper is sometimes sewn in cotton of a particular color, according to the *marabout*'s prescription. Elements besides the written paper may be put inside the amulet. In Africa, gris-gris are worn around the neck, arm, waist, ankle, knee; under women's headdresses; and in pockets. They are put over doors, under beds, and around a favorite animal's neck. Some are invisible: a common Muslim gris-gris, for instance, consists of a written piece of paper that the client puts into water and, after the ink has dissolved, washes with. The mixture can also be drunk. Sometimes the writing is done on a wooden slate—the type used in Koranic schools—and the water that washes away the letters is absorbed, as described by a *marabout* in nineteenth-century Bahia: "The clean [slate] had already been washed of its letters . . . , so that the water could be drunk as a *mandinga*, but after it had been written on twenty times."[68]

Muslims and non-Muslims use Islamic gris-gris. It is a tradition in West Africa for non-Muslim rulers, such as the *asantehene* in Ghana, to have a profusion of Islamic gris-gris attached to the symbols of their authority and to their clothes. An Ashanti king in the 1820s wore "a large white cotton cloth which partly covered his left shoulder, [and] was studded all over with Arabic writing in various coloured inks."[69] This practice is still customary for the Ashanti leaders. Through the power of the written word, thought to confer a unique efficiency to the amulet, Muslim clerics often exercised a strong influence on the animist or fetishist rulers. They also got rich, as an amulet-covered coat of the type used by the Ashanti chiefs of Ghana could cost as much as thirty slaves.[70] Given their extreme importance in Africa, it is not surprising that gris-gris made their way to the Americas.

Antoine Le Page du Pratz, director of the plantation of the Company of the Indies in Louisiana, acknowledged the widespread use of gris-gris. The slaves, he wrote "are very superstitious and attached to their beliefs and to trinkets that they call gris-gris; and they must not be taken from them nor can one talk about them, otherwise they would think themselves lost if these things were taken from them."[71] In Brazil, the amulets are called *bolsas de mandinga* ("Mandingo purses," because they are often carried in a leather pouch), or simply *mandingas*, and the men who make them are called *mandingueiros*. In Argentina, Uruguay, Peru, and Mexico, *mandinga* means "sorcery," as well as "rebellious." The Mandingo's occult skills are reputed in West Africa, and very rightly, a European who traveled to Senegambia to buy slaves in 1746 remarked that they were "magicians or southsayers, in which practicesis they shew wonders to these deluded people."[72] The Mandingo were among the first Muslims to be deported to the New World, where they kept their reputation intact to the degree that, although every African culture uses charms, talismans, and amulets, only the Mandingo left an indelible, linguistic mark in the domain of the occult.

Most of the amulets the slaves used were made in the Americas, but many Africans arrived with their gris-gris. Even though the Africans were shipped naked, they kept small personal ornaments such as rings, earrings, and bracelets. The presence in the Americas of Islamic gris-gris made in Africa is confirmed by the description of a freshly disembarked group of recaptives in Trinidad in the 1840s. Most of the 441 men, women, and children "had amulets very neatly sewn up in leather, suspended either round their necks or loins."[73]

One could argue, the mere fact that they had been enslaved and shipped overseas should have convinced the Africans that the Muslim gris-gris were not as protective as they believed. By extension, one might conclude that the gris-gris had no chance of even surviving in America. But this line of reasoning is not relevant in the Islamic world, where every human being has to submit to his or her fate. Enslavement was recognized as the fate of the Africans who were deported. Within the perimeter of this fate, however, some arrangements were possible. In other words, in the Americas and the Caribbean, even more than in their homeland, the Africans needed protection. They had to be protected from the whims, cruelty, and hatred of an owner or overseer. They had to make sure they would succeed in staying at large when they ran away. They had to protect their families against sale, separation, humiliation, punishment, and the envy or bad intentions of other slaves. They had to ward off diseases and brutal death at the hands of the slave owners or during revolts. The enslaved men and women also used the power of the gris-gris against their enemies: slave owners, slave dealers, overseers, and slave drivers. Native slaves actively sought the assistance of the Africans when they needed a gris-gris, as in the case of Francisco, second overseer of an indigo plantation on the German Coast in Louisiana, who asked Carlos, a Mandingo from "Guinea," to give him a gris-gris with which to kill the first overseer. Francisco and Carlos were tried on June 12, 1773, in New Orleans; Carlos died in jail.[74]

Gris-gris to protect oneself and to defeat the enemy seem to have been widely used by the insurgent slaves of Saint-Domingue, as a French colonel who fought them recalled:

> During the wars I was obliged to do against the blacks, we often found written papers in the bags or *macoutes* of the few negroes we killed. The patriots used to yell, when the soldiers brought those papers: *see, this is the Aristocrats' correspondence.* Those writings were understood by nobody. It was Arabic.[75]

The papers were likely protections against death, and they seem to have worked in many cases, since Colonel Malenfant notes that the French killed very few blacks! It is also possible that part of the "aristocrats' correspondence" was indeed correspondence—not amulets but writings relating to the revolt, as will be discussed further. If the papers were amulets, their owners were in all probability Muslims, because even though gris-gris can be worn by non-Muslims, the latter should always sew them in leather or cotton so that the holy words of the Koran do not come into contact with an "impure" person.

During their revolts, the Brazilian Muslims also used antideath protections. When they planned their first rebellion, in May 1807 in Bahia, the Muslims had "certain magical compounds they make use of, which they call *mandingas* and which they believe, make them invulnerable and immune to all pain and injury."[76] Some Islamic gris-gris, found by the Bahian police after the 1835 revolt were examined by the Hausa *marabout* and translator Albino, who explained that one "had been written more than a year and a half ago to protect the body from all weapons and had prayers which after having been written on a slate had to be washed away with water and drunk to be protected from the arms."[77] After the inquest, the chief of police, Dr. Francisco Goncalves Martins, informed the president of the province that "the leaders persuaded the unfortunate wretches that pieces of paper would protect them from dying, and this is why a lot of those papers were found on the dead bodies and in the rich and exquisite clothes probably belonging to the chiefs seized during our house searches."[78]

In the Americas as in Africa, Islamic gris-gris were an integral part of the warriors' panoply, and their very existence galvanized the fighters, enabled them to be bold, daring, and unafraid. They were as vital as weapons, and by providing antideath protection to the insurgents, the *marabout*s played a significant role in the slave revolts, whatever may be thought about the efficiency of their products. At a practical level, the making of amulets required an intense work as well as much paper and ink. Each fighter received a protection that would consist in the repetition of a special formula, dozens, hundreds, and even thousands of times. The preparation of a rebellion by the Muslims was thus a long process. Nevertheless, the conspirators were usually successful at remaining undetected, as has been mentioned by contemporary observers such as George Gardner, who believed that the Muslims were "more united among themselves than the other nations, and hence are less liable to have their secrets divulged when they aim at a revolt."[79] The literacy that the *marabout*s brought and preserved was an integral and essential part of the rebellious movements led by the Muslims.

Besides its role in the occult, literacy in Arabic was used in a temporal manner that was equally lethal. Arabic was used to disseminate the plans of insurgents. Documents of this nature were confiscated in Bahia: one paper seized during the revolt of January 1835, for example, was a call to take the country and kill the whites. Another stated, "Everyone should come out between 2:00 and 4:00 A.M. stealthily, and after doing what they could, they should gather at Cabrito opposite Itapagipe, in a large hollow there. There would be people from another nearby engenho [plantation], because they had been alerted. In the event they did not come, they would proceed to the engenho, taking considerable care in steering clear of soldiers so as to take them by surprise, until they had all left town."[80] This was a sketch of the basic plan for the uprising, and because it was written in Arabic, it could be easily circulated.

Individuals, too, were making their own plans during the Bahia revolt. A note that Albino translated had been sent by a man named Allei to a certain Adao, enslaved by an Englishman, in the Victoria neighborhood. Allei was making his own arrangements for his and Adao's participation in the revolt, stating that he would come at 4 A.M. and that Adao should not leave without him.[81] Another paper was a call for the people to assemble. It affirmed that nothing bad could happen to them on the way, was marked with diverse signs, and was signed by Mala Abubakar.[82] According to an *alufa* who spoke years after the revolt, Mala Abubakar— or rather *Mallam*, a title conferred to learned leaders in central Sudan— was the "chief of the imams" in 1835. Not one of the Muslim prisoners mentioned his name, and he remained unknown to the police. The police also discovered a sort of map that mixed topography and occult spirituality. It was "found covered with earth, [it] shows roads underlined and a circle. It stated that on all the roads they had to take and in all the encircled places no harm would befall them, and the earth symbolized the dirt of the road."[83]

The Muslims went to war truly protected: halfway between the gris-gris and the exhortation to war were papers that the French representative in Rio received, whose translation, he said, was "In the name of God the merciful, the compassionate! May God have compassion on our lord Mohammed! Praised be the name of the giver of salvation = blood must be shed: we must all have a hand in it = Oh God! Oh Mohammed! Servant of the Almighty! We hope for success if it be God in the highest's will. Glory be to God! Amen."[84] This is clearly a call to insurgency that could be discreetly passed along because non-Muslims could not decipher it. Representative de la Rosière stated that the versicle on the shedding of blood was repeated 210 times on forty-two different lines of each piece of paper carried by each one of the rebels. In Islamic numerology, twenty-one and its multiples correspond to *Al-Fatiha* and have a powerful and protective function.

Part of the "aristocrats' correspondence" found on the dead Haitian insurgents could have been exhortations of the Bahian type or documents directly relating to the revolt. One may also speculate about other papers written in Arabic that were found in Essequibo, British Guiana (now Guyana), in 1807. According to a slave who exposed the plot, some slaves had planned an uprising for Christmas Eve. After his denunciation, twenty people were arrested. One "piece of evidence brought forward at the trial was a letter in Arabic addressed to the slaves of Essequebo but, as no one in the Court could read it, its purport was only guessed at."[85] Nothing more has transpired about this paper, but the suspicion of the court that condemned nine men to be executed can be well understood. It was confronted with the unknown, the unintelligible, and that in itself was threatening.

Even if most of the planning for the insurgencies was done orally, the Muslims who revolted, in their ability to read and write in an unknown language, had a unique and efficient additional weapon at their disposal. Literacy in Arabic, coupled with a high concentration of organized believers, could be not only dangerous but deadly.

Communication through the Written Word

Through writing, African Muslims also carried out communications of a more sedate nature. Though the classical Arabic of the Koran is a dead language, West Africans have used it to communicate for a thousand years. Scholars, family members, traders, and rulers exchanged letters and documents. Non-Muslim monarchs who were illiterate employed *marabouts* as scribes. Writing was limited only by the scarcity of paper, imported at great cost first from the Maghreb and the Middle East and later from Europe through the French and British trading posts. It is not surprising to find the same impulses toward written communication among the Muslims in the Americas, within the limits that servitude imposed on the Africans. For a Muslim to want to write a letter would have been a reflexive gesture.

Perhaps the most moving attempt at communication through writing is that of Omar ibn Said. Shortly after he ran away from his owner's rice plantation in South Carolina, he was captured as he was praying and thrown in jail. Unable to communicate in English, he tried to do so in the only other way he could think of: he wrote. "Knowing nothing of the language as yet, he could not tell who he was, or where he was from," explained a pastor some years later, "but finding some coals in the ashes of his room, he filled the walls with piteous petitions to be released, all written in the Arabic language."[86] Omar had no way of knowing that in nineteenth-century Fayetteville, North Carolina, nobody could read Arabic; as a literate man, his first reflex was to express himself through writing. Though they were not understood, his words ultimately had the desired effect: "The strange characters, so elegantly and correctly written by a runaway slave, soon attracted attention, and many citizens of the town visited the jail to see him."[87] Finally, after Omar had been put on sale by the jailer to pay for his keep, he was bought by General Owen of Wilmington, North Carolina, who had gone to the jail specifically to see the man write. This was the end of Omar ibn Said's existence as a beast of burden. From then on, because his literacy had gained him curiosity, interest, and sympathy, he lived an easier life as a house servant and gardener. Though he remained enslaved, Omar ibn Said had improved his situation because he was literate. A few other Muslims were even more fortunate.

About a century before Omar ibn Said's momentous plea in Arabic, Job ben Solomon used his literacy to get out of his own predicament. As stated earlier, Job had been kidnapped in 1731 by Mandingo slavers as he was going back to Bundu after a trade mission in the Gambia, where he had been selling two slaves and buying paper. In Maryland he had run away and been treated fairly well by his owner after that flight. Nevertheless, he did not accept a "benign" type of enslavement. What he decided to do to put an end to it is typical of a Muslim. As his biographer Thomas Bluett explained, "he therefore wrote a letter in *Arabick* to his father, acquainting him with his Misfortunes, hoping he might yet find Means to redeem him."[88] Only a Muslim could send a letter to his family in Africa, and only the Muslims routinely redeemed their coreligionists when they happened to be captured by Christians. In America, Job, who had remained faithful to his religion steadfastly, used the tools it gave him to the hilt. He was a pure product of the Islamic and aristocratic tradition and, as such, was a model of self-esteem, self-confidence, and insuperable faith. He was also smart and used his observations and understanding of the workings of the trans-Atlantic trade in slaves to his best advantage.[89] He arranged for his letter to return to his homeland along the same route he had taken from Africa to Maryland. The letter was sent to Vachell Denton, a factor for slave dealers, with the instruction to remit it to Captain Pike. Denton had sold Job to his owner on behalf of Captain Pike, the slaver who had bought the young Senegalese from his Mandingo captors. It was a bold move: Job was using the same people who had enslaved him and treated him as a merchandise in order to gain his freedom. He may have let them know that they would make money out of the transaction. Pike having already left for England on the third leg of one of his many triangular voyages, Denton sent the letter to Captain Hunt, who was instructed to give it to the slaver. Unfortunately, when the missive reached London, Captain Pike had once again left for the west coast of Africa, to load his ship with African men, women, and children. Hunt showed the letter to the deputy governor of the Royal African Company, James Oglethorpe, a former member of Parliament and a philanthropist. His curiosity piqued, Oglethorpe forwarded it to Oxford University to be translated by John Gagnier, who held the chair of Arabic. On reading the translation, Oglethorpe decided to buy the freedom of the young man.

In June 1732, after eighteen months of servitude, Job was purchased from his owner for forty-five English pounds. He owed his freedom to two distinctively Muslim traits: his faith and his literacy. First, the fact that he had presented himself as a Muslim when taken out of jail made an impression on the men who were trying to find out who he was. Second, because, as a Muslim, he was literate—and very much so, as he was able to write three copies of the Koran—he could use a tool that was out of the reach of the mass of the enslaved Africans.

As some European writers emphasized, for an African to write in the Arabic of the Koran was akin to a European writing in Latin. Whereas Europeans did not routinely write their correspondence in Latin, however West African Muslims did write theirs in Arabic, even those enslaved far from their land. Fortunately, Job had written in Arabic, not in Pulaar, which could not have been deciphered at Oxford. For Job ben Solomon, literacy meant the difference between a life of servitude in America and a free life in Senegal.

One may wonder what would have happened if Hunt and Oglethorpe had not gotten involved. Would Job's letter have reached his father? Would gold have been sent from Senegal to Maryland? Could that have set a precedent for some men and women—most probably Muslims—to be bought back by their families? This scenario is far from being unrealistic. An old man from Timbo, for example, asked a group of Swedish travelers to help him find his son, Amadu, who had been shipped to the West Indies; he "said he would willingly pay any ransom for his son."[90] Men and women who had bought their freedom and were on their way back to Africa mentioned that once there, with the help of their families, they planned to send money to redeem their loved ones in America.[91] This was the plan devised by the grandparents of famous abolitionist and Harvard-educated physician Martin Delany. His grandfather, who was said to be a Hausa or a Mandingo, became a mariner in the West Indies in order to reach Africa more easily. Once home, it was agreed, he would send money to his wife, Graci, to pay for her passage and that of their daughter, Pati.[92] Ibrahima abd al Rahman's life story attests that the strategy could well work. While in Liberia, after gaining his freedom, he sent a letter to Timbo informing his family that he needed money to redeem his children. They sent seven thousand dollars in gold.

The road to freedom had opened up for Ibrahima a few years earlier when, enslaved in Mississippi, he had decided to send a letter to his family.[93] On October 3, 1826, his friend Andrew Marschalk sent Ibrahima's letter, written in Arabic, along with a cover letter to Thomas B. Reed, a United States senator from Mississippi. In his own letter, Marschalk noted that Ibrahima's epistle, as stated by the writer, was to inquire about his family, hoping to join them. Marschalk also mentioned that Ibrahima claimed to belong to the royal family of Morocco. This, obviously, was not the truth. Andrew Marschalk may have purposely invented that story; by claiming that Ibrahima was related to the reigning family of Morocco, he was almost certain to attract attention and fast action on behalf of his friend. Whereas the United States had diplomatic relations with Morocco, it had none with Futa Jallon, Ibrahima's own region.

Six months later, Ibrahima's and Marschalk's letters reached Thomas Mullowny, the U.S. consul in Tangiers, Morocco. The Moroccan authorities took the matter seriously: they told the U.S. consul they were eager to have their coreligionist freed and would pay for the expenses. Mullowny wrote to Secretary of State Henry Clay, urging for the release of Ibrahima. Clay forwarded the consul's letter to President John Quincy Adams, who devoted a passage to the matter in his diary on July 10, 1827. The president asked that the price of Ibrahima be ascertained and, if he could be purchased, that he be sent to Morocco. Two days later a letter was sent to Andrew Marschalk to inquire about Ibrahima's price. Ibrahima's owner, Thomas Foster, was finally cooperative and agreed to sell him. The involvement of the president of the United States certainly had had some effect on him. But Foster had one condition: Ibrahima abd al Rahman should not remain in the United States because it would have a negative effect on the old man's children, who were to remain Foster's property.

In February 1828, eleven months after he had decided to write home, Ibrahima was freed. As with Job, a letter in Arabic was his key to freedom. A senator, a consul, a Moroccan king, a secretary of state, and finally a president of the United States had been implicated in that saga. Many letters across the United States, the Atlantic, and the African continent followed Ibrahima's first, fateful letter.

Still another enslaved Muslim owed his freedom to his literacy. Abu

Bakr al Siddiq had caught Richard Madden's attention in Kingston, Jamaica, when Madden saw him sign his name in Arabic. His curiosity aroused, the magistrate asked for Abu Bakr's story and determined to free him completely by raising money to buy the four years left on his contract as an apprentice.[94]

Literacy in Arabic clearly made a huge difference in Job's, Omar's, Abu Bakr's, and Ibrahima's lives. Job, Ibrahima, and Omar actively sought their freedom through the means of the written word. They used their ability to write deliberately for that purpose. Three of the four men, and perhaps others, owed their freedom—and in Omar's case, his improved situation—to their writing abilities and were able to go back to West Africa. Ironically, even though writing in Arabic could not possibly help in forging documents to be used for escape, it did, in some cases, achieve the same result: freedom.

Literacy was also an important element in the lives of a group of Muslims from Trinidad who engaged in a correspondence with the king—and later the queen—of England and the British administration. They were freemen and wanted to be repatriated to Africa at Great Britain's expense, since they had been transported against their will in the first place. (See chapter 5.) Their first letter to King William IV, dated January 5, 1833, was written in English, but it opened with a Muslim incantation: "Alla huma. Sally Alla Mohamed. Wallah Shad Mohammed. Salla La Hu actahre wa salla ma,"[95] or "May God greet Muhammad and may God greet Muhammad and his apostles with his blessing." The cowriters signed their names in Arabic. Their leader was the *imam* John, or Jonas, Mohammed Bath.

This group of men, who acted in the name of the Mandingo Society in Port of Spain, could have sent a regular letter to the king, but they chose to open theirs with Islamic incantations and end it with Arabic writings. By so doing, they not only emphasized their religious background and stressed its importance but also presented themselves as men of higher learning, used to the written word long before their enslavement. Their first letter was followed by a second to Queen Victoria in January 1838, still on the subject of repatriation. There again, they emphasized their Muslim background by ending their letter with "The merciful God of the Mohammedans and of the Christians will be pleased to grant their Most Gracious Sovereign the blessings of a long, happy and generous reign."[96] It is worth noting that the Trinidadian Mandingo spoke of the God of the Mohammedans first and of the Christians second. They addressed the queen with courtesy but remained firmly entrenched in their religious specificity, even flaunting it, and making sure the queen understood that, though they represented a minority, the Muslims somehow had precedence over the Christians.

As with the first letter, the petitioners signed the second one in Arabic. This display of education and knowledge did not go unnoticed. James Stephen from the Colonial Office stated in March 1838, "This is a case which should receive prompt attention. The petitioners are able to sign their names in Arabic and are probably therefore persons of some education and rank in Africa though it may be reasonably guessed that they have no knowledge of anything more than the general meaning of the Petition they have signed."[97] Though Stephen was condescending, nevertheless he was impressed by the fact that the Mandingo could write in Arabic. The Free Muslims had achieved what they wanted: they were taken seriously as men of stature, which was conferred to them by their literacy and their religion.

Communication was not limited to the outside world, and Muslims communicated with one another through the medium of the written word. Job ben Solomon sent several letters from England to his father in Senegal before going back to Bundu. Once home, he continued to write in Arabic to the British traders with whom he had commercial relations. In Liberia, Ibrahima wrote to his family in Timbo while awaiting departure. Omar ibn Said and Lamine Kebe exchanged letters before the latter went back to Africa in 1836, as did Mohammed Kaba and Abu Bakr in Jamaica prior to Abu Bakr's return to Mali. Omar ibn Said's letter to Lamine Kebe opened with "In the name of God, the compassionate,"[98] and continued with apologies for his forgotten Arabic before proceeding to matters of his earlier Islamic education. Kaba started his letter to Abu Bakr in the same manner: "In the name of God, Merciful omnificent, the blessing of God, the peace of his Prophet Mahomet."[99] When Abu Bakr answered, he mentioned in the first sentence that he had "finished read the Coran in the country of Gounah."[100] The format of both letters was purely Islamic. Even though the writers were living in an alien culture, they kept their own frames of reference intact. Other letters written by Muslims may still exist. Madden mentioned in 1834 that he had "a great many addressed to me by negroes, both in English and Arabic."[101]

An interesting case of communication between Muslims can be found in Brazil. In 1849 the police in Rio were alarmed because the Mina had secret associations and corresponded with other Muslims in Bahia, São

Paulo, and Minas Gerais. The police conducted a search of the Africans' houses and found "an infinity of written papers . . . in unknown characters; some books also manuscripts."[102] Because of their literacy in Arabic, the Muslims were able to keep in touch with coreligionists hundreds of miles away. This is another indication that the Islamic networks were widespread and tightly knit.

Autobiographies in Arabic

Religious writings, gris-gris, and letters were all traditional forms of expression for the Muslims, but in the Americas, some became involved in a totally new writing exercise: the autobiography. The slave narrative, consisting of autobiographies or partial autobiographies, became a literary genre in the United States much more than in Latin America or the Caribbean, where the former slaves' production has been extremely limited. From 1703 to World War II, about six thousand slave narratives were recorded in North America. About half were written during slavery and the rest after Emancipation. Yet among these are very few testimonies by Africans. True African narratives were authored by William Ansa Sasraku (1750), James Albert Ukawsaw Gronniosaw (1785), Olaudah Equiano (1789), Venture Smith (1798), Ibrahima abd al Rahman (1828), Omar ibn Said (1831), Abu Bakr al Siddiq (1834), James Bradley (1835), Mahommah Gardo Baquaqua (1854), and Mohammed Ali ben Said (1867). Among these ten Africans, five were born and raised as Muslims. (Bradley, who was shipped at age two or three, cannot possibly have remembered the religion of his parents.) African-born slave narratives generally were not sought after by the abolitionists, who were the main force behind the slaves' narratives, for propaganda reasons. With the exception of Equiano, whose book was a success, the Africans may have seemed too foreign and thus less likely to attract interest and compassion than native-born former slaves. The disproportionate number of Muslim writers among the Africans can be attributed to the fact that as "non-Africans"—that is, as pseudo-Arabs—they were accorded more consideration than the "real" Africans. Also, their background as intellectuals probably encouraged them to seize opportunities to express themselves with the written word.

Two documents written in Arabic are of singular interest for what they reveal about the Muslims' outlook on life as slaves and their literacy. Both were written at roughly the same time: 1831 for Omar ibn Said and 1834 for Abu Bakr al Siddiq. Omar, who was about 59 years old when he wrote, had been a slave for twenty-four years, and Abu Bakr, who was forty-five, had been enslaved for thirty years. Both men came from neighboring areas of West Africa: Omar had grown up in Futa Toro on the Senegal River, and Abu Bakr in Timbuktu and Jenne on the Niger River. Their manuscripts are remarkably similar. Omar ibn Said's autobiographical notice opens with a long religious text; he then states that he has forgotten much of his own language, as well as Arabic, and asks for forgiveness. The first significant relation of his life deals with his education: "I sought knowledge under the instruction of a Shaykh called Mohammed Seid, my own brother, and Shaykh Soleiman Kembeh, and Shaykh Gabriel Abdal. I continued my studies twenty-five years and then returned to my home."[103]

In a striking parallel, Abu Bakr opens his autobiography by stating his name and his place of birth. He then continues, "I acquired the knowledge of the Alcoran in the country of Gounah, in which country there are many teachers for young people: they are not from one country, but come from different parts, and are brought there to dwell for their instruction."[104] Then follow the names of six teachers. Only after he has given this list does Abu Bakr mention his father's and uncles' names.

Interestingly, another Muslim, who wrote in English, followed the same pattern. Mohammed Ali ben Said, a teacher in Detroit and a Union soldier, starts the fifth sentence of his autobiography thus:

> These nations (Fellatah and Bornu) are strict Mohammedans. . . . Different languages are found in each nation, some written and some not, but the Arabic is very much in use among the higher class of people. . . . Especially the Koran is written in Arabic, and in my country no one is allowed to handle the Sacred Book unless he can read it and explain its contents.[105]

Contrary to what might be expected, Abu Bakr al Siddiq, Omar Ibn Said, and Mohammed Ali ben Said did not begin their works with reminiscences of the parents, siblings, wives, children, and—because these have a very special place in African culture—uncles they had left behind. Their first concern was to write about the extent of literacy in their countries and of their own studies. Evidently, formal education was of the utmost importance to the three authors. Abu Bakr and Omar knew that nobody in Jamaica or in the United States had heard about the type of learning they had been pursuing or about the scholars who had taught them. Nevertheless, they made a point of naming their teachers—to show gratitude, certainly, and to acknowledge the important role they had played in their formative years. With this unexpected emphasis on formal education, the writers established from the start they had been brought up as Muslims, could read and write, and had studied for a long time; that they were men of faith and accomplishments who had been not always mere beasts of burden but intellectuals, who had suffered a terrible reversal of fortune. The two autobiographies in Arabic go on to describe the capture of the authors (both were prisoners of war), and Abu Bakr writes at length, and very accurately, about the politico-religious situation of northern Ghana at the time of his enslavement.

Omar left very little information on the servile life he had to endure for almost three decades. From an African perspective, this omission may have been a matter of pride and dignity, of not wanting to mention the abjection he had to go through. But in Abu Bakr's case, another reason clearly existed for his discretion. In the first version of his autobiography, which Abu Bakr translated to Richard Madden, he alluded to his enslavement in these terms: "We were three months at sea before we arrived in Jamaica, which was the beginning of bondage. —I have none to thank but those who brought me here."[106] It is impossible to know whether this is the actual translation Abu Bakr gave to Madden or whether the magistrate took liberties and shortened what Abu Bakr was dictating to him. The original Arabic document was discovered in a box at the office of the Anti-Slavery Society in London one hundred years later, was translated by Dr. Charles Wesley of Howard University, and was published in 1936. It agrees almost word for word with Madden's translation, except for the spelling of African names and localities. But the part relating to the writer's enslavement says, "We were three months at sea before we arrived in Jamaica, which was the beginning of bondage until this day. But for the bitterness of bondage, I have more to thank but those that brought me here."[107] Whereas Madden's version makes no reference to the hardship of bondage, the original does; and both versions "thank" the captors for the captivity.

The last version of the autobiography, written in London after Abu Bakr was free, is similar to the others in all aspects but this passage, where it is strikingly different: "This was the beginning of my slavery until this day. I tasted the bitterness of slavery from them, and its oppressiveness. But praise be to God, under whose power are all things."[108] Not only was enslavement bitter and oppressive, but "them" points firmly at those responsible for the ex-slave's misery. There are no thanks to the captors, only praises to Allah. As long as he was not completely free and had to count on the help of whites to go back to Mali, Abu Bakr was ready to compromise and omit from his text whatever could remind them of their society's cruelty and guilt. He played the "good African" to the hilt, thanking his enslavers for the chance they gave him to get out of the "darkness." As soon as he could, however, he made a point of stating the truth.

Omar and Abu Bakr both concluded their narratives by highlighting the main principles of Islam, expressing thereby the importance they attached to their religion and to having its fundamental tenets properly explained to the unbelievers. The two writers definitely expressed a pedagogic concern. At the same time, being indebted to Christians, they were careful not to assert their own beliefs too clearly. Abu Bakr hid behind the statement "My parents' religion is of the Mussulman,"[109] while Omar, distancing himself completely, stressed, "Before I came to the Christian country, my religion was the religion of Mohammed, the Apostle of God—may God have mercy upon him and give him peace."[110] Omar's autobiography is an interesting balancing act. Although he opened it with the Islamic formula "In the name of God, the merciful, the gracious—God grant his blessing upon our Prophet Mohammed," he ended it with the doubtful assertion he was no longer a Muslim; yet he felt compelled, as he wrote that very sentence, to give his benedictions to Muhammad.

Omar stated that he had been asked by "*Shaykh* Hunter" to write his life; in other words, he wrote on command, and he devoted many lines to laudatory comments about his owner and his family. This part of the narrative, showing a happy slave content with his life and thankful to his masters, appears constrained. Like Abu Bakr, Omar had to compromise. It is possible that a new translation would shed a different light on the manuscript. In any event, it must be stressed that Omar wrote his manuscript while still a slave, whereas writings in the genre of the slave narrative were, understandably, written by former slaves who had escaped, bought their freedom, or been emancipated in 1865. Omar ibn Said may have been the only person who actually wrote—openly—an autobiography while still enslaved. The fact that it was in Arabic could act as a buffer between him and his potential readers, but he still had to be very much on his guard.

A striking feature of the Muslims' autobiographical sketches is their austerity. They are very different from the other slave narratives, which incorporated many elements of adventure and suspense, terrifying descriptions, and examples of cruelty. When writing about his life in Africa, Abu Bakr chose to relate details about his family that were neither interesting to the stranger nor exotic. He also wrote at length about an intricate African political situation and gave an overview of his religion. In the same manner, Mohammed Ali ben Said described an austere society bent on education and religion and examined the politico-religious differences between Usman dan Fodio and Mohammed el Kanemi, whom he called the "Washington of Bornoo." The writers clearly intended to relay information on Africa as they knew it, not as it was being imagined. Their preoccupation may have been the same as that of Lamine Kebe, who told Theodore Dwight, "There are good men in America, but all are very ignorant of Africa. Write down what I tell you exactly as I say it, and be careful to distinguish between what I have seen and what I have only heard other people speak of. They may have made some mistakes; but if you put down exactly what I say, by and by, when good men go to Africa, they will say, *Paul told the truth.*"[111]

For obvious reasons, neither Abu Bakr nor Omar needed an editor, whereas editors generally handled the narratives of escaped slaves, whose autobiographies were often commissioned, revised, and published by the abolitionists. The degree of involvement of the editors in such writings has been the subject of debate. But no editor could have been involved with the Muslims' Arabic manuscripts. What is significant and distinctive is that those texts were not interpreted by anyone. That they were written in a foreign language inaccessible to almost everyone kept pristine, unaltered, what the authors wanted to say, including their potential self-imposed censorship.

In the Americas, Muslims were engaged for more than three hundred years in reading and writing exercises that covered the production of religious texts, occult protections, correspondence, plans for uprisings, and autobiographies. They preserved their literacy with imagination and determination and made use of it in the various ways accessible to them. A long tradition of literacy, which in some parts of West Africa was already five hundred years old at the beginning of the slave trade, could not be erased, even in the most intellectually damaging environment. Knowledge acquired for religious and intellectual purposes in Africa was turned into a tool and a weapon in America by men and women who deliberately preserved and expanded it. The literate Africans used their knowledge not only to remain intellectually alert but also to defend and protect themselves, to maintain their sense of self, to reach out to their brethren, to organize uprisings, and, for some, to gain their freedom.

5

Resistance, Revolts, and Returns to Africa

Frugal, serious, and dedicated to hard work in order to get their freedom or reach the upper echelons of the slave structure, the African Muslims may have appeared, at first glance, to be "model slaves." These characteristics, however, represent only one facet of their experience in the Americas, that which drew on their education and discipline in Africa. They also brought with them a tradition of defiance and rebellion, because as Muslims, they could be only free men and women. They proved antagonistic toward their captors from the very beginning, and from a few years after the arrival of the first Africans in the New World, anti-Muslim measures were being implemented repeatedly to protect the colonies from their assault.

As early as 1503, one year after he had been appointed governor of Hispaniola, Nicholas de Ovando asked the Spanish Crown to put a complete stop to the importation of Africans, because they fled, joined the Indians, and taught them "bad customs."[1] Nevertheless, Africans continued to be shipped, and in ever greater numbers; and the Muslims among them caught the colonists' attention. On May 11, 1526, Spain passed the first item in a series of anti-Muslim legislation. A royal decree (*cédula*) specifically forbade the introduction of "Gelofes" (Wolof) from Senegal, *negros* from the Levant, blacks who had been raised with the Moors, and people from Guinea.

Muslim Rebels and Maroons in Spanish America

The Wolof were the only African population targeted by name. The Spanish settlers had reason to be familiar with them, because the Senegalese had just led the first slave revolt by Africans in the Americas. In 1522, Wolof revolted on the sugar plantation of Admiral Don Diego

Colon—Christopher Columbus' son—in Hispaniola, in the territory of what is today the Dominican Republic. As they went from plantation to plantation trying to rally other Africans, they killed a dozen whites.[2] Wolof had also rebelled in San Juan, Puerto Rico; in Santa Marta, Colombia; and in Panama. It appeared as if they were establishing a trend, and so, six years after the first *cédula,* the Crown issued another, which made reference to uprisings having resulted in the deaths of several Christians and stressed the danger still posed by the Wolof. They were described as "arrogant, disobedient, rebellious and incorrigible."[3] This attitude is consistent with men who, as Muslims, thought themselves free. They could not accept being enslaved by Christians or being forced to convert. Their complete refusal of their new situation translated into disobedience and rebelliousness and, as noted by the legislators, could not be "corrected." The arrogance is equally typical of men who, as Muslims, would think themselves better than "infidels" and Christians. The Wolof, in addition, were accused of fomenting trouble by preaching insubordination to the other nations, which were "more pacific and of good habits."

The royal decree also excluded mulattos, Jews, *gente bereberisca* (a blanket name for Muslims), and *moriscos,* or Muslims (often Moors from Spain) who had been forcibly converted to Catholicism. These last were considered especially dangerous, an indication that they profoundly resented their conversion and were possibly disposed to go to great lengths to return to their former faith.

Still another piece of legislation was issued on August 14, 1543. It stated that Muslim slaves and free Muslims who had recently converted to Catholicism, as well as their children, were prohibited in the colonies because they had occasioned much "inconvenience" in the past. Unfortunately for the colonists, the situation did not improve, and on July 16, 1550, new instructions were given to the Casa de Contratación that again prohibited blacks from the Levant and Guinea, because they were "mixed with the Moors"—in other words, Muslims. The interdict was not respected, however, and the authorities in the Caribbean Islands, as well as in Mexico, Peru, and Chile, continued to protest the introduction of African Muslims.

No fewer than five pieces of anti-Muslim legislation were issued by the Spanish authorities in the first fifty years of Spain's establishment in the New World. Though the decrees issued prohibitions concerning Jews and mulattos, only Muslims were targeted repeatedly and with extraordinary vigor. The Spanish Crown was worried for two reasons: it feared the expansion of Islam in America, and it was confronted with deadly rebellions fomented by Muslim slaves and maroons.

The inconvenience alluded to in the *cédula* of 1543 was indeed serious. At that time in the Spanish territories of the Americas and the Caribbean, Indians were still the majority population, even though their numbers had been decimated, and they lived in villages not too distant from the plantations and the mines. It was easy enough for the Africans who fled slavery to find refuge among the natives. In the West Indies, they had formed maroon communities under the protection of the Caribs and were particularly destructive.[4] Throughout the colonies African maroons, such as the three hundred men led by Antonio Mandinga in Panama, raided the plantations, killing, stealing livestock, destroying crops, and "abducting" slaves.[5] In addition to the nagging and dangerous presence of the maroons, the Spaniards had to face full-blown revolts from Africans allied to the Indians. Such rebellions occurred in Hispaniola (1522–1532), Mexico (1523), Cuba (1529), Panama (1550–1582), Venezuela (1550), Peru (1560), Ecuador (1599), Guatemala (1627), Chile (1647), Martinique (1650), and much later, Florida (1830–1840).[6] Repeatedly, the Spanish settlers and officials blamed the Muslims for their pernicious influence on the Indians. Confronted with a perilous situation, the colonists reacted with ferocity. Very early on, the presence of an African among the Indians was considered a major crime. For having been found in an Indian village in Costa Rica, Pedro Gilofo, a runaway who, being a Wolof, may have been a Muslim, was condemned to death on September 1, 1540; he was boiled alive.[7]

The colonists had a genuine fear that the Muslims would proselytize among the Indians. These concerns may not have been rooted in reality, but they were strong enough to make the Spaniards try to enforce a rigid segregation of Indians and Africans. Islam did not spread, but the Muslims may have made some attempts to reach out. Accusations and condemnations do not indicate that a deed or offense has been committed, but in 1560 the mulatto Luis Solano was condemned to death and the "Moor" Lope de la Pena to life in prison for having practiced and spread Islam in Cuzco, Peru.[8]

The Inquisition was very active in the new colonies and vigilantly condemned to death what it called "sorcerers." Many Africans who dealt in the occult were among its victims. There is little doubt that *marabouts* involved in the making of protective and offensive amulets, as well as in divination, were killed by the church as a result of their activities. Just overtly retaining Islamic beliefs could lead a person before the Inquisition tribunal. Such was the case, for example, of many Wolof enslaved in Portugal during the sixteenth century, who were denounced for expressing their faith in the superiority of their religion. There is reason to believe that similar cases may have happened in the overseas colonies.[9]

Disobedience, rebellion, real or potential proselytizing, arrogance, and sorcery—the colonists had to contend with a series of problems that the Muslims posed. An additional one was their use of horses. As horses were unknown to the Indians and the Central Africans,[10] cavalry gave a decisive advantage to the conquistadores and the slaveholders' patrolmen. But African Muslims had been handling horses for centuries; they bought them from Arab merchants, who traded the animals against slaves.[11] The *Buurba Jolof*, or emperor of Jolof, for example, had a cavalry of eight thousand to ten thousand mounted men, according to the Portuguese who visited the region between 1504 and 1506.[12] Some of these cavalrymen were later enslaved in the Americas, having been taken prisoner when the Jolof Empire collapsed. Ironically, it was the colonists who had asked for the recruitment of Muslim horsemen. They needed men who were used to cattle raising and the handling of horses, and the slave dealers found such men in the Wolof, Mandingo, Tukulor, and Fulani areas of Senegambia.

The Wolof who rose up on Diego Colon's plantation in Hispaniola were used to cavalry warfare, as is indicated by their behavior in front of the Spaniards. They did not panic when the horsemen charged but opened their ranks, let the horses pass, and regrouped to face the countercharge. By the 1540s, Wolof maroons had created their own cavalry with stolen horses and harassed the plantations of Hispaniola. The danger posed by these Africans who went "always on horses" and proved to be "skilled and audacious, both in the charge and the use of the lance"[13] was stressed in a letter to the Spanish king written on June 28, 1546. The Wolof horsemen of the Spanish possessions impressed some of their white contemporaries, and Spanish poet Juan de Castellanos (1522–1607), who resided in Puerto Rico, saluted their dexterity:[14]

> Destos son los Gilosos muy guerreros
> Con vana presuncion de caballeros
> (The Wolof are skillful and very warlike
> With vain presumptions to be knights)

It goes without saying that not all runaways and rebels were Muslims; but the fact that between the sixteenth and the eighteenth century the Muslims were the only ones targeted with specific legislation, which attempted to prohibit their importation, indicates that they must have been numerous and influential in the ranks of the rebels. That bloody rebellions and aggressive maroon communities were trademarks of the Muslims is not surprising. They were used to fighting for their faith, and they were without a doubt indignant at being made the slaves of Christians. The policy of forced conversion that the Catholics launched could only have added to their resentment and hatred toward their enslavers. Warriors of the faith were not disposed to reject a religion for which they had fought, nor to accept their total subjugation by men they probably felt were morally inferior. As a minority, they understood they would not be able to defeat the slaveholders by themselves, that they had to find allies in the non-Muslim Africans and the Indians; they had to persuade others to join their ranks. Hence the accusations made by the Spanish colonists that the Muslims taught the "more pacific nations, bad customs."

Another indication of the fear that Islam and the rebellious Muslims inspired in the Spaniards, as well as of the diversity of measures taken to control them, can be found in the *Moros y Christianos*. This was a special type of anti-Muslim play that the colonists imported from Spain and Portugal. The settlers made the slaves in the Americas play out the struggle between the Moors and the Christians in Spain which ended with the eviction of the former. The story was a good illustration to the bondmen of the superiority of the Christians over the Muslims. If the Moors, who had conquered parts of the Iberian Peninsula and dominated the Spaniards and Portuguese for seven centuries, finally had been subjugated, then it should have become evident to Muslim slaves that they could not hope to accomplish much in the Americas with their violent opposition to their Christian masters.

If the Spanish colonists were suspicious of and negatively disposed toward the Muslims for historical reasons, the French, for whom Islam and its followers were only a faint memory—they had defeated the invading Arabs on French soil in 732—had no qualms about introducing them into their new territories. The records of the Jesuits and other missionaries show that the French were well aware that Senegambian Muslims were living among them. They even acknowledged the presence of *marabout*s, as Father Jean Mongin, stationed on the island of Saint Christopher, did in a letter in May 1682: "There are even some who have marabouts among them, which is what mahometan priests are called."[15] A century later, Colonel Malenfant reported from Saint-Domingue, that "mahometan blacks" and "even dervishes"[16]—probably Sufis involved in mystical practices and rituals—were living on the island. The French missionaries denounced the reluctance of the Muslims to embrace Catholicism, but they did not seem to have any other complaints.

The Muslim Factor in the Haitian Revolution

What the French did not realize was that their most profitable colony, Saint-Domingue, was fecund ground for Muslim maroons and rebels. The island had always had numerous maroon communities, and an average of a thousand runaways were advertised every year. The notices posted by the plantation owners, who listed the disappeared give a measure of the place of the Muslims among the maroons. Although large numbers of Muslims had been forcibly baptized, some had retained their original names, and Ayouba, Tamerlan, Aly, Soliman, Lamine, Thisiman, Yaya, Belaly, and Salomon appear in the notices. Female runaways, such as Fatme, Fatima, and Hayda, are also mentioned. The Africans left individually and, more usually, in groups. For instance, twelve Mandingo men, aged twenty-two to twenty-six, fled one night in 1783 from their owner's house in Port-au-Prince.[17] They were all professionals—masons, carpenters, and bakers.

It is not known if some maroon communities were entirely composed of Muslims, but major communities had Muslim leaders. Yaya, also called Gillot, was a devastating presence in the parishes of Trou and Terrier Rouge, before he was executed in September 1787. In Cul-de-Sac, an African Muslim named Halaou led a veritable army of thousands of maroons.[18]

These Muslims were well known and feared, but the most famous of the pre-Revolution maroon leaders was without a doubt François Macandal. Macandal was a field hand, employed on a sugar plantation. One day, as he was working the sugar mill, one of his hands got caught in the wheel and had to be severed. As he could no longer cut the cane, he became a cattleman, later running away. For eighteen years Macandal was at large, living in the mountains but making frequent incursions on the plantations to deliver death. He organized a network of devoted followers and taught the slaves how to make poison, which they used against their owners or against other slaves in order to ruin the slave-holders. His reputation was such that a French document of 1758 estimates—with much exaggeration, no doubt—the number of deaths he provoked at 6,000 over three years.[19] In eighteenth-century Saint-Domingue, poison was called *macandal*.

An African born in "Guinea," Francois Macandal was in all probability a Mandingo. He came from an illustrious family and had been sold to the Europeans as a war captive. He was a Muslim who "had instruction and possessed the Arabic language very well,"[20] emphasized nineteenth-century Haitian historian Thomas Madiou, who gathered information through the veterans of the Haitian Revolution. Macandal was most likely a *marabout*, for French official documents describe him as being able to predict the future and as having revelations.[21] He was also well known for his skills in amulet making—so much so that gris-gris were called *macandals*. In addition, he was said to be a prophet, which indicates that he was perceived as having a direct connection to God. Thus besides being a *marabout* he may have been a *sharif*, a descendant of the Prophet; but this is only speculation, as no evidence exists to confirm or inform this hypothesis.

François Macandal was much more than simply a maroon leader. He had a long-term plan for the island and saw the maroons as the "center of an organized resistance of the blacks against the whites,"[22] stressed an eighteenth-century French document. He used practical symbolism to explain his vision for Saint-Domingue. One day, in front of a crowd, he put three handkerchiefs in a water container: one was yellow, one white, and one black. He took the yellow one out and said, "Here are the first inhabitants of Saint Domingue, they were yellow. Here are the present inhabitants"—and he showed the white handkerchief—"here, at last, are those who will remain the masters of the island; it is the black handkerchief."[23]

To turn this prophecy into reality, Macandal planned to poison the wells of the city of Cap-Français. Once the slaveholders were dead or in the middle of convulsions, the "old man from the mountain," as Macandal was sometimes called, followed by his captains and lieutenants, would attack the city and kill the remaining whites. Before he could launch his assault, however, a slave betrayed him and he was caught. Tied up in a room with two guards, he somehow managed to escape. If he had killed the men with the pistol that lay on a table between them, Macandal may have been able to remain at large. But he did not. The guards gave the alarm, and he was caught again, this time by dogs.

On January 20, 1758, Macandal was burned at the stake. The pole he was tied to collapsed, and the crowd saw this incident as a sign of his immortality. He had told his followers that as he was put to death, he would turn into a fly and fly away. The executioner asked to kill him with a sword as the coup de grâce, but his request was denied by the attorney general. Macandal was tied to a plank and thrown into the fire again.

The maroon leader Macandal can best be described as a *marabout-warrior*. He used his occult knowledge and his charisma to gain allies to wage war against his enemy, and he participated in the action personally.

Another popular leader who attained quasi-mythical status in Haitian history was Boukman. Very little is known about him. He was not born in Saint-Domingue but came from Jamaica, smuggled by a British slaver. As a slave, he became a professional and rose to the rank of driver, later becoming a coachman. Using a position that allowed him to travel from plantation to plantation, as well as his charismatic personality, he had built a network of followers in the north. He definitely entered Haitian history when he galvanized a large assembly of slaves gathered on the night of August 14, 1791, in a clearing in the forest of Bois-Caiman. During this voodoo ceremony, Boukman launched the general revolt of the slaves with a speech in Creole that has remained famous. He denounced the God of the whites, who asked for crime, whereas the God of the slaves wanted only the good. "But this God who is so good, orders you to seek revenge," he pounded. "He will direct our arms, he will assist us. Throw away the image of the God of the whites who is thirsty for our tears and listen to freedom which talks to our hearts."[24]

A week later, two hundred sugar estates and eighteen hundred coffee plantations were destroyed by the slaves, who were said to have cut the throats of a thousand slaveholders. At the beginning of November, Boukman was shot dead by an officer as he was fighting a detachment of the French army with a group of maroons. His severed head was fixed on a pole and exposed on a public square in Cap-Français.

There are indications that Boukman was a Muslim. Coming from Jamaica, he had an English name that was rendered phonetically in French by Boukman or Bouckmann; in English, however, it was Bookman. Boukman was a "man of the book," as the Muslims were referred to even in Africa—in Sierra Leone, for example, explained an English lieutenant, the Mandingo were "Prime Ministers" of every town, and they went "by the name *bookman.*"[25] It is likely that Boukman was a Jamaican Muslim who had a Koran, and that he got his nickname from this. As many Muslims had done, and would continue to do, he had climbed the echelons of the slaves' power structure and had reached the top. He was a trusted, professional slave. He was also at the top of the slaves' hierarchy in another way: he was recognized as a priest. He has passed down in history as a voodoo priest, but this does not mean that he was such. Because the Muslim factor largely has been ignored, any religious leader of African origin in the Caribbean has been linked to voodoo or obeah.[26]

There is thus compelling evidence that two major leaders in Haitian history—Macandal and Boukman—were not only Muslims but also *marabouts*. They were not the leaders of Muslims, they did not embark on a *jihad*, but they were the leaders of the slave population, irrespective of religion. What they provided was military expertise coupled with spiritual and occult assurance that the outcome of the fight would be positive. Both skills were of extreme value, each in its own way; but put together, they conferred on these leaders the aura of mythical figures. Because of their *marabout* knowledge they could galvanize the masses, push them to action and to surpass themselves.

Other *marabouts*, and the Muslims in general, played a crucial role in the Haitian revolts and ultimately in the Haitian Revolution through their occult skills, literacy, and military traditions. The *marabouts* provided protections to the insurgents in the form of gris-gris, as Colonel Malenfant recorded, and the Muslims used Arabic to communicate during uprisings. Though their role and contribution have not been acknowledged, the Muslims were essential in the success of the Haitian Revolution.

The Muslim Revolts in Bahia

Brazil was another fertile ground for Muslim unrest. The country was a principal importer of Africans, and starting at the turn of the nineteenth century, as indicated in chapter 1, the *jihad* of Usman dan Fodio in northern Nigeria provided vast cohorts of Hausa and Fulani Muslims to the Portuguese colony. In addition, the Yoruba country to the south was a theater of Muslim expansion, and large contingents of Muslim Yoruba (Nago) were shipped to Brazil. In 1807 alone, 8,307 Hausa, Nago, and Ewe were introduced to Bahia. The same year saw the first attempt, by mostly Muslim Hausa slaves and freedmen, to organize an uprising. Like many others, the insurrection did not take place, because a slave loyal to his master betrayed the plot. House searches led to the discovery of bows, arrows, knives, pistols, rifles, and gris-gris written in Arabic. The two Hausa leaders—one slave, one freed—were executed, and eleven conspirators received 150 lashes each.[27]

A year later, on the day after Christmas, Nago and Hausa men fled their sugar plantations of the Reconcavo (the Bay of Bahia). Another group soon joined them, and a party of several hundreds attacked the town of Nazare das Farinhas, but they were defeated after a fierce battle. About a hundred men were taken prisoner. For months the remaining maroons roamed the surrounding area, assaulting plantations, setting houses on fire, stealing, and killing.

Another major revolt took place on February 28, 1814, when about six hundred Africans under the leadership of a maroon Hausa *marabout* hit the fisheries where they had been employed and the town of Itapoan. Their group was diverse because they had succeeded in establishing efficient networks linking the slaves and freedmen of the Reconcavo to those on the island of Itaparica (ten miles from Bahia) and to the maroons living in the vicinity. The insurgent Africans, poorly armed, left fourteen whites dead and lost fifty-eight men, mostly Hausa. The repression that followed was commensurate with the gravity of the event: four men were hanged, a dozen died in prison, and twenty-three freedmen were flogged and sent for life to the prisons of Angola and Mozambique. The rest of the captured men were whipped and handed back to their owners.

Public punishments were no deterrent, however. Less than a month later, another revolt broke out and was quelled in Iguape, an area of large sugar plantations. No fewer than seventeen uprisings, all but one on the sugar plantations surrounding San Salvador de Bahia, erupted between 1816 and 1830. Muslims were clearly identified as leaders in at least five—and participants in all—including the first one to take place in the heart of the city of Bahia.

On April 10, 1830, about twenty Africans later recognized as Nago attacked three hardware stores, where they seized twelve swords and twelve long knives. They then proceeded to a slave market, where they freed newly arrived Africans and killed or wounded eighteen who refused to join them. The group was now more than a hundred strong and set upon a police station, where the insurgents killed one man. As reinforcements arrived, the Africans were met with rifles. Many were wounded and forty were taken prisoner, while soldiers and the crowd lynched more than fifty. Some managed to escape and took refuge in the bush outside the city. This was the first revolt to have actually taken place in Bahia, and it shook the town. The response was swift and ferocious. It took another five years before Africans dared to launch an attack on the city.

In the early morning hours of January 25, 1835, Africans sporting white pants, white shirts, and white caps and turbans took to the streets of Bahia armed with knives, lances, swords, and a few pistols. To the sound of beating drums, they assaulted the National Guard barracks, the city jail, and the police barracks and fought against the cavalry. When day broke, seventy Africans and about half a dozen whites lay dead. Some insurgents died later from their wounds, and others committed suicide.

Within a few months of the 1835 rebellion, at least five hundred Africans had been tried, four men had been executed, forty-five had been flogged up to a thousand times in the course of three months, thirty-six had been deported, and twenty-four had been sentenced to jail or hard labor. The fate of other defendants is not known. Most were Nago (199), thirty-one were Hausa, ten Ewe, and thirteen Bornu. All were Muslims. They had also rallied ten Bantu from Congo and Angola, who may have been converts; fourteen West Africans from diverse nations; and five native-born slaves. While 186 were slaves, 115 defendants, or 38 percent, were free. There were fourteen women among the prisoners.

Hundreds of Africans, enslaved and freed, took part in the best planned and most daring slave uprising in American history, after the Haitian Revolution. The Bahia rebellion was not the first time that Muslims had risen up, but it was by far the most widespread, best organized, and most devastating urban insurrection they had staged. Their plan was to set buildings on fire, and while the police and the army were busy putting the fires out, the Africans would attack. The rebels would be joined by others from nearby plantations, and together they would leave the city, once taken, and proceed to conquer the rest of the bay.

Even had it been executed as planned, the plot might not have had much chance of success. As it was, the Africans were forced to launch their offensive precipitously; two freed Nago women betrayed them, the husband of one of whom was taking part in the uprising. Three hours after the denunciation, the police started searching the houses of the Africans. At 2 Ladeira de Praca, they came upon a meeting of the conspirators. It was 1 A.M., and the uprising had been scheduled to start a few hours later. Discovered, the insurgents decided to give the assault anyway. One conspirator was immediately bludgeoned to death by a neighbor helped by two young slaves, a Creole and a Nago. Numerous papers in Arabic were found on his body.

Divided into two groups, the men took to the streets and tried in vain to liberate the prisoners held in the city jail. Licutan, an esteemed religious leader who was called "the sultan," had been held there since November 1834 as a guarantee for a debt contracted by his master. After their unsuccessful attempt at a jailbreak, the rebels attacked the artillery and police barracks, killing a few soldiers; they were joined by Africans coming from the Victoria neighborhood. Because their original plan had been disrupted, they had to alert their coconspirators that the fight had already started. "Different groups of armed blacks spread out through the main streets of the city whooping and hollering," stated the president of the region, "beating on their cohorts' doors entreating them to join in. The only opposition they encountered was from patrols who shot at them from time to time."[28]

The insurgents continued their march and attacked the National Guard and the police barracks on Lapa Square. Besides getting rid of the soldiers and policemen, their objective was probably to help themselves to their weapons. They did not succeed in entering the barracks but were not subdued by the troops. After some skirmishes, during which men on both sides were killed, they proceeded toward Itapagipe Peninsula, where rebels from the plantations were supposed to join them. But at Agua de Meninos, midway to the peninsula, the infantry and the cavalry were waiting for them. "It cannot be denied that the Malês [a generic term for Muslims in parts of West Africa, Brazil, and the West Indies] were prodigiously valorous,"[29] admitted Father Etienne Ignace, who was not sympathetic to their cause. According to Ignace, the chief of police was so impressed by their courage that he asked them repeatedly to surrender. None accepted, however, and nineteen Africans were killed in the intense fight that ensued; others drowned or were shot as they jumped into the bay. Thirteen Muslims were taken prisoner, and many others fled to the woods. Meanwhile, in Bahia, six armed men dressed in white got to the streets at dawn, as originally planned. At Agua de Meninos, the small group was entirely wiped out by the troops.

The rebellion was frightening to the white citizens. The rebels had been bold, unafraid. They repeatedly had dared attack the well-armed soldiers. But after the first shock passed, the whites were in for a second one, when the magnitude of the conspiracy was discovered. As the police chief pointed out, "the insurrection had been contemplated for a long time and the planning was better than what might have been expected, in view of their brutality and ignorance."[30]

It became clear to white Bahians that, with their schools, books, rings, mosques, multitudes of papers written in a foreign language, antideath amulets, and religious uniforms, the African Muslims truly constituted an unknown, secretive, mysterious, and dangerous group that had to be completely crushed. Scores of freed men and women were expelled from the country, many slaves were sold outside the province, and numerous prisoners died in jail. Others were whipped in a display of horrific brutality. Suspicion was enough to condemn a man to the lash. The whites considered Licutan, who was jailed at the time of the uprising, a leader because the Muslims deferred to him. The Muslims had repeatedly visited his cell, kneeling and asking for his benedictions. The failure of the uprising devastated him, a freed African working at the jail testified: "On that same Sunday he bowed his head and never raised it. He became upset and cried when the other negroes taken prisoners that morning were brought in. One of them brought him a book, or a folded piece of paper with letters on it, like those that have been found lately, and Pacifico [Licutan] read it and began to cry."[31] Though nothing could be proved against him, he received fifty lashes a day on four days in April, eleven days in May, and five days in June—one thousand lashes in all for the elderly religious leader. Forty-four other men received the same treatment, and one died from his whippings. When they were strong enough to be sent back to their masters, the Africans had to wear an iron collar with a cross around their necks and chains and shackles on their legs.

Of the eighteen men who were condemned to death for their part in the uprising, four were executed. An unexpected problem arose, however: the authorities could not find anybody willing to hang them. As late as a day before their scheduled execution, a reward representing a four-month salary was offered to prisoners who would agree to work the gallows. It was to no avail, and a baffled warden explained, "I have offered the job to the inmates, and no one will take it. I did the same thing today at the Barbalho and Ribeira dos Gales jails, and no one will take it for any amount of money; not even the other blacks will take it—in spite of the measures and promises I have offered in addition to the money."[32] Solidarity; respect; a sense of honor; fear of reprisals—overt or occult—

from other Muslims or Africans; and despair at another failed uprising were certainly among the reasons that pushed blacks, both African- and native-born, to refuse to take part in the execution. Their passive resistance, which proves that the Muslims were not alienated from the rest of the black population, was successful. Jorge da Cruz Barbosa (a free Hausa whose real name was Ajahi) and Joaquim, Pedro, and Goncalo (Nago slaves) were executed by a firing squad of policemen on May 14. They were killed like soldiers, not common criminals.

The Muslim uprising has been widely studied and analyzed, and many interpretations of its nature have been given. Afro-Brazilian scholar Manoel Querino, who associated with the Muslims of Rio at the turn of the century, denied that Islam played a role in the revolt. Querino, who probably wanted to present the Muslims in the best light possible, went so far as to maintain that no Muslims took part in the uprising.[33] Raymundo Nina Rodrigues, Etienne Ignace, Roger Bastide, and Pierre Verger, in contrast, have placed Islam at the rebellion's very core.

The Bahia rebellion of 1835 was the most visibly Muslim uprising of all, but many previous revolts were launched in the same spirit. This has been pointed out by Raymundo Nina Rodrigues, who met several African Muslims in Bahia:

> For the chroniclers at the beginning of the last century, these revolts were only the manifestation of the pervert and cruel dispositions of the blacks, which provoked their utmost indignation; for the more benevolent spirits, they were only just reprisals exercised by brutalized beings against inhuman masters; the more liberal writers saw in the blacks' insurrection a noble revolt of oppressed people against the usurpation of their freedom, which they reclaimed by this heroic and courageous example. There may have been a little of all of this in these revolts, but they were forgetting the most important factor, the basis of all these uprisings, which in reality was the presence of Islam in Bahia.[34]

Roger Bastide went further and stated that the revolt "represented a real holy war waged by the Mussulmans against the Christians."[35] Pierre Verger had a slightly different take on the events: the revolts were, he explained, "the direct repercussion of the warring events that were taking place in Africa"; Usman dan Folio's "holy war continued in Bahia in the form of slave revolts, and even free Africans' revolts."[36] According to these authors, the Muslims had launched a *jihad* in Bahia, whatever their reasons for doing so. These scholars viewed Islam as a fanatical religion whose favored mode of opposition was expressed by the holy war. The most balanced and best documented study on the famous rebellion is Joao Jose Reis's *Slave Rebellion in Brazil: The Muslim Uprising of 1835 in Bahia.* Concerning the role of Islam in the uprising, Reis concludes, "In a nutshell, this was a *Male* plot but an *African* uprising."[37]

Strictly speaking, a *jihad* could not have taken place in Bahia because the conditions were not met. A *jihad* must follow four rules: the Muslims must be oppressed to the point that they cannot follow their cult; they must be half the number of their oppressors; they must have the same weapons; and their territory must have been invaded. Only the first condition was met in Bahia. At first glance, the part played by the Islamic clothes, rings, gris-gris, and documents in Arabic can lead one to assert that religion played a leading role. While this is true, it does not mean that the revolt was a religious war. Islam, for a Muslim, permeates every aspect of life, from the way one bathes to what one can drink and wear. Everything that a devout Muslim does is done in reference to religion. It is inconceivable to start any important enterprise without asking for God's blessings, without protective amulets, or without consulting a *marabout*, who will go into a *khalwa* (a retreat during which he will fast, pray, and do *dhikr*) to see the outcome of the endeavor. The clerics will perform special prayers for guidance, called *salat al-istikharah*, particularly in situations that may have a dramatic outcome such as military operations. Everything—material, spiritual, and occult—that will ensure a positive outcome is used: from astrology to numerology, from the recitation of the Koran to the symbolism of certain colors and the choice of a special date. This is especially true in Sufism.

The Africans in Bahia put every chance on their side. They chose to act during Ramadan, a sacred and blessed month; they wore white clothes, the symbol of purity and heaven; they had ample reserves of gris-gris; they had war drums, doubtless fitted with special amulets. Does this mean they were engaged in a *jihad*? At no point at all did the insurgents refer to freedom of the cult or to an action against the Christians or the unbelievers. The enemy was not defined in terms of religion. The insurgents did not take arms to defend the purity of Islam, as the *shehu* Usman dan Fodio had done, nor did they indicate any willingness to convert the infidels. It is a mistake and a stereotype to view every military action or uprising by Muslims as a *jihad*.

What the Africans said they wanted to do was "kill the whites." Pedro, a wounded prisoner, testified during the trial that the conspirators had invited him to be ready to kill whites, and Belchior da Silva Cunha had heard people talk of waging war against whites. Another source mentioned that not only the whites but also the mulattos and the native-born blacks would be killed. One of the women who betrayed the plot, Guilhermina Rosa de Souza, said that her husband had heard talk of killing the whites, the Creoles, and the blacks who would not join the rebels and of sparing the mulattos to use them as slaves. Not much credit should be given to this last piece of hearsay, which sounds like the fabrication of somebody who wanted to present herself as having saved every living soul in Bahia. The men and women who had carefully planned their uprising, extended their bases through networks all over the Reconcavo, and been involved in or witnessed a few failed revolts should be credited with more sagacity. All the Africans put together represented 34 percent of the Bahian population, while the native-born blacks and mulattos made up 38 percent, and the whites 28 percent. Being such a minority, the African Muslims certainly would not have been willing to take on everybody, including those of their own who would not join them. As a matter of fact, even the supposed white killing spree was not reality, because the insurgents did not kill indiscriminately. The president of the Province acknowledged that "there is no evidence that they robbed a single house or that they killed their masters on the sly."[38]

What the insurgent Muslims did was attack the strategic buildings—the police, National Guard, and army barracks—where they could destroy the defenders of the slaveholders and get much-needed arms and ammunition at the same time. After their professional protectors had been killed or disarmed, the whites, who were a minority, could have counted only on themselves to stand up against the insurgents. Some slaves likely would have defended them, but the same cannot be said of the majority. By presenting the purpose of the uprising as the killing of whites, the conspirators may have wanted to attract as many antiwhite blacks as possible—and those could be recruited among the Muslims, the animist Africans, and the native-born slaves—all the while knowing that the mass of rebels would be controlled by the Muslim leaders, who defined the objectives and determined the unfolding of the events. The Bahia rebellion was a Muslim plot and an African uprising, but going further, it can be suggested that the African insurgents who had a few native-borns in their ranks—probably also counted on the support of the rest of the blacks, without whom they could not hope to accomplish much. This support may not have been expected to come initially but rather at a later stage, when the African insurrection had succeeded in gaining momentum.

Although the uprising could not unfold as planned, it nevertheless involved as much as 5 to 7 percent of the African population in Bahia. As Reis points out, this percentage of men and women sentenced, if reckoned in today's figures for a city of 1.5 million inhabitants, would number twelve thousand. The number of those sentenced and the number of people who actually took part in the plot and the insurrection clearly did not match—the latter number was probably higher—meaning that a total number of about two thousand participants should be considered. In today's terms, this would be comparable to about thirty-six thousand people, an extremely high figure even for a city of a million and a half.

Because nobody talked about, confessed, or explained the reasons of the uprising, questions and speculations abound. One question is why there was a conspiracy to begin with. It may simply be that the Africans wanted their freedom. Though this undoubtedly was true, it does not explain why so many free Africans took part in the plot and the uprising. A better answer may be that what the Africans wanted was real freedom, not the nominal type that came with paying a master for their own bodies but having to defer to and obey any white. That freedom included, but was not limited to, the right to practice one's religion at will. With the end of the white rule would come the end of humiliation and oppression and the possibility of reestablishing an African social order, based on African values. In their own sphere, the Muslims lived according to their African and Muslim values, beliefs, customs, and conventions; but they also had to live in the other world and go through the trauma of adapting to it every time they had to leave their African universe. They were not acculturated; they had not internalized the white, Christian, European American culture, and having to endure it must have proved nearly unbearable, as the African Muslim world they had re-created was very much present for them. With the help of a revolt, that world could become the only one.

One can wonder why the Muslims were more successful than some of the previous rebels in carrying out at least part of their plan, and why they were the leaders. Islam was an excellent organizing force, if only for its own preservation. Makeshift schools and mosques had to be opened, maintained, equipped, staffed, and kept secret. Dates for the holy days, based on the lunar calendar, had to be calculated and communicated to all the believers. Baptisms, circumcisions, weddings, and funerals had to be arranged according to Islamic customs. Dues for the *esusu* had to be collected, special clothes sewn, rings made, prayer beads imported. *Halal* dinners had to be prepared. The Muslim community of slaves, freedmen, and maroons had to be kept informed not only in Bahia but also in the Reconcavo, the countryside, and the remote areas where the *quilombos* (maroon villages) were hidden. Just by virtue of being Muslims and wanting to remain so, the Africans had to be well organized and particularly discreet. Their ability to communicate by writing in Arabic or with Arabic characters was of considerable help. Thus, more than other groups, the Muslims had practical experience in organization and discretion. In addition, a large proportion had been shipped to Bahia as a result of their involvement in Usman dan Fodio's *jihad* or in other Islamic-inspired movements, and so they had military experience. There is little doubt that the events in Central Sudan had an impact on the history of Bahia, but it was more the technical aspect of the *jihad* than its religious ideology that played out in the New World.

Islam was also a galvanizing force. It reinforced a sense of self-worth in human beings who were brutalized and constantly humiliated. It even instilled or strengthened a feeling of superiority over the "Christian and *kafir* dogs." Muslims certainly thought that their religion was morally far above any other. Their daily interactions with the Christians could only reinforce this certitude. Furthermore, to be a Muslim was prestigious because of the literacy Islam emphasized, and because it gave personal power to men and women who chose to impose a discipline on themselves rather than to submit to another people's discipline. To be a Muslim meant to be part of a close-knit, upwardly mobile community that looked after its members, offered them diverse activities and services, and was charitable and well organized. It was a world in itself, with its own particular sets of beliefs that did not depend on the slaveholders' view of the world. To be light skinned had no value; to be a house slave or a field slave meant nothing. A free man in this context was not superior to a slave. Learned slaves were the teachers of free men; enslaved and jailed clerics were the spiritual leaders of the community. Islam was democratic and progressive in a society that was despotic, repressive, tyrannical, and racist.

In retrospect, the chance that a slave revolt would have succeeded in Bahia seems very slim, as the slaveholders could depend on well-armed militia, the police, and the army. But it is necessary to look at the context to understand why the Muslims were certain they could be victorious. At the time of the first attempted revolt, in 1807, two important uprisings of the downtrodden had already been successful in these Africans' history. In central Sudan, where most of the Muslims came from, Usman dan Fodio's *jihad*, which counted many slaves among its combatants, was triumphing. Some years later, during the other Bahian revolts, the Muslims were reaping victories all over central Sudan. The Africans had been kept abreast of the events through the continual arrivals of prisoners. They learned the latest political and military developments in their homeland as wave after wave of warriors disembarked in Brazil.

In the Americas, too, the former slaves of Saint-Domingue had defeated Napoleon Bonaparte's army, killed or sent away thousands of once seemingly invincible whites, and established the second independent country in the Western hemisphere, after the United States. What had happened on the Haitian island sent shock waves throughout the slaveholders' world. It was known and commented on by the slaves and freemen as well as by the whites. Hardly a year after Haiti's independence, according to a document of 1805, blacks in Rio de Janeiro were wearing pendants with the effigy of the black general Jean Jacques Dessalines,[39] who had assumed the title of emperor of Haiti after Independence. Right after the Bahia uprising of 1835, a motion by the provincial assembly of Rio stressed, "It is obvious to all that the Haitian doctrines are preached here."[40] It is not a coincidence that the number of slave revolts increased all over the Americas after the Haitian Revolution. A dozen years before the Brazilian Muslim uprising, Denmark Vesey in Charleston, South Carolina, asked for the assistance of the Haitian president as he was planning a general revolt against the whites. The Haitians themselves were actively involved in recruitment, trying to entice free blacks to settle on the island. With the victory of slaves over their masters and the example of a working black republic in the New World, as well as news of Muslim ascendancy in the Old, the final separation of the two antagonistic worlds created by American slavery was seen as a distinct possibility.

Returning to Africa

Separation from the white Christian world was achieved not only by revolt but also by running away. As already stated, it is not known if the Muslims formed maroon communities of their own. However, the description of a maroon village in Jamaica gives some clues that can be interpreted as relating to Muslims. The settlement was called Moore Town, which may mean that its inhabitants were Moors or Muslims. They were "a fine race of people, tall, and elegant in person, with features more European than the negros generally possess. . . . Some of the women are decidedly handsome, and except their complexion, more like gipsies than negros."[41] This description, reminiscent of the portrayal of Muslims by other European Americans (as seen in chapter 3) would perfectly fit Wolof, Tukulor, or Fulani individuals but not other maroons on the island, who were mostly people from the Gold Coast (Ghana). In any event, although Muslim maroon communities have not been documented, it is probable that they existed, given the asserted leadership of Muslims in mixed runaway communities.

Another way for the Africans to escape the world of slavery was to leave it completely. The return to Africa was a recurrent theme in the slave cultures, expressed in folktales, funeral practices, and songs. On the Sea Islands, for example, slaves buried their dead near the water so that they could more easily cross the ocean. In the same spirit, tales of flying Africans leaving for their homeland abounded all over the Americas and the Caribbean. And for a small minority of former slaves, going back to Africa became a reality.

As assessed in chapter 4, Muslims, because of their religion, may have had an added incentive to liberate themselves; for the same reason, once free they may have been more eager to leave the countries of their enslavement. This propensity is exemplified in an anecdote that Colonel Malenfant reported in 1791. After he had a conversation with Tamerlan, the teacher and *marabout* enslaved in Saint-Domingue, he wrote, "He is the only slave whom I found willing to go back to Africa; more than thirty to whom I talked about this, said that they preferred Saint-Domingue."[42] Malenfant added wisely, "Were they telling the truth?" Maybe not; but it is significant that only an identified Muslim, among some thirty slaves, clearly stated his desire to go back home. Tamerlan was still a slave and could not act on his wish, but freed African Muslims in different parts of the New World tried to, and some actually did, return to their native land.

The first widely documented—if not the first actual—case of an African going back home is that of Job ben Solomon. After eighteen months of captivity, he left Maryland for London, where he was used as an Arabic translator by Sir Hans Sloane, the president of the Royal Geographical Society. Touted as a curiosity for his writing ability, noble birth, and regal behavior, Job met the royal family and was the toast of the salons. He finally set sail to his native land, with letters from the Royal African Company that recommended to its factors in the Gambia to use him "with the greatest respect and all the Civility you possibly can."[43]

Having landed on August 8, 1734, at Fort James, Gambia, Job ben Solomon started his journey back to Bundu in Senegal in the company of British factor Francis Moore. In an extraordinary coincidence, on the first evening of their trip Job came across the very men who had kidnapped him three years before. "Job, tho' a very even-temper'd Man at other times," wrote Moore, "could not contain himself when he saw them, but fell into a most terrible passion, and was for killing them with his broad Sword and Pistols, which he always took care to have about him."[44] Instead, the former victim engaged his abductors in conversation. He inquired about their king and learned that "amongst the Goods for which he sold *Job* to Captain *Pyke* there was a Pistol, which the King used commonly to wear slung about his Neck with a String . . . , one Day this accidentally went off, and the Balls lodging in his Throat, he died presently." Job fell to his knees and "returned Thanks to *Mahomet* for making this Man die by the very Goods for which he sold him into Slavery." There was much to be thankful for, as Job ben Solomon was only the second man, as a Pulo remarked to Moore, "ever known to come back to this Country, after having been once carried a Slave out of it by White Men."[45]

Job's father had died before his son's arrival, but he had received his letters from England and knew that his son was free and on his way home. Job "wept grievously" at the news of his father's death. But his four children were well. One of his two wives had remarried, but he was philosophical about it. The woman and her new husband, he said, "could not help thinking I was dead, for I was gone to a Land from whence no Pholey ever yet returned."[46] There is no information on the man who preceded Job back to Bundu, but a third man soon returned. During and after his enslavement, Job did not forget Lamine Ndiaye (variously spelled Lahmin Jay, Loumein Yoai, Lahamin Joy, or Loumein Yoas in contemporary documents), the unfortunate Wolof companion who had been abducted with him. While in England, he had asked for Ndiaye's release. On returning to Maryland, Thomas Bluett had found Ndiaye, and with funds provided by the duke of Montague, the man was redeemed in 1737. After a few weeks in London, he sailed back to Gambia in February 1738.

Job ben Solomon—or rather, as he was called again, Ayuba Suleyman

Diallo—remained in Bundu but kept a close relationship with the British. They had hoped that with him as their ambassador, and through his connections, they would have easy access to the gold-rich Galam region and the gum-rich Ferlo savanna. Diallo made several trips with officials from the Royal African Company to prospect trade possibilities. The results were disappointing, but he maintained contact with the company and its successor, the Company of Merchants Trading to Africa, for forty years. He died in 1773 at age seventy-two.

Starting a few years after Job's return, there was a steady, if not large, stream of men and women of African descent leaving the Americas for Africa. In the United States, as also in Great Britain and later in Brazil, the movement that sent blacks to Africa was concerned with protecting slavery by expelling the free blacks. The American Colonization Society (ACS), founded by whites in 1816, had for its objective, as defined by secretary of state and supporter Henry Clay, "to rid our country of a useless and pernicious, if not dangerous portion of its population." It was expected that the free blacks, useless in America, would be useful in Africa, as they would "civilize" and Christianize the continent and develop the natives' taste for American goods. Through the society's efforts, fewer than seven thousand emancipated and free blacks out of a population of about four hundred thousand, which represented 12 percent of the black community, settled in Africa between 1816 and the beginning of the Civil War.

Most free blacks' organizations were opposed to African colonization, seeing it as a racist, proslavery scheme. Their reasons ranged from their unwillingness to separate themselves from those who were still enslaved, to fear that their departure would make the institution of slavery more secure, to a sense of alienation from Africa. In fact, more than twice as many free men and women chose to emigrate to Canada as to Liberia. Very few Liberians coming from North America were first-generation Africans because the manumission laws in the United States, different from those in effect in the French, Spanish, and Portuguese colonies, were restrictive and more favorable to the native-born slaves. Also, the African-born population was smaller in the United States than it was generally in Latin America and the Caribbean. Therefore, the overwhelming majority of U.S. blacks who went "back" to Africa were, in fact born in America.

Given its general lack of success, the American Colonization Society was very eager to help anybody who wanted to leave. That was exactly

Ibrahima abd al Rahman's wish. Not only did he want to go back to Timbo, but his departure was a condition of his emancipation, insisted on by his former owner. It was therefore only natural that the man and the organization would work together.

Ibrahima and his wife, Isabella, were anxious to leave the United States, but one major problem prevented them from doing so immediately. When he had said his good-byes to Natchez, Mississippi, and forty years of servitude, Ibrahima had left, in the words of President John Quincy Adams "five sons and eight grandchildren—all in slavery, and he wishes that they might be all emancipated, and be sent with or to him."[47] If he were to go back to Timbo without them, emphasized the desperate father, he would not survive long. When President Adams turned down his request for help, Ibrahima found the support of the American Colonization Society. The society would not pay to free the family—this was contrary to its principles—but agreed to help him raise funds through its networks of friends, agents, and benefactors.

The society had its own agenda, however, and placed high hopes in the old man. It hoped that once he was restored as a ruler of Futa Jallon, Ibrahima could be of help to the ACS in Liberia, about three hundred miles from Timbo. Moreover, as was envisioned with a flourish in the *African Repository*, the organ of the ACS, Ibrahima might "become the chief pioneer of civilization to the unenlightened Africa— . . . armed with the Bible, he may be the foremost of that band of pilgrims who shall rock back the mighty waves of darkness and superstition, and plant the cross of the Redeemer upon the furthermost mountains of Kong!"[48] (Kong was a Muslim trading enclave in what is today the Ivory Coast.)

Ibrahima was not given any handouts. He worked himself to release his family. In full "Moorish" regalia, with subscription book in hand, he attended events and parades and met members of Congress and government—including, once again, President Adams, who declined to subscribe—as well as the general public, for whom he wrote *Al-Fatiha* in the hope of raising the $8,500 demanded by Thomas Foster. He patiently sat through patronizing, ignorant, condescending speeches that described him as a former barbarian and pagan and Africa as a "dark region" thirsty for the gospel of Christ.

In the course of his continued efforts to take his children and grandchildren back with him to Africa, Ibrahima met two men who became instrumental in the elder man's quest. The first was the Reverend Thomas Gallaudet, father of deaf-mute education in the United States. Gallaudet at first was shocked at the African's criticism of the Christians and sent him a Bible in Arabic. He, too, had grand designs for the Muslim, envisioning him as the envoy of Christ to Africa. With age Ibrahima had mellowed, the pastor thought; enslavement had softened him, and maybe divine grace had touched him. To Gallaudet, these were all good reasons for Ibrahima's having had to remain a slave for so long. Had he returned to Africa sooner, Gallaudet conjectured, Ibrahima would have done so with "his Moorish disposition and his Moorish sword."[49] The pastor saw Ibrahima's and Africa's redemption in the old man's forty years of servitude and expected him to be the instrument of evangelization in the "interior of Africa."

Ibrahima humored Gallaudet in his expectations. He sent the pastor a letter, assuring him that he would "get many to become Christians." He went as far as to state that when he had left Futa Jallon forty years earlier, almost all the youngsters were Christians—an obvious lie. In fact, the letter in its entirety is woven with lies and deception. But Ibrahima's reasons for deception can be found in the postscript: "I have five sons and eight grandchildren. I am sorry to go to my own country and leave them behind in slavery. If I can find any way to get them, I shall try to get them before I go to my own country."[50] Ibrahima was trying to sell himself as a missionary in the hope of raising sympathy for his only cause: the liberation of his family and their moving to Timbo.

Not only was Muslim Ibrahima to be a Christian missionary, but he was also to be the spearhead of a major commercial enterprise. His second helper was Arthur Tappan, a wealthy importer, an abolitionist, and New York's foremost philanthropist. A supporter of colonization, Tappan envisioned a commercial venture that would send immigrants and goods to Liberia and import African products. His project was to use Ibrahima's connections and influence as a member of a ruling family to open up trade with the hinterland.

Ibrahima abd al Rahman had suddenly become a precious asset to the ACS and was viewed as the main figure in its colonization scheme. But his financial, and therefore familial, needs remained unfulfilled. His efforts notwithstanding, Ibrahima and his wife left without their sons and grandchildren. On February 7, 1829, they boarded the *Harriet* with 150 settlers bound for Liberia. They arrived in Cape Mesurado on March 18, and Ibrahima immediately turned to the only God he had known. He had left a Muslim and come back a Muslim. Tragically, the old man, who had been sick during the rainy season, died in Monrovia on July 6. He was sixty-seven and had been a slave for forty years. Ibrahima never saw Timbo again, but he made sure that his manuscripts in Arabic were sent to his family.

Ibrahima's life was tragic to the end. Even though his dream of going back to Africa had materialized, it was bittersweet. He never saw his family or his country. All his descendants were still enslaved. For a full year he had tried to raise money in Cincinnati, Washington, D.C., Philadelphia, Boston, and New York. He had met powerful and wealthy men, but in the end, his efforts had brought him only $3,500, less than half the amount requested by Thomas Foster. Nobody in America, not even the rich philanthropist Tappan, was willing to participate in the redeeming of Ibrahima's children. Yet as soon as his family in Timbo heard about his children's predicament, they sent him a caravan loaded with $7,000 in gold dust. In another bitter twist of fate, the porters learned of Ibrahima's death before they reached Monrovia and turned back.

Two months after Ibrahima passed away, Thomas Foster died. His heirs were willing to sell the slaves he had bequeathed them. Tappan used the $3,500 Ibrahima had raised to redeem Lee; Simon; Simon's wife, Hannah; and their five children. In December 1830 they landed in Monrovia, where they were reunited with their mother. Ibrahima and Isabella's three other sons, daughters-in-law, and three grandchildren remained enslaved in Mississippi. When their parents had left them in slavery almost three years before, promising them their freedom, the sons, according to Andrew Marschalk, had had "a look of silent agony in their eyes."[51] One can only imagine the horror and despair that those who were forced to remain must have felt. At least three generations of Ibrahima's descendants remained slaves.

A few years after Ibrahima abd al Rahman made his way back to West Africa, another famous Muslim, Abu Bakr al Siddiq, left Jamaica, the country to which he had been deported as an adolescent. Years earlier the duke of Montebello had tried to redeem him, but his owner, Mr. Anderson, had refused to let him go because his ability to keep the property's records in Arabic was of great value. On Richard Madden's insistence, however, and with a compensation of twenty pounds raised by sympathetic inhabitants of Kingston, Anderson agreed to dispense with the four years of apprenticeship Abu Bakr still had to serve under British law. After thirty years of slavery Abu Bakr was free, but he had one more wish: he wanted to go back to Africa.

Madden had hoped that the Royal Geographical Society could use

Abu Bakr as a guide and facilitator in its African explorations. The society, however, thought he was useless. The area he knew, Timbuktu, had been a mystery years before, but as the secretary explained in a letter to Madden, much had been learned in the past few years, and what were presently needed were accurate surveys and scientific examinations, "for which an uneducated native is quite unsuited."[52] Moreover, continued the secretary, having left thirty years before, Abu Bakr had become a stranger, and if he was indeed of noble birth, as he claimed to be, he would be even more useless, as political changes had affected the power structure. As a last straw, the society, displaying its ignorance of African culture, advised Abu Bakr to stay in Kingston where he had friends, because nobody in Africa would care for him.

Fortunately for the forty-five-year-old descendant of Muhammad, friendly men were willing to help. Another magistrate took Abu Bakr from Jamaica to London, and Madden recommended him to John Davidson, who was preparing a private expedition to Timbuktu. In September 1835, Abu Bakr sailed to Gibraltar and from there to Morocco. As soon as he set foot on African soil, orders came "from the palace to treat him with respect, as he was a Mulay (prince),"[53] or descendant of the Prophet. Moreover, it was learned that one of his relatives was presently the "sheik of Tomboktu."

After a year in Morocco, the expedition finally left for the Niger River in November 1836. Three weeks later it was attacked, and John Davidson was killed. In 1841, Richard Madden was appointed on the Gold Coast and made inquiries about Abu Bakr's fate. In June the British vice-consul at Mogadore relayed to him the information that Abu Bakr had reached Jenne—about 250 miles south of Timbuktu—but that nothing else was known of his whereabouts.

Abu Bakr al Siddiq, like Job ben Solomon, and Ibrahima abd al Rahman, went back to Africa on an individual basis. Strong wills, a religion that excited curiosity and gave them moral strength, noble origins, and a cortege of sympathetic whites helped these men achieve a unique feat for slaves: going back to their families. The three men were redeemed by whites who saw in them a unique opportunity to advance their own projects in Africa, whether missionary, economic, political, or educational. Living among the Christians, even in the terrible conditions of slavery, had somehow "civilized" the Africans in the eyes of their benefactors, and they could thus be used as facilitators. As far as the Westerners were concerned, the slaves' release was not the end of their adventure; they still had to be useful. Job was a willing participant, but it is clear that Abu Bakr just wanted to be left alone. Lamine Ndiaye disappeared from the records and probably chose to stay clear of the British. As nothing is known about the "Pholey" who had gone back to Bundu before Ndiaye and Job, chances are that he, too, preferred to remain anonymous. What Ibrahima would have done is a matter of conjecture, but his behavior in Monrovia leads one to think that once his family had been redeemed, he would have had nothing more to do with the Americans. Another Muslim, Lamine Kebe, who went back to West Africa in 1835 after being a slave in the American South, left no trace of his whereabouts.

The "philanthropic" policy, with its underlying self-serving goals, that sent some African Muslims back to Africa was not successful. It was an arrogant and stupid miscalculation on the part of the British and the Americans to think that these men could become the agents of Western acculturation in Africa. They all had demonstrated a fierce cultural resistance during their years of enslavement, at a time when they were completely subjected to the power of their owners; therefore, it should have seemed doubtful that they would, once free and at home, engage in a process that would lead to the Christianization of their homeland.

Because of the whites' involvement in their saga, Job, Ibrahima, and Abu Bakr became celebrities of sorts. But there were anonymous Africans who succeeded in going back to their native land through their own efforts, and whose stories have not been told. What they accomplished was more difficult than what the three men did. They first had to liberate themselves, working overtime and saving money to buy their own bodies. Then they had to save again, to pay for their passage to West Africa. As they shared a communal life in America, worshiping together and being bonded by religion, they usually left together. Examples of these group departures appear in Baron Roger's novel *Kélédor*, which well describes the chain of events that led Africans from enslavement to freedom and back to their countries.

In Puerto Rico, where Kélédor was living after the Haitian Revolution, Roger's hero met a group of Senegalese Fulani who introduced him to coreligionists, among whom were men who, like himself, had fought in the *almami* Abdel Kader's army. They informed him that they had formed the project of going back "to the fields of Senegal." Eager to join them, Kélédor worked hard to get enough money to pay for his passage. Soon the group made up of twenty-nine men and women was able to charter a ship for the Canary Islands. They were encouraged by the fact that two previous expeditions of the same type had been successful, news that Kélédor and his companions may have learned from newly arrived slaves or from black mariners. Baron Roger specifies that in 1819 and 1822 two groups of Senegalese, formerly from Cuba, went back to their native land. The second contingent was made up of thirty-two individuals who had sailed from Havana to Tenerife, where they had boarded a French vessel that transported them to Senegal. Several groups of Africans whose religious affiliation has not been recorded also left Cuba for Africa, but in the three cases Roger mentions, the returnees were Muslims, and those who had been converted to Catholicism went back to Islam.

Other groups from other countries certainly succeeded in their endeavor. A particular Muslim community's efforts at repatriation have been well documented. Alternatively called the Free Mandingo of Trinidad, the Mandingo Society, and the Free Mohammedans, the group was made up of former slaves who had bought their freedom and of recaptives. As discussed in chapters 2 and 3, they made a concerted effort at keeping their traditions alive, and their common religion was the cement that kept them together as well as the axis around which they built their community of successful men.

It was a logical step for the Free Mandingo to wish to go back to their land: "We cannot forget our country," they wrote to the king of England. "Death alone can make us do."[54] Hence, in 1831, they asked the governor to be repatriated; but when they did not obtain satisfaction, they petitioned the British government directly two years later, asking it to buy up their properties and to repatriate them to Senegal or Gambia. They were businessmen and made clear in a letter to the king that they would not leave without being compensated for the property they would leave behind and without being able to pay their debts:

> We know you can send us in your ships to our country, but permit us to say according to the law of Mahomet which we revere, a person who owes money and cannot pay is a slave. We owe money here. We want to sell our cocoa and coffee plantations and our slaves, and our houses in town. But there are no purchasers to be found here. We, therefore beg your Majesty to buy them for a fair price so that we may pay our debts, which we cannot do otherwise.[55]

The *imam* Jonas (John) Mohammed Bath, leader of the society, who wrote the petition, attributed the Mandingos' success to their cultural and religious principles; but those very religious principles that had helped them become free were now an obstacle. It was because of Islam's requirements concerning debts that they could not leave. Ironically, besides their natural longing for home, the possibility of living their religion freely was undoubtedly an incentive to go back to Africa, but the willingness to respect the Koranic teachings in Trinidad could prevent them from actually setting foot in their native land. In January 1834, their request for payment and repatriation was denied.

Four years later the men once again appealed to the government. This time they stressed that they needed an armed ship to avoid falling into the hands of the slave dealers, still very active despite the official abolition of the international slave trade by most European and American nations. The British authorities denied their request once again. The governor summoned Bath on April 23, 1838, and informed him that the administration in London wanted the men and their families to know that they would face danger in going back to Africa, including the possibility of being enslaved again. Two days later, the Mandingo sent a determined and somewhat ironic letter to the governor:

> We respectfully beg leave to inform your Excellency that we have communicated with our tribe, and have resolved to brave all dangers and run all risks, if the British government will only afford us a passage to Sierra Leone. Those dangers and risks, we do not apprehend to be either as serious or numerous as the philanthropic Secretary of State for the Colonial Department in his anxiety for our safety and welfare seems to anticipate, as some of our tribe have already performed the journey from our country to Sierra Leone overland. On our arrival at that settlement we shall meet with a number of our brethren, and we shall then make such arrangements as will ensure us a safe journey across the Country. This of course will be done at our own expense from our own resources. We never thought of taxing the generosity of the British government so far as to require an escort from the Sea Coast.[56]

The Mandingo of Port of Spain were well informed of the political situation in West Africa. They may have obtained the information from recaptives settled in Trinidad or perhaps, given the precision of their knowledge and their plan, from letters entrusted to black sailors by their "brethren." They knew they could count on their coreligionists and compatriots to take them home safely—another indication that Islamic networks were functioning very well on both sides of the ocean.

No further mentions were made of the Mandingos' efforts at repatriation. It appears they were promised free passage at some point, but the cost of chartering a boat and the precedent it would set finally convinced the British government not to grant their request. John Mohammed Bath died in September 1838, in Port of Spain. Another prominent member of the society, Mohammedou Maguina, whose signature appears on the 1838 petition, died in 1852 at one hundred years of age. Others, however, may have managed to go back to Africa after the collective plan finally failed, as some had done on their own while the rest of the group was still engaged in its repatriation efforts. At least three men sailed to England with their families to appeal directly to the government. One, Mohammedu Sisei, a former Koranic teacher, was a recaptive who had served in the Third West India Regiment for fourteen years. When discharged, he should have received a plot of land or a pension. As neither was provided to him, he brought his case to the Colonial Office in London, asking for his pension and free passage to Freetown. Sisei, Mohammed Houssa (Hausa)—who, according to Bath, met with Queen Victoria—and a third Muslim named Jackson Harvey finally sailed to Sierra Leone, whence they proceeded to their respective countries.[57]

Though a few individuals achieved their goal, the Trinidadian Muslims as a group were not successful in their efforts to go back to their native land. A combination of factors may explain their failure. Besides the religious argument concerning their reluctance to leave without paying their debts, they may indeed have faced serious obstacles. Because they had invested their money in houses, slaves, and coffee plantations that they could not sell, they may not have had enough cash to charter a boat. Ironically, less successful freed Africans may have had a better chance at leaving because their assets were not tied up in immovable investments.

At the same time that the Trinidadian Muslims were launching their repatriation campaign, scores of their coreligionists were actually sailing back to Africa. In the aftermath of the failed insurrection in Bahia, hundreds of free Africans, most of them Muslims, were expelled from Brazil or went back to their homeland voluntarily. In November 1835, two hundred suspected men and women were deported to Whydah, in present-day Benin. But public opinion wanted more. All free Africans, it was proposed, should be sent back to where they came from. A decree authorizing the deportation of the suspects—even if they had not been sentenced—was issued in March, and it was made law two months later.

When the first contingent of deported Africans arrived in Whydah, it was well received by the local authority.[58] The deportees, many of whom were masons and carpenters, were given a piece of land where they erected their own village and started to cultivate. The Muslims expelled from Bahia were doing well, and when word of the welcome they had received reached their former town, hundreds of freed Africans decided to sail home.[59] Within a few months, more than seven hundred asked for passports. Two free Africans who were described as rich, Antonio da Costa and Joao Monteiro, chartered a British boat to take them, their families, and 150 other free Africans to their native land. They arrived safely and disembarked in the ports of Elmina, Winnebah, and Agoue in April 1836. Another group, of two to three hundred individuals, also chartered a British boat to take them back to Lagos, whence they had been taken in the first place. Their leader was a wealthy freed African who, in order to finance the operation, sold all his property and some of his slaves and liberated six others, who accompanied him. Interestingly, this man had been through the Middle Passage in 1821, and sixty of the individuals he took back to Africa had traveled with him on the same slave ship.[60] They all had acquired their freedom within fifteen years. A complete solidarity existed among them, which had started on the slave ship or perhaps before—they may have been taken as prisoners of war at the same time—and lasted during and after their enslavement. They are a perfect example of the type of community built by the Muslims: a close-knit group made up of hard-working and successful people.

When these Africans left Brazil, Bahia was in the midst of a vicious anti-Muslim and anti-African fervor. For six months the Muslims who had been condemned to be flogged were whipped publicly, until their sentences of up to a thousand lashes were completed. Searches and arrests lasted for months. The repression was so violent and blind that the chief of police denounced soldiers who were killing and wounding "peaceful blacks." Without a doubt, this hostile atmosphere contributed to the numerous departures of African Muslims.

The repatriation movement lasted until the abolition of slavery in 1888, with peaks between 1850 and 1860. In 1852 a delegation of Mina from Rio de Janeiro told representatives of the English Society of Friends that they, too, wanted to go back to Africa, but they wished to know if the coast was really free of slavers. They informed the missionaries that another group of sixty-three Mina had left the year before for the Bight of Benin. The shipbroker they had retained procured a copy of the charter for the Quakers; it showed that the group of free Africans, which included women and children, had paid $4,000 for the passage and had landed safely. As a token of their appreciation for the Quakers' interest, the Mina of Rio gave them "a paper beautifully written in Arabic by one of their chiefs who is a Mohammedan."[61] The Mina were still involved in repatriation societies in the late 1860s, as reported by the Count de Gobineau.

Some Brazilian Muslims settled in the Gold Coast and became the avant-garde of the fast-growing Muslim neighborhoods in Cape Coast and Winneba.[62] Another group of returned Muslims was made up of soldiers who had been forcibly recruited by the Dutch, after the close of the international slave trade, to serve in the Dutch West Indies and in their Asian possessions. They, too, established themselves in the Gold Coast, between Elmina and Cape Coast.[63] There were many Hausa among them. The vast majority, however, relocated in Dahomey, Togo, and Nigeria.

The returned "Brazilians," or *Brésiliens*, were generally successful. A British traveler to Dahomey in the mid nineteenth century described their achievements:

> The country ten or twelve miles round Whydah is very interesting, the soil good, land level, and in many places well cultivated by people returned from the Brazils. . . . Many of them were driven away from Brazil on account of their being concerned in an attempted revolution amongst the slaves there, who turned against their owners. These people are generally from the Foolah and Eya countries. Many, it appears, were taken away at the age of twenty or twenty-four years, consequently they can give a full account of their route to Bagadry, where they were shipped. They are by far the most industrious people I have found. Several very fine farms, about six or seven miles from Whydah, are in a high state of cultivation. The houses are clean and comfortable, and are situated in some of the most beautiful spots that imagination can picture.[64]

In another example, hundreds of miles away from Whydah, in the heart of the Sokoto caliphate, a returned Pulo, drawing on his painfully earned experience in Brazil, had built a sugar mill and a refinery.[65] The Brazilians were used to the ways of both the Africans and the Europeans, and some capitalized on this knowledge: they served as a sort of go-between. Souleiman Paraiso, for instance, whose father had been transported to Bahia as a child and had returned to Africa in 1848, became a powerful businessman and the adviser of King Toffa of Porto-Novo. His signature appears on the treaties signed between France and Dahomey.[66]

As they had been in their country of servitude, the Muslim Brazilians who returned to Africa remained a close-knit and devout community. In Whydah they formed their own neighborhood, called Maro. Those who settled in Porto-Novo erected the large central mosque. In Lagos, one of the main mosques was built by a returnee who went back home in the 1880s.

After the abolition of slavery, some returnees went back and forth between Africa and Brazil, strengthening the commercial, religious, and social ties that had existed long before Emancipation between Muslims on both sides of the Atlantic. An interesting case illustrates this continuing relationship between Brazil and Africa. The Nago Muslim Paulo Jose Ferreira, who was born in Bahia in 1886—two years before Emancipation—traveled to Lagos with his parents and sisters when he was three. As a young man he went back to Brazil, leaving his parents, siblings, and children behind in Lagos and Kano. He was fluent in Yoruba, Arabic, and Portuguese and made a living selling African goods in Rio and giving "confidential advice to blacks and whites on love, health, and religion."[67] Paulo Jose Ferreira may have been a *marabout*, genuine or otherwise. In any event, the large income he derived from his activities helped his children live very comfortably in Nigeria.

Because the Brazilians had returned to Africa as nominal Catholics, the priests who were stationed on the coast were eager to count them among their flock. Their Christian names notwithstanding, the Muslims did not display any intention of keeping a faith that had been imposed on them. They had remained secretly faithful to their religion overseas, and they went back to practicing it overtly once in Africa. The priests were puzzled and accused them of being deceivers, who had presented a facade to the white society of Brazil while retaining their old habits.[68]

By running away from the mines and the plantations; by organizing and leading revolts; and by insisting, once free, on going back to Africa, the Muslims firmly established their opposition to the Christian world of their enslavement. They were indomitable opponents whose antagonism was rooted in the normal hatred the enslaved feels for the enslaver, in the ordinary longing from freedom, but also in religious certitude and cultural self-confidence.

Even though they were far outnumbered and had little, in material terms, to help them assault and weaken the power structure, the Muslims were persistent and oftentimes successful in their endeavors. The manner in which they pursued their objectives was unique, in that they used all the advantages and tools Islam gave them: fortitude, faith, literacy, occult protection, common language, sense of community, organization, frugality, and hope.

6

The Muslim Legacy

With a documented presence of five hundred years, Islam was, after Catholicism, the second monotheist religion introduced into post-Columbian America. It preceded Lutheranism, Methodism, Baptism, Calvinism, Santeria, Candomble, and Voodoo to name a few. All these religions are alive today and are followed by the vast majority of the Africans' descendants, but in the Americas and the Caribbean, not one community currently practices Islam as passed on by preceding African generations. Where orthodox Islam exists in America it has been reintroduced by immigrants from the Middle East, southern Europe, Asia, and, recently, West Africa again. The United States is the only American country with a native Muslim population of African descent, but there is no indication so far that the African American Muslims of today inherited Islam from the Muslims of yesterday.

The orthodox Islam brought by the enslaved West Africans has not survived. It has left traces; it has contributed to the culture and history of the continents; but its conscious practice is no more. For Islam to endure, it had to grow both vertically, through transmission to the children, and horizontally, through conversion of the unbelievers. Both propositions met a number of obstacles.

Barriers to the Vertical Growth of Islam

The transmission of a religion to one's progeny presupposes, of course, that there is a progeny. Yet the very structure of the slave trade, with the disproportionate importation of men, the physical toll that enslavement took on the Africans, and the selling off of family members, placed tremendous obstacles in the path of the constitution and perpetuation of families.

There was, to begin with, a significant imbalance between the number of African males and females shipped from Africa. Among the Africans in the eighteenth-century Americas, for example, 72 percent of Senegambians were male and 28 percent female.[1] The figures for the central Sudanese are even worse, with about 95 percent men.[2] On any given plantation the demographics could be even more slanted, with some planters buying males exclusively when they needed sheer strength and adding a few women over the years for reproductive and domestic purposes. Because of this policy, a large number of African men could not form families. Language barriers and differences in cultures and religions among the Africans added another layer of difficulty in the finding of a mate. Among the native-born population, the sexual distribution was natural, and the sexes tended to be of equal numbers; but there are indications all over the slave world of a tendency to endogamy, with native-born slaves marrying and living among themselves and the Africans who could doing the same.

For both African and native-born men and women, the low fertility rate and the high infant and adult mortality rates were another hindrance to the development of families. And at the end of this obstacle course loomed the ever-present possibility of the sale of family members, which could forever destroy the unit and any possible cultural continuity. Therefore, the chances for a Muslim man to find a Muslim spouse, have children, and keep them long enough to pass on the religion were indeed slim. Muslim women fared better in the first and second parts of this process, but the third was out of their control. If the lives of the well-known Muslims are any indication, about half did not have children. By choice or out of necessity, it appears that Omar ibn Said, Abu Bakr al Siddiq, Yarrow Mahmout, and Job ben Solomon did not have descendants in America.

In contrast, Ibrahima abd al Rahman, John Mohamed Bath, Salih Bilali, and Bilali Mohamed did have children. There is no indication that Ibrahima's children, who had Christian names like their mother's, were Muslims; but one of Salih Bilali's sons, named Bilali, apparently was a Muslim and kept alive the female West African tradition of the distribution of rice cakes as an Islamic charity (*saraka*). He married the daughter of a *marabout*, but their children, who grew up seeing Muslims around, nevertheless had no understanding of Islam, at least as recorded by the WPA. In general, the grandchildren of Muslims recalled the exterior manifestations of Islam, such as prayers, but do not seem to have had precise ideas about the religion and, as far as can be ascertained by the published interviews, did not mention the religion by its name. It is not impossible that they knew more about Islam and the Muslims than they revealed but did not wish to confide in white Christian strangers—some of whom were the grandchildren of former slaveholders—asking them personal questions in Jim Crow South.

For the Muslims who had children, conformism on the children's part and difficulties with literacy may have coincided to prevent the passage of Islam from generation to generation. As a minority religion, Islam was surrounded by cults and religions with a much larger following that may have been more appealing to youngsters in search of conformity and a sense of belonging. To be a Muslim was to singularize one's self. Moreover, it was an austere religion that manifested itself through rigorous prayers and additional privations, propositions that may have handicapped its acceptance by a second and a third generation. The lack of interest of the youngsters in the religion of their parents, who had gone to great lengths to preserve it, was deplored by the Muslim clerics of Trinidad. A religious leader regretted that their youngsters "were in danger of being drawn away by the evil practices of the Christians."[3] The laments were the same in Bahia, where the clerics complained of the ungratefulness of the children who turned to fetishism, Candomble, or Catholicism.[4] After the repression of 1835, the *malés* became extremely discreet, private, and secretive, and this forced isolation was probably not appealing to the younger generations. And if the passing on of Islam was difficult when both parents were Muslims, it must have proved an even more daunting task to the Muslim who had a Christian or animist companion.

In addition, as much as literacy in Arabic was a force and an anchor for the faith, it was also most likely a hindrance to its propagation in the particular circumstances of American slavery. African children were educated in Islam through the Koranic schools, which were much more than the Sunday schools of the Christians. Islam demanded study and dedication on the part of the children every day of the year, for many years. In the Americas, the most parents could do was to teach their children in an informal way or, where possible, send them to the more elaborate schools that functioned in some urban settings. Further, it is one thing to maintain one's literacy in Arabic, but it is quite another to acquire it from scratch in the absence of time, adequate structures, and tools, as was true in most cases. Even if a book or Koran in Arabic was available, doubtless a slave child could not have found the amount of time necessary to learn how to read it.

The only alternative Muslim parents had to teaching Arabic and the Koran through schools and written media was to pass on orally what they knew. This mode of transmission works for Christians because images, icons, statues, wood carvings, stained glass, and wall paintings act as support and explanation. They are the illiterates' books. But iconography does not exist in Islam. Whatever was passed on may have been close enough to orthodoxy for the second generation, but by the third, the risks of approximation and misinterpretation would have been high and finding a reference person difficult. With the definitive end of the trans-Atlantic slave trade in the 1860s and the passing away of the African-born population, the number of people who could actually read and write Arabic, who were knowledgeable in the religion and could interpret it for the novices, was very much reduced. With some variation in time depending on the country, by the first or second decade of the twentieth century, there were no more African Muslims who could read and write Arabic in the Americas.

Barriers to the Horizontal Growth of Islam

If passing on their "religion of the Book" to their progeny was an arduous task for the Muslims, then spreading the faith among their companions proved equally daunting, if the Muslims even tried. In Africa, proselytizing was mostly done through example, by the mystic Sufis, the merchants, and the clerics and teachers who settled among the "infidels." Active recruiting was usually not part of their activities. Proselytizing in the Americas would certainly have followed the same unobtrusive pattern, only it would have met with more difficulty, because while Africans from different parts of the continent shared the same fate in the Americas, their customs, education, and culture were alien to one another. Their languages were mutually unintelligible and their mastery of the colonial languages only acquired over time. To hold religious discussions and to successfully convert under those conditions would have been very improbable. The Central Africans had had no contact with Islam in Africa, and their linguistic and cultural differences with the West African Muslims in the Americas may have been an insurmountable barrier. The West Africans constituted an African group that might have represented a source of potential recruits, as they had already been in contact with Islam in their homeland. But those who had refused conversion in Africa were probably not likely to change their minds in the Americas, particularly if they had been enslaved and sold by Muslims.

Some proselytizing did occur, as the cultural make-up of the men and women condemned for the 1835 uprising in Bahia seems to indicate. Some Central and West Africans who were certainly not Muslims in Africa took part in the revolt and may have been converts. Undoubtedly there were some conversions, but indications are strong that conversion of unbelievers was far from being a priority for the Muslims. It is remarkable that among the thousands of slave testimonies recorded in the United States, there is nothing but silence concerning the Muslims: no description of their particular rituals, comments about their habits, mention of their religion or of their eagerness to share it. When references to Islamic rituals emerge, as in the Sea Islands interviews, the believers are said to have been praying to the sun and the moon. The practitioners of Islam obviously had not told their non-Muslim companions who reported these observations anything about the religion. Charles Ball noticed this lack of communication: "I knew several," he wrote about the Africans, "who must have been, from what I have since learned, Mohamedans; though at that time, I had never heard of the religion of Mohamed."[5] Clearly, the "Mohamedans" he knew were not involved in proselytizing. Ball talked at length with one, "the man who prayed five times a day," but at no point in the narrative did the Muslim mention the particulars of his religion, which is never quoted by name. Given Ball's precise descriptions of the Africans' state of mind, in which traces of Islamic philosophy concerning life and death can be detected, he must have had extensive talks with more than one Muslim. Yet none, not even his own grandfather, tried to impress his religion on him. Nor is there any indication that Salih Bilali, Ibrahima abd al Rahman, and Bilali, for example, were involved in proselytizing. Preserving their faith, respecting its exigencies, maintaining a religious community, and trying to pass on their beliefs and knowledge to their children must have proved challenging and absorbing enough to the Muslims, who may have preferred to devote their time, resources, and energy to these tasks rather than to getting involved in missionary work. Reaction to external forces, such as fear of retribution from the slave masters, who would not have accepted seeing Islam spread, may also have played a role.

Islam survived in the Americas due to the continuous arrival of Africans—including the recaptives and the indentured laborers after the abolition of slavery in the British and French islands—and not to con-

version. It therefore remained orthodox, unadulterated by foreign elements. Unorthodoxy and tolerance of foreign elements, in contrast, are
characteristic of the successful African religions that are still alive today.
They became creolized, borrowing features from a diversity of religions
and cults and synthesizing them. Even though, in Africa, Islam and traditional religions are not exclusive, there are limits to what Islam can ab-
sorb. Syncretism is not acceptable; or as historian Lamin Sanneh explains, Islam "is syncretist only as a phase or for want of knowing better,
not as a permanent state."[6] In the Americas, it could hardly accommodate such traditional African elements as the concept of multiple deities
or of trances as a means of communication with the spirits. These traits
were heretical, and some would have been considered blasphemous.
Shirk, the belief that God's divinity may be shared, is, according to the
Koran, the most heinous and unforgivable sin. As far as Christianity was
concerned, orthodox Islam had already stated quite clearly what was acceptable in it and what was not. To introduce other crucial elements,
such as the belief in the Trinity or that Jesus was the son of God, would
have been sacrilegious. Since syncretism was not an option and the possibilities of transmission of the orthodoxy were extremely limited, only
one avenue was left for African Islam in the Americas: it could only disappear with the last Africans, enslaved, recaptives, or indentured laborers.

Islamic Survivals in Other Religions

The last decades of the nineteenth century were a decisive period for
Islam in America. In addition to the Muslims who had remained faithful
to their religion and their descendants who had turned to other faiths, another group was evolving, midway between the two. Some children of
African Muslims who were Muslims themselves, officially and voluntarily, belonged to Christian fraternities and associations. In Bahia, the So-
ciedade Protectora dos Desvalidos and the confraternities of Our Lady of
the Rosary and Saint Benedict the Moor counted many members who
were Muslims. One was Djibirilu, also known as Manoel Nascimento de
Santo Silva. The son of a Nago *alufa* and a Muslim himself, Djibirilu was
active in the Catholic confraternities.[7] When he passed away in 1959, he
was considered to be the last practicing orthodox Muslim in Bahia.

A similar phenomenon was recorded in the Sea Islands of Georgia. According to one of Bilali's descendants, a great-granddaughter of Bilali,

Harriet Hall, was a Muslim at least until 1866, when the First African Baptist Church came to Sapelo Island.[8] Information given by her descendant suggests that she may have remained a Muslim secretly while being active in the church until her death in 1922.

Being overtly a Christian had distinct advantages. In Brazil in particular, belonging to the church black associations distracted the attention of the authorities, which had become actively anti-Muslim after the 1835 rebellion. In the United States, black churches started to blossom and recruit forcefully after Emancipation, and everywhere in the Americas, the church and its associations created and strengthened solidarity in the black population as a whole—an important outcome in a hostile environment. After Emancipation, adherence to Christianity on the part of the Muslims may have been a way of disguising and protecting their true faith while taking advantage of positive and useful structures.

Islam practiced by the children of African Muslims was still Islam, but this situation soon became exceptional, for orthodox Islam died out. Yet it did not wholly disappear; parts of the religion survived as a number of its traits were incorporated into other African religions with which it had existed side by side. These religions had been tolerant, adaptable, and opportunistic from the start, so logically, as had been the case in Africa, they borrowed Islamic features and integrated them into successful syncretic cults.

For various reasons, such as concentration of followers in the slave population, ongoing contact with Africa, adaptability, and tolerance of syncretism, a number of African-based or African-derived religions have remained. They have expanded and stopped being the religion of a particular ethnic group to become the religion of peoples of different origins, all of whom brought something to the new creed and liturgy.

No systematic research has been conducted yet on Islam's contribution to the syncretic religions of black America, and how some of its elements found their way into Candomble, Santeria, Voodoo, and other rituals is not known. The observation of similar phenomenon in Africa may shed light on what happened in the Americas. In Africa, in the contact zones between animists and Muslims, where they share the same villages, for example, interaction and a definite interdependence between the groups have always existed. The animists, as already mentioned, from the early days of Islam have made great use of Islamic amulets. Animist village chiefs—and in earlier times, rulers—are acknowledged by the Muslims, who are part of their inductions and give their benedictions.

The *asantehene* Osei Tutu Kwame, the non-Muslim king of Ashanti in early nineteenth century, testified to the efficiency of Islam and the usefulness of the Muslims, saying, "I know that book [the Koran] is strong, and I like it because it is the book of the great God, it does good for me, and therefore I love all the people that read it."[9]

Even though there is close interaction between Islam and traditional African religions and real ecumenism among the adherents, each group remains faithful to its beliefs, with the non-Muslims appropriating with pragmatism whatever they find useful and efficient in the Islamic practices. The borrowing of Arabic words, perceived as words of power, is widespread, and sometimes Allah is considered one of the deities in the polytheist pantheons. There is an Allah Bango (Allah of the writing board or slate) among the Gwaris of northern Nigeria and another deity called Mamman (Muhammad).[10] As in some cases the contact has been going on for several centuries, a number of Islamic traits have made their way into animist cults and are permanent fixtures that would remain with or without the presence of Muslims. Muslims do not integrate animist elements into their liturgy but have kept pre-Islamic practices that they resort to in certain circumstances, and some consult animist healers or diviners when the *marabout* has not been able to help them.

In the Americas, as traditional African religions were being reconstructed, adapting to local conditions, they integrated Islamic and Christian features as well as tenets from a diversity of African cults. There was no fusion but rather coexistence, juxtaposition, or symbiosis. In some religions, Islamic traits are recognized as such by the believers, who make direct references to Allah, the Muslims, or Arabic. In others, the origin of such traits seems to have been forgotten, but they are present and almost as visible.

Religions that have integrated Islamic traits in an overt manner are the Bahian Candomble and the Cuban Santeria, introduced by the Yoruba. The Yoruba religion had begun to integrate Islamic elements in Africa. Its first deity, Orishala or Obatala, is said to be *Oba-t-Alla*, or "Lord Allah."[11] His day is Friday, the Muslim Sabbath, and his color is white. The *Ifa* divination system used by the Yoruba was introduced by the first *babalawo* (master of divination), whose name was Alaba or Araba. He is said to have come from Arabia. The system itself is viewed by some scholars to be partly derived from Islamic geomancy.[12]

The Yoruba religion was not merely transposed to Brazil and Cuba; it adapted to a new set of conditions—the enslavement of the adepts and their forced conversion to a foreign religion in particular. In the Americas, it incorporated Christian elements and more Islamic references into its liturgy. Allah was called on, as is attested in the following two songs heard, at least until the 1930s, in some Bahian *terreiros* (places of worship):

> *Allah!*
> *Allah! de Deus!*
> *Allah!*
>
> *Allah!*
> *Olo Allah!*
> *Baba quara da!*[13]

Allah himself found a place in the Candomble pantheon, not under the name Obatala but under his own. Given the prestige of Islam and the high regard that Islamic divination, healing, and protection making enjoyed among non-Muslims, to invoke the God of the Muslims was an attempt to attract efficient benedictions and divine interventions.

Islamic elements in Candomble can also be seen in the description of a cult active in the state of Alagoas, Brazil, in the first decade of this century. The principal god was *orixa-alun* or *orixa-allah*. The priest was not called *pae* (father) *de terreiro*, as in Candomble, but *alufa* (from *alfa*, a Muslim leader). The faithful wore *mandingas*, and the walls of the place of worship were decorated not with representations of the *orishas* and their corresponding Catholic saints but with what a witness described as "arabesques."[14] In addition, a chant contained this verse:

> *Edure, edure, alilala*

which probably derived from the *shahada*: *La-ilaha ill-Allah*, or "There is no God but God." The presence of these Islamic traits notwithstanding, *orishas* such as Oya, Oxun, and Shango were honored.

The Muslims themselves appear in some of the rituals and creeds of the non-Muslims. A Candomble song recorded in 1934 stated that the *orisha* Ogun, the bellicose god of iron and war, was somehow linked to the *malés*:

> *Ogun menino e de male*
> (Little Ogun is of the *malés*)
> *Nu-e, nu-e!*
> *Ogun menino e de male*
> *Nue-e, e-re-re-re!*[15]

The Muslims are acknowledged further in an African-derived Carioca cult, the Macumba, that mixes Yoruba, Bantu, Gege (Ewe, from ancient Dahomey and Togo), and Native American beliefs. They are called Mussurumin, Mussuruhy, or Massuruman. The *linha de Mussuruhy*, or "line of the Muslims," is made of gunpowder that encircles pins, bottles, cigars, and chickens. As the powder is lighted and explodes, the angry and vengeful spirits come down. In keeping with their Islamic origin, the *paes de santo* of the Muslim lines are called *pae alufa* or *tio alufa*.[16]

The memory of the Muslims is also kept alive in Umbanda, a spiritualist cult that developed from the Macumba. It arose in the 1920s and counts about 20 million followers. In this cult, the spirits of the black and Indian ancestors form armies, led by *orishas*. The *orisha* Omulu, god of medicine and smallpox, leads the line of the skulls, souls, Indian sorcerers, and Muslims (called variously Mussurumin, Massuruman, Massurumin, Mussuruhy, or simply *malés*.[17]) This line of spirits of the dead represents the souls of the native and Muslim medicine men. The association of Muslims and medicine is not fortuitous. Popular Islam has a long tradition of herbal, faith, and religious medicine performed by *marabouts*, who use herbs, amulets, animal sacrifices, prayers, and incantations to treat their patients. Their reputation transcends their Muslim communities, and they have always been consulted by non-Muslims.

Generally speaking, the Brazilian syncretic cults are made up of—according to a classification proposed by anthropologist Arthur Ramos—Gege, Yoruba, Muslim, Bantu, Indian, spiritist, and Catholic elements, all of which can be readily identified.[18] Some cults combine all these elements, while others use only three or four. Out of seven such combinations, only two do not contain Islamic features.

In Cuba, the Santeria priests and priestesses, though they are of Yoruba tradition and use Yoruba terminology in their rituals to this day, greet the faithful with the Arabic words *Salam ualeikum*, to which the latter respond with *Mualekum salam*.

Medicine and occult powers that appear to be linked to Islam are at the center of a cult in the Dominican Republic. The Morenos (the blacks) family, who are recognized as having special healing powers, trace their roots back to Isidro, a Haitian born at the turn of the century. With his father and three brothers, he left for Santo Domingo around 1830. The others eventually went back to Haiti, but Isidro remained. Starting with Isidro and continuing to this day, the leaders of the Morenos use supernatural powers to cure their followers and wear a trademark white turban.[19]

In nearby Haiti, Islam and the Muslims appear in voodoo. Voodoo came to the island of Saint-Domingue from Dahomey, carried by the Fon and Ewe. Their religion, in Africa, had already assimilated elements of other peoples' beliefs, including those of the Yoruba. In the Caribbean, it absorbed the contributions of still other religions and cultures. The Voodoo pantheon has one supreme god, called Mawu in Benin and Papa Bondieu (Father God, in French and patois) on the island, and deities or spirits, called *loas*. The *loas* serve the same function as the *orishas*. Most *loas* come from Africa, but many are creoles, having originated in the island. The African deities are called *loas Guinin* and are divided into *nanchons* (nations) that represent the different African ethnic groups. There are *loas* Congo, *loas* Ibo, *loas* Nago, and so forth.

When the *loas* are called by the *houngan* (priest) and the assembly, they descend on the participants and "ride" them, expressing themselves through the believers in the manner specific to their nation. Tellingly, the *loas* Senegal speak Arabic: they say, "Salam! Salam Malekoum! Salay' salam ma salay,"[20] or "Peace! Peace be with you! Prayer, peace, prayer." To this day, in some *houmfors* (Voodoo temples), when a particular *loa* appears and is recognized by the congregation and the *houngan* as being a *loa* Senegal, the *houngan* greets him with the words *Salam, salam*, then kneels and raises his hands above his head, as Muslims do when they pray.[21] In addition, the name Allah can sometimes be heard in the prayers.[22]

Islam and the Muslims are thus acknowledged and invoked by the followers of the most successful neo-African and African-derived cults in the New World and are integrated into their rituals and creeds. Their belief in one God, their Arabic literacy, their bellicose spirit, and the efficiency of their learned men are the traits that seem to have most impressed their non-Muslim companions. Their acknowledgment is another indication of the important place they held in the slave community, in disproportion to their numbers. It is also an indication of the positive manner in which the non-Muslims perceived them. Contrary to Christianity and its saints, Islam was not imposed on them. They freely chose to integrate some of its elements. In their own indisputable way, the non-Muslims rebuked the assertion that they had strained relationships with the Muslims in the Americas. In addition, these religions confirm that Islam was a unifying force that regrouped different nations into one global community. In effect, the Muslims entered the non-Muslim rituals as Muslims, not as Hausa, Mandingo, or Fulani. In Voodoo, for instance, the Arabic-speaking *loas* are not designated by their ethnic origin; they are called collectively "*loas* Senegal." They are the only ones grouped under a geographic terminology, whereas the other *loas* were integrated on an ethnic basis.[23]

Islamic elements also appear in American and Caribbean cults that do not seem to have retained a conscious memory of the origin of these borrowed rituals. One example can be found in Toco, a village at the extreme north of Trinidad. Officially outlawed in 1917, the cult nevertheless continues to operate and was observed by anthropologists Melville and Frances Herskovits in the 1940s.[24] The scholars never linked what they were studying to Islam, which has typically been the case with researchers of Africanisms in the Americas. The fact that there is no reference to Islam and the Muslims in their work may mean that the congregation itself was not aware of the origin of some of its rituals, or it may have been but did not mention these origins to the Herskovitses.

The adepts of the cult, called "Shouters," are Spiritual Baptists, part of a Protestant revivalist movement that spread throughout the British islands between the late eighteenth century and the late nineteenth century. Their clergy is composed, among many officiants, of a preacher; a teacher who, like a *marabout*, interprets dreams and visions; a divine healer who, also like a *marabout,* has the power of faith healing; a prophet who see things in the past and in the future through astrology; a fortune-teller, whose function is to "read" the faithful; and a judge. Many of the functions that the *marabout* normally holds seem to have been redistributed among the clergy.

Other Islamic traits can be detected. The faithful are barefoot in the church, as the Muslims are in a mosque; they kneel on a piece of fabric in the same manner as the Muslims do on a rug when they pray; and they use a particular ceremonial handshake. This ritual handshake consists of three downward shakes of the right hand, followed by the elevation of the hands above the head as in a Muslim prayer. Next comes the touching of the left breast by one, then the other participant—a typical trait of the handshake exchanged by Muslims the world over. Further, as noted in chapter 2, the Shouters turn around a special altar built in the center of the church, different from the regular one located at the front of the building. This may represent another example of Lorenzo Dow Turner's theory that the "shout" is, in essence, an Islamic survival linked to the *shaw't*, or circumambulation of the Kaaba in Mecca.

In Toco, the Shouters are not alone in their use of Islamic features. For all segments of the population, important ceremonies such as weddings and funerals always include the consultation of the ancestors, which is preceded by an offering of food and drinks called *sakara*. The word may refer to a type of traditional music found in some areas of West Africa or, rather, it may be a slight corruption of the Arabic word *sadakha*, or freewill offering. The *sakara* in Toco is offered to all the ancestors, including those left in Africa. At midnight, an old man takes the food and drinks outside, and speaking in a language that, according to the participants, is like "Yarriba" (Yoruba), he says, "All a me people from Guinea, all you come. Come, this are we own food. . . . Who a drink rum, drink. Who a drink beverage, drink."[25] Interestingly, the beverage referred to in the *sakara* ceremony is nonalcoholic, and its mention alongside the alcoholic libation is probably a reference to the Muslim ancestors, who do not drink rum or any other alcohol. The ancestors receive *sakara* during the ceremonies marking the ninth and the fortieth day after a funeral. This practice may have its origin in the Islamic tradition of marking the eighth and fortieth days of a person's death with prayers and a meal.

In the islands of Carriacou and Grenada, people of African origin give offerings of food to the spirits of their ancestors during a dance called the Big Drum Dance, the Nation Dance (African nations), or *saraka*.[26] The dance proper consists of different dances performed by the descendants of African nations such as the Mandingo, Koromantin, Arada, Temne, Ibo, Congo, and Chamba.

Saraka and *sakara* appear to be linked to the cult of the ancestors, but, if the Islamic hypothesis is correct, the connection is only indirect. As no such cult or even celebration exists in Islam, it is clear that the communities that perform these rituals would not have adopted the name as part and parcel of a Muslim ceremony. One explanation for the survival of the word is that the Muslims in Trinidad, Grenada, Carriacou, and other areas impressed the rest of the slave population with their almsgiving. Islamic precepts demand that *sadakha* be given to the needy, and it is probable that non-Muslim slaves, too, were the recipients of the Muslims' charity, which expresses itself in food, money, cloth, or whatever the donor can afford. In a situation of abject deprivation, the Muslims' gesture would have created positive feelings and made a lasting impression on the slave community, which would have associated offerings with the Muslims. As the non-Muslims developed their own ceremonies, they adopted the word—which was not connected with any particular ethnic group—to describe offerings. Since most offerings given by the followers of traditional cults are directed toward the ancestors or the deities, *saraka* in the Americas became identified with the cult of the ancestors, even though such a ritual is unknown in Islam. Another, explanation for the survival of the word is that the non-Muslims attributed a special strength to the offerings made by the Muslims. In Africa, the polytheist Bambara of Mali, for example, use the word *sadakha* to describe offerings to their gods.[27] They borrowed it from the Muslims, and just as they use the word *bismillah* (in the name of Allah) in their religious invocations, they attribute a special power to the word *sadakha*, linked to the effectiveness of the Muslim rituals.

Another association between Islam and a funeral ritual was observed at the end of the nineteenth century in Penedo in the state of Alagoas, Brazil, where a feast of the dead that took place twice a year contained numerous Islamic features. This particular ceremony, held by "Africans," was preceded by a period of abstinence from meat, cereals, and alcohol. The male participants wore a white cap and white clothes, and the priest and his aides had garments "similar to the costume of the Sahara desert and the sands of Oman."[28] They spent the first night praying and reciting incantations. At dawn, they slaughtered sheep in the Muslim manner, by letting the animals bleed. The women, wearing head wraps and fabrics from Africa, placed food on the ground and under rocks for the departed souls who would come and eat during the night— an un-Islamic rite. The feast ended with music and dance for the community at large. The religious group, however, did not take part in this segment of the ceremony. What took place in Penedo was probably a common ritual involving Muslims and non-Muslims, with each group performing its part according to the precepts of its religion.

This association of Muslims and non-Muslims in a particular event meant to reinforce the cohesion of the community as a whole is evident in a festivity that took place on the Sea Islands, during slavery. Elderly men and women have described it as an important affair that marked harvesttime. Its function was to "thank for the crops"; it was a propitiatory rite as exists in most agricultural societies. The Sea Islands former slaves mentioned to the WPA that the festivity included prayers and dance, and that the celebration lasted all night. Though everyone agreed on this framework, some variations can be detected in the recollections of the respondents.

Rachel Anderson, whose great-grandmother was a Muslim, remembered that the slaves did the shout all night, and at sunrise, they prayed and bowed low to the sun. Another descendant of Muslims, Rosa Grant, whose grandmother Ryna prayed three times a day and made the *saraka*, also said that they shouted all night, and at sunup they sang and prayed.[29] Harvesttime for the Muslims appears to have been spent chanting all night, a widespread Muslim tradition, and to end with a prayer at sunrise as is customary in all Islamic celebrations.

Former slaves who were not associated with Islam gave a different version of the feast. Nero Jones of Sapelo Island remembered that they prayed and sang all night, and when the sun rose, they got out and danced. Hettie Campbell and Henry Williams of Saint Marys both said that the people shouted and sang all night and started to dance when the sun rose. Catherine Wing stated that they went to church with their first crop, prayed, and danced.[30]

The three versions of the same event attest that even though the community as a whole commemorated harvesttime, each group did so in its own way. The Christians went to church, the followers of traditional African religions celebrated with prayers and ritual dances at daybreak, and the Muslims chanted and prayed to the east at sunrise. Despite differences in the celebrations, all shouted, a rite that may have been created by the Muslims and borrowed by the rest of the slaves. They may also have borrowed another Islamic feature: the First African Baptist Church on Sapelo Island is built so that the congregation prays turned toward the east.[31] In addition, the dead are buried with their head to the west and their feet to the east, therefore "looking" east, a practice not restricted to the Sea Islands but found among other African American communities. Muslims bury their dead lying on the right side, their hands under their head, their eyes facing east. There is a possible Islamic retention or loan in the American practice, but east may also symbolize Africa, not Mecca.

An Islamic tradition that has survived the demise of the African Muslims and made its way into other communities is the gris-gris. In Cuba, the followers of the African-derived, or neo-African, religions wear leather or fabric pouches containing protections around their necks, along with Catholic medals. In Brazil, the *mandingas* worn by the Catholics are called *patuas*. Exactly like their Islamic counterparts, they consist of prayers and cabalistic signs written on a piece of paper that is inserted into a leather or cloth pouch.[32] In both Cuba and Brazil, black and white Catholics influenced by the Muslims write prayers on pieces of paper that they glue to their windows or doors to protect their house from thieves.[33] The Brazilian *figa* may also be linked to Islam. It is a small hand, worn around the neck to protect against evil spells. In Islamic numerology, the number 5 is of particular significance: it refers to the Five Pillars, the five prayers, and the five holy persons (Muhammad, Ali, Fatima, Hasan, and Useyn). Their names are often written on a gris-gris shaped like a hand with its five fingers, to protect the bearer from the evil eye.

Islamic Survivals in Music

African Islam has left traces in other ways. A Gullah song, for example, carries the memory of the *saraka* into the twentieth century:

> Rice cake, rice cake
> Sweet me so
> Rice cake sweet me to my heart.[34]

It is, fittingly, a children's song, since slave children were the beneficiaries of the Muslim women's charity. Their Islamic gesture of goodwill and community spirit clearly made a lasting impression. Other songs in Latin America and the Caribbean also relate to the Muslims and Islam. The expression *Salam ualekum* appears in a song sung by the Peruvian blacks.[35] Another song, part of the folklore of the black Peruvians of the coast, contains the words *moce male*, which, according to linguist Fernando Romero, could be a corruption of *voce male*, meaning "you are a *malé* [a Muslim]" in Portuguese.[36] The song may have been brought to Peru by slaves whom the Portuguese sold or by immigrant freed Africans.

Cuban Tapa or Nupe speakers sang in "languages" well into the 1950s,[37] and being Muslims, they undoubtedly used Arabic terminology. Similarly, in Trinidad, informants interviewed for a research project in the 1960s were familiar with songs and phrases in a few African languages, including Arabic.[38] Another research project has shown that prewedding songs collected from an eighty-two-year-old Hausa woman in Gasparillo, Trinidad, in the 1970s contain Arabic words.[39]

Arabic words and expressions appear in almost all songs the Muslims in Africa sing, including the nonreligious songs. Expressions such as *Lailaha ill-Allah Muhamadu rasul Allah* (There is no God but God and Muhammad is his Messenger), *Allahu Akbar* (God is the Greatest), or "It is Allah's will" are found routinely in Wolof, Tukulor, Hausa, Mandingo, and Fulbe songs of praise or love and in historical pieces. These songs were transported to the Americas and sung on the plantations, just as other songs from other cultures were remembered and kept alive.

Besides these secular songs, Muslims have a repertoire of religious songs and recitations from the Koran, consisting of the chanting of the *surah*s. Both the secular and religious genres constitute an important part of the musical creations of West African Muslims.

Islamic-influenced music is quite distinctive. The traits that distinguish it are found in the call to prayer, which the muezzin sings five times a day, every day of the year. It is a simple melody with long, decorated, swooping notes. Musical recitations of the Koran have the same characteristics and use falsetto, yodel, trembling of the voice, and guttural and nasal sounds. This style has influenced the traditional music of West African Muslims, who have incorporated these techniques and the melodic element particular to Islamic music into their creations. Naturally, much cross-pollination has occurred between the music of West and of North Africa: free and enslaved black Africans lived among the Arab and Berber populations of the Maghreb, and their musicians were particularly valued. The music of the Maghreb has thus been influenced by the music of sub-Saharan Africa, and this new type of music in turn went south of the desert to be absorbed by the Muslim populations, who brought it with them to the New World.

Music, which is viewed as a means to bring an individual or a group closer to God, is an integral part of Sufi life, following the injunction of the *Hadith*: "Adorn the Koran with your voices." The members of the Sufi orders routinely chant the Koran and religious hymns in a group during secular ceremonies and religious feasts, funerals, holy days, pilgrimages, and at night during Ramadan. Sufi *dhikr*, in contrast, are always sung solo. Supplications are also a genre, consisting of prayers chanted in an emotional way. Another genre is the high art of *tilawat*, the musical recitation of the Koran, performed by specialists who follow strict rules of pronunciation and intonation and always chant solo.

The music of the African Muslims in the Americas was markedly different from the musical styles carried over by the Yoruba, the Congolese, and the Angolans, with their strong reliance on rapid drumming, call and response, group singing, and short melodic lines. The typical song coming from the Sahel was a solo, moaning kind of song that blues expert Alan Lomax calls a "high lonesome complaint."[40] George Washington Cable, whose description of Congo Square in nineteenth-century New

Orleans has remained famous, had already noted this singularity. As he was strolling the square, he spotted a girl, tall and straight, "a Yaloff [Wolof]. You see it in her almost Hindoo features, and hear it in the plaintive melody of her voice."[41]

The ornamented, unaccompanied, lonesome complaint is, according to Lomax, emblematic of the kingdoms and empires where absolute power reigns. It is found, among other places, in the Middle East, the Mediterranean, North Africa, and Islamic West Africa. The American South, Mississippi in particular, having a long tradition of absolute tyranny, was fertile ground for the blossoming of the style. Other musicologists have seen in the Islamic-influenced music of the West Africans the origin of the quintessential African American musical creation: the blues.

An incident that occurred in Sierra Leone in the eighteenth century may well describe what gave birth to the blues. In the slave yard on the coast was a Muslim man of thirty-five years, who could read and write Arabic. He was in irons, awaiting departure and "sometimes he would sing a melancholy song, then he would utter an earnest prayer."[42] The melancholy song was in all probability the recitation of the Koran. Muslims like him would sing in the same manner as a consolation, time and again, on the plantations of the South, and their lonesome "song" probably became what is known as the blues.

Blues expert Samuel Charters recalls in his study *The Roots of the Blues: An African Search* that when blues was first introduced to European audiences, comments were made about similarities between this African American music and Rom (gypsy) flamenco music from Spain. Flamenco certainly did not influence the blues; but when the musicologist listened to Muslim Mandingo musicians in the Gambia, it became clear to him "that the West African musicians had already been influenced by Arabic music just as gypsy singers and instrumentalists had been along the Mediterranean. The influence hadn't come from the Gypsies to the Mississippi blues men. There had been earlier Arabic music that had influenced them both."[43]

In the American South, even though Africans from Senegambia and the rest of the Islamic belt were outnumbered by men and women from the forest area, their music had a better chance than that of other Africans of being preserved. Because drums were outlawed in the South, musicians who traditionally relied less on them and more on string and wind instruments were at an advantage. Moreover, as musicologist Paul

Oliver points out, the slaveholders used these musicians, who could easily adapt to fiddles and guitars, in their own balls, so they could continue to exercise their talents openly.[44] They were usually exempted from work in the fields and had time and the necessary instruments to continue developing their skills. Drummers and percussionists, in contrast, had few opportunities to keep in practice. Sahelian Islamic-influenced music, through its musicians and their knowledge of string instruments, thus had a good chance to survive in the South.

A close study of the musical particularities of the blues confirms the hypothesis of an African Islamic-derived music. The string-playing techniques of the savanna are similar to the techniques used by blues guitarists. The *kora*, a twenty-one-string harp, the Mandingo instrument par excellence, is "played in a rhythmic-melodic style that uses constantly changing rhythms, often providing a ground bass overlaid with complex treble patterns, while vocal supplies a third rhythmic layer," states musicologist John Storm Roberts, who concludes that "similar techniques can be found in hundreds of blues records."[45] The same holds true for the vocals. The "long, blending and swooping notes" of the blues, explains Roberts, are "similar to the Islam-influenced styles of much of West Africa."[46] In addition, the "bending of notes"—which produces quarter tones at the third, fifth, and seventh of the scale—a major feature of vocal blues, is another characteristic of Islamic-influenced music, as is producing a note slightly under pitch, breaking into a vibrato, or letting the note trail off and finishing it above what is expected. These techniques used in the blues are present, notes Roberts, "in Islamic African music and hardly at all in other styles."[47]

Even complete songs seem to have been transported from one side of the Atlantic Ocean to the other. The holler "Tangle Eyes," for instance, has been found to have a match in Senegal. "As one listens to this musical union," stresses Alan Lomax, "spanning thousands of miles and hundreds of years, the conviction grows that Tangle Eye's forebears must have come from Senegal bringing this song style with them."[48]

Even an untrained ear can recognize the similarities that exist between the blues and Islamic-influenced West African music; but parallels are as strong between some blues pieces and the musical recitation of the Koran, an area that has not been explored by musicologists. A good example of these similarities can be found in a blues recording from the penitentiaries of Mississippi and Louisiana, made by Alan Lomax. The cut "Levee Camp Holler" could easily be juxtaposed to a recitation of the Koran: it features the same ornamented notes, tortuously elongated sounds, pauses, nasal humming, simple melody, and impression of human lonesomeness. Joint research by experts on African Islamic music and specialists of the blues is needed to delineate with more precision the Muslims' contribution to the musical creations of the Americas. As the overall influence of the Muslims is recognized, light will be shed on perplexing parallels and "coincidences."

The Disappearance of the Enslaved Muslims from American History

Although they have left a mark on the religious and cultural landscape of African America, the Muslims for the most part have disappeared from collective consciousness and have been overlooked by scholarly research. An obvious reason may be that Islam and the African Muslims died out, and having thus completely disappeared from sight, they also disappeared from awareness. In the British and French possessions, the last African Muslims must have passed away in the 1880s or 1890s, and the indentured laborers shortly thereafter. In the United States, Brazil, and Cuba—where the slave trade and slavery lasted longer—the last Muslims probably disappeared between 1920 and 1930. The followers of voodoo, Santeria, and Candomble, in contrast, still exist, and their religions therefore cannot be forgotten.

The decades after Emancipation were difficult times for the former slave population, who had to adapt to new and disappointing circumstances after the euphoria that freedom brought, while trying to fit in a larger society that looked down on them, their history, and their customs and that ultimately rejected them often violently. In the United States, descendants of Muslims who could have kept their memory alive were engaged in mainstream religions that had little tolerance for other faiths. Their forefathers' religion was of no relevance or particular significance to them. In addition, there are indications, if the Sea Islands are taken as an example, that these descendants related their family's religion to sun and moon worship, because the Muslims prayed at sunrise and sundown. A determination to distance oneself from "primitive" African practices, a lack of understanding and knowledge, a desire to conform, and fear of retribution from the white and Christian establishment all may explain why the Muslims' descendants remained silent about the religion of their parents and grandparents.

In the United States, this silence of the "humble" was paralleled by the silence of the elite. Some famous African Americans may have been the descendants of Muslims, but none ever claimed such a filiation. Some scholars see Muslim origins in the families of a few personalities, but the evidence is questionable. Martin Robinson Delany, a Harvard-educated physician, the first black major in the U.S. Army, an abolitionist, and a black nationalist, was the grandson, through his mother, of a man who has been described as an African "captured when young, during hostilities between the Mandingoes, Fellatahs [Fulani], and Houssa," and a Mandingo grandmother.[49]. His grandfather's name, however, was not Mandingo, Fulbe nor Hausa: he was called Shango, like the Yoruba *orisha*. His grandmother said she was born near a "great river called Yolla Ba."[50] It is evidently the Niger, or the Djoliba (great blood), as the Mande people—and not the Yoruba—call it. To complicate matters, she used to sing a song whose first verse was *oja batta batta*,[51] or "the rain falls down," but the language is not Mandingo but Yoruba (*ojo kata kata*). Her name, Graci, is neither Mandingo nor Yoruba. Thus evidence suggests that Delany's maternal grandfather was Yoruba, and not Mandingo, and that his grandmother was either a Mandingo whose family settled among the Yoruba or a mixed Yoruba-Mandingo. From the available information, it is difficult to assess what their religion was.

Delany's friend and fellow abolitionist Frederick Douglass may have been—according to one of his biographers—the descendant of Muslims. His great-great-grandfather's name was Baly, and Douglass's own name at birth was Frederick Augustus Washington Bailey—after his mother, the slave Harriet Bailey. The name leads biographer William McFeely to theorize that, Bailey being possibly a corruption of Bilali, Frederick Douglass may have been the offspring of Muslims.[52] The descendants of Bilali Mohammed from Sapelo Island are now named Bailey, and there is no reason to think that they are the only family whose original name underwent this transformation. But in any event, Douglass could not have been a descendant of this particular Bilali, because the Bailey name in his family preceded the arrival of Bilali Mohamed in the United States.

Elijah Muhammad is another celebrity who, according to historian Michael Gomez, may have had Muslims in his family. Gomez claims that Muhammad's father, a Baptist preacher, was named Wali, which means "saintly man" in Arabic. But in reality his name was William, and the only Wali that Muhammad was close to was Wally Fard, the founder of the Nation of Islam, whose origins are particularly controversial.

No Islamic link has ever been presented for Harriet Tubman, and she herself never claimed any Muslim origins, but her name may reveal some connection. Her grandparents were Africans and she was a second-generation American whose name at birth was Araminta Ross.[53] While Araminta is not a Muslim name, it may be a corruption of Aminta, Aminata (an Africanized rendition of Muhammad's mother's name), or Aramisa (Thursday).

In other parts of the Americas and the Caribbean, such as Haiti, Brazil, Jamaica, and Trinidad, the Muslims and Islam were integrated into the religious life of the black population just as any other African religions were. They were not accorded a special status but were not forgotten either; they just became another component of the religious and social world. Whereas in the United States the Muslims' lack of visibility developed from omission, in the rest of the Americas it stemmed from their being taken for granted. Yet the memory of the Muslims has lingered on in some of these areas, and some families can still trace their origins to a particular Muslim ancestor or population. There are families in Colombia and Cuba, for example, whose last name is Mandingo, Mandinga, or Mina. (There is only one such case in the United States: in southwestern Louisiana, a Creole family bears the name Senegal and evidently had ancestors who were Tukulor, or Wolof Muslims shipped from Saint-Louis.) In Trinidad, John Mohamed Bath, the chief of the Free Mandingo Muslims, is very much alive in the mind of his family, as attested by his descendant Dr. Patricia Bath, an eye surgeon now living in California.

African Muslims have also been the victims of academic oversight. Most of what is known about the African Muslim slaves was produced during slavery, and very few contemporary scholars have relayed their story into the twentieth century. Those who did wrote almost exclusively about Brazil. Studies devoted to the Muslims in that country have been published by Raymundo Nina Rodrigues (1900); Manoel Querino (1906); Etienne Ignace (1909); Gilberto Freyre (1933); Arthur Ramos (1934); Edison Carneiro (1936); and Roger Bastide, Vincent Monteil, and Rolf Reichert in the 1970s. The research culminated with two major works by Pierre Verger (1968) and Joao Jose Reis (1994). In other parts of Latin America and in the Caribbean, notably in countries where the Islamic presence was strong, such as Haiti, Martinique, Guadeloupe, the

Guianas, Trinidad, Peru, and Jamaica, research and writing on slavery issues in general are not as developed as they should be. In those conditions, the Muslims fare no better in terms of recognition than the rest of the slave population.

In the United States, in contrast, scholars have a keen interest in the history of slavery and in African cultural and religious survivals, and more studies on these subjects have been produced in the United States than anywhere else in the Americas. Nevertheless, Muslims have been conspicuously absent from works relating to African Americans. There is no mention of Islam or Muslim Africans in any of the major works on the slave trade and slavery. No reference to their story, contributions, or mere presence can be found in publications on African American culture or religion. Only in the 1990s has there been, from time to time, an allusion to or a few words on the Muslims in scholarly works.

Lack of resources cannot explain this phenomenon, because an abundance of published records exist on eighteenth- and nineteenth-century Muslims in the United States. Additional material was made available in the early twentieth century. Newbell Puckett, for example, produced a list of hundreds of African names, many of them Islamic, in 1926. Dr. Lorenzo Dow Turner's book on Gullah, published in 1949, evidenced a number of Islamic names used in the Sea Islands. In 1940 the WPA published the reminiscences of former slaves, many of whom described habits of their companions or grandparents that could be identified as Muslim without too much effort; and the *Journal of Negro History* put out the first study of the *Ben-Ali Diary* in the same year. By the end of the 1960s, Philip Curtin had edited *Africa Remembered: Narratives by West Africans from the Era of the Slave Trade*, which—although its focus was not the Muslims—presented information on Job ben Solomon, Abu Bakr al Siddiq, Salih Bilali, and the recaptive Ali Eisami Gazirmabe. Terry Alford's excellent biography of Ibrahima Abd al Rahman, published in 1977, did not generate new research; nor did a somewhat patronizing book on Job ben Solomon. Even though these last two stories are significant, they nevertheless focused on individuals and did not draw attention to the larger Muslim community.

Writers and artists, for their part, have given the subject of Muslim slaves in the Americas scant attention. Alex Haley did not make Islam a meaningful element of his ancestor's life, as it most probably was, and made no mention of Muslim populations in the United States. Toni Mor-

rison's "Song of Solomon," in her novel by the same name, contains the
verses:

> Solomon and Ryna Belali Shalut
> Yaruba Medina Muhammet too.
> Nestor Kalina Saraka cake.[54]

with no explanation and no other reference to Muslims. (This recitation
of Bilali's family names and the allusions to *saraka* and to Kalina, another known Muslim from Sapelo, are woven into a song created by
Morrison herself, who set her story in Virginia.) Although Julie Dash's
beautiful movie *Daughters of the Dust* (1991) opens with the praying of
an old Muslim man, an overt acknowledgment of the Muslims of the Sea
Islands, it does not pursue their story any further. Steven Spielberg's
Amistad (1997) features a few Muslims; however, this poorly researched
movie, which is particularly offensive to Africans, shows them only for a
split second, praying on the ship deck. Strangely, most of the men and
girls in *Amistad* wear turbans, which are a Muslim trademark and are
never worn by non-Muslims or by Muslim young men who have not
gained the right to do so. In addition, at no point in Spielberg's movie is
there any mention of religion or any display of religious behavior or attitudes among the prisoners, except when it comes to the Christian convert. In this fanciful and stereotypical rendition of Africans, the Muslims
again are poorly served. Muslims indeed were on the *Amistad*, as has
been documented by Richard Madden, who testified on behalf of the
Africans in Connecticut on November 11, 1839. He

> spoke with one of them and repeated in the Arabic language a Mo-
> hammedan form of prayer and the words "Allah Akbar" or "God is
> Great" were immediately recognized by the negro, and some of the words
> of the said prayer were repeated after him by the negro. That deponent ad-
> dressed another negro, standing by the former, in the ordinary terms of ori-
> ental salutation "salaam Aleikoum" or Peace to you and the man immedi-
> ately replied "Aleikoum Salaam" or with you be peace.[55]

One of the young men, Ba-u, whose name must have been Ba (a Pulo
name), said that his father was a *marabout*.[56] There is little doubt that
these Muslims—and their non-Muslim shipmates, for that matter—
would have acted and behaved very differently than the mass of animal-
istic Africans depicted in Spielberg's movie.

On a more serious note, some recent scholarship has recognized the
presence of Muslim slaves in the United States but has minimized their

importance. Gwendolyn Midlo Hall, who has written a very detailed study of the Senegambians and Malians who formed the basis of the Creole population of Louisiana, devotes twenty-five lines out of 422 pages to Islam among the Mandingo of Senegambia and remains silent about the religion of the Wolof and Fulani. Hall rightly states that two-thirds of the men and women whom the French imported into Louisiana came from Senegambia. Among the Senegambians introduced by Spain after 1763, she emphasizes, 29 percent were Mandingo, 10 percent Fulani, and 22 percent Wolof. But Hall does not mention that the three populations were already largely Islamized; and when giving a list of names, many of which are Islamic, Hall feels compelled to state that "Islamic names do not necessarily mean that these slaves were Muslims."[57] Contrary to what the writer affirms, Islamic names in West Africa are given only to Muslims. Overall, Gwendolyn Midlo Hall's strenuous effort to deny any relevance to the Muslims in Louisiana is difficult to understand, in light of the overwhelming evidence.

The first comprehensive study devoted to African Muslims in the United States was done by Allan Austin, a professor of English and Afro-American Studies at Springfield College in Massachusetts. His rich 759-page sourcebook *African Muslims in Antebellum America,* published in 1984, presents *in extenso* the autobiographies, biographies, and related documentation concerning Omar ibn Said, Job ben Solomon, Ibrahima abd al Rahman, Salih Bilali, Bilali, Yarrow Mahmout, Abu Bakr al Siddiq, Mohammed Ali ben Said, Mahomma Gardo Baquaqua, and some other, lesser known individuals. A fifty-page introduction and copious notes put the Muslim slaves in historical perspective.[58]

Coming after this pioneer book, about half a dozen articles in scholarly journals and a deconstructionist study of Omar ibn Said's and Bilali's manuscripts have not added significantly to the knowledge about the enslaved Muslims. One book on Elijah Muhammad, published in 1997, has given scant attention to them; and another on African American Islam, published the same year, sums up in one chapter the stories of individual Muslims such as Ibrahima abd al Rahman, Yarrow Mamout, and Job ben Solomon.[59]

Considering the number of books on slavery published in the United States in the past thirty years, the research on Muslims enslaved in the Americas is strikingly limited. This is all the more remarkable because studies on slavery, Africanisms in America, and Afrocentrism are numerous. In addition, the United States is the only country in the New World with a native Muslim population of African descent. Ironically, these may be the very reasons for the widescale neglect of the subject of African Muslims in the Americas. Continuing a line of thought started in the nineteenth century in the United States, some scholars appear to think that the Muslims were not authentic Africans. The reason is not racial but cultural: the West African Muslims may be seen as "true blacks" instead of Moors or Arabs, but their culture and religion are viewed as foreign, Arab.

It is significant that Islam is rarely, if ever, mentioned in studies on or references to African religions. After one thousand years of continuous presence, dissemination by the sub-Saharan Africans themselves, accommodations to the local cultures, and an overall record of voluntary conversion rather than imposition, Islam is still considered a non-African religion by most American scholars. For some, to see Islam's influence on and importance to Africans in both Africa and the New World acknowledged is almost a belittling of what they think are authentic African cultures and Africans. Islamic influence is wrongly perceived as Arabization and a reflection of the supposed weakness of traditional cultures in the face of foreign entities. Interestingly, Chinese, Indonesian, and Albanian Muslims are not seen as being Arabized; only sub-Saharans are viewed as acculturated, which seems to indicate that some advocates of African cultures have internalized the anti-African prejudices they are fighting in other settings. In this mindset, to celebrate the so-called real Africa, or what is perceived as being the real Africa, Islam and the Muslims have to be denied or minimized. The reality is that traditional African religions have usually been favorably disposed toward Islam and the Muslims and have taken from them what they deemed useful to their own preservation and continuity. However, in a mythical and false reconstruction of African cultures as static, millennial, untouched, and uninfluenced except by force, Islam has no place.

Aside from the cultural prejudice, a religious bias may be observed. The insistence on the Christianity of the slaves and on the foundational role of the Christian church in the black communities sometimes appears to have obscured objective research. A careful reading of the slave narratives and testimonies, as well as of the writings of missionaries, shows that Christianity was not widely diffused among the slaves, who counted numerous followers of African religions, including Islam. Christianity became a relevant and important feature in the existence of Americans of African descent only in the nineteenth century, and singularly so after

Emancipation. To overstate its role and magnitude is to minimize or plainly to ignore the diverse components of the slaves' religious life.

Lastly, a political component is likely present in the array of reasons that have rendered African Islam invisible in the United States: a certain reluctance to explore a subject that seems to be linked to a controversial contemporary situation. Because today's Black Muslims and Islam in general are oftentimes the objects of contention and controversy, it may be seen as safe not to delve into a topic that might be viewed as giving credibility and legitimacy to claims of widespread historical conspiracies and cover-ups.

The African Muslims and the "Black Muslims"

Ironically, in contrast to the remnants of Islam in syncretic religions in Latin America and the Caribbean, there is no evidence in the United States of any Islamic continuity in the twentieth century. Though there were still Muslims and their children alive at the turn of the twentieth century, and though African American Muslims today number between one and two million, no hard evidence so far shows any direct connection between the two groups.

The emergence of twentieth-century Islam among the African American population can be traced to 1913.[60] That year, Timothy Drew, who was born in 1886 in North Carolina, took the name Noble Drew Ali and founded the Moorish Holy Temple of Science in Newark, New Jersey. He recruited mostly among recent immigrants from the South in Philadelphia, Pittsburgh, Detroit, and Chicago. Little is known about the man and how he acquired some notions of Islam. He is said to have worked in a circus with a "Hindu fakir" and, given the success of the show, may have decided to start his own order, which was a mixture of beliefs drawn from systems ranging from Freemasonry to Buddhism to Islam.

Noble Drew Ali's teachings were essentially the basis of a black nationalist movement that extolled black pride and a sense of confidence by linking a disfranchised, humiliated, and exploited people to the conquering and cultured Moors of the Middle Ages. He portrayed himself as a prophet ordained by Allah. The claim was in total opposition to a crucial tenet of Islam, which considers Muhammad the last prophet. Ali, who also called himself Mohammed III, based his cult on a sixty-four-page Koran he had written. Such a creation, as well as his assertion that before a people can have a God, it must have a nationality, ran contrary to the most basic beliefs of Islam. He died in 1929 in unclear circumstances, as his cult was suffering serious internal strife that had led to the killing of one of its leaders.

The few African Muslims who were still living in the early years of his movement would not have recognized what Noble Drew Ali presented as Islam. The only Islam they would have been familiar with was the orthodox religion that was reintroduced into the United States in the early twentieth century by immigrants from the Middle East, southeastern Europe, and Asia. Just as the Africans had done before, the Muslim immigrants lived their faith within their religious community and did not attempt to proselytize. Also like the Africans, many did not marry or have children, for lack of Muslim women. The children of those who took Christian or Jewish spouses usually followed their mother's faith.

There was one exception to the generally nonproselytizing attitude of the foreigners: the Ahmadiyah movement, founded in India by Mizra Ghulam Ahmad in the last decade of the nineteenth century, sent missionaries to the United States in 1920. After having tried in vain to convert white Americans, they concentrated their efforts on the black community. Many of their recruits were nationalists and Garveyites. Far from being a legitimate Islamic movement, the Ahmadiyah is considered heretical by most Muslims. It claims that Muhammad was not the last prophet and mixes an infinity of diverse elements with Islam.

The Ahmadiyah probably influenced the founder of the Nation of Islam, Farad Mohammed, also known as F. Mohammed Ali, Wallace D. Fard, Waly Fard, Wally Farad, and W. D. Fard. His origin has remained unknown. He claimed to have come from Saudi Arabia and to have been a descendant of Muhammad. However, some believed he was a Syrian Druze, an Iranian, or a Turk. The Federal Bureau of Investigation (FBI) and the police suspected he was born in Portland, Oregon, or in New Zealand, from British and Polynesian parents.[61] Having served three years in San Quentin Prison for drug dealing, Fard first made his appearance in the black community of Detroit in the summer of 1931, as a silk peddler. While selling his wares, he preached to the Southern immigrants what he presented as Islam and sold them his books, *The Secret Ritual of the Nation of Islam* and *Teaching for the Lost-Found Nation of Islam in a Mathematical Way*. After he disappeared—quite literally, as nothing is known of his whereabouts—in 1934, Elijah Muhammad, his trusted lieutenant since 1931, succeeded him. The new leader had been born Elijah Poole in 1897 in Sandersville, Georgia. Before disappearing, Fard had claimed that he was God and Elijah Muhammad was his prophet.

Even though the scholar Eric Lincoln, an expert on Islam in the United States, insists that the early Nation of Islam was "proto-Islamic" and Claude Andrew Clegg III states that it was "arguably a legitimate Muslim sect given its marginal adherence to central tenets of the Islamic faith,"[62] its fundamental doctrine—and this is also true of Noble Drew Ali's Moorish Temple—was more consistent with Islam's major unpardonable sin. According to Islam, nothing is more unforgivable and heinous than *shirk*, the association of others—such as Waly Fard—with the worship of God. Likewise, to believe that other prophets—such as Noble Drew Ali and Elijah Muhammad—follow Muhammad cannot be reconciled with orthodox Islam. These affirmations are not differences of interpretation; they are contrary to the most fundamental teachings of the religion.

Because of the nature of these cults, it is highly improbable that the last African Muslims in the Americas would have been involved in them. There is no documented continuity between the Islam brought by the African Muslim slaves and the early twentieth-century movements that claimed to be Islamic. Neither Noble Drew Ali nor Elijah Muhammad mentioned that he was an heir to an Islamic tradition passed on by his parents or grandparents; in fact, Muhammad's father, William, was a Baptist preacher. For their part, the syncretic cults of the West Indies and Latin America that incorporated Islamic elements taken from the orthodox Muslims are not and never claimed to be Islamic. In contrast, cults in the United States that mixed some Islamic tenets with elements drawn from other philosophies, some of which were in opposition to orthodox Islam, were proclaimed by their founders to be purely Islamic, thereby calling upon themselves the label of heresy and, by the same token, demonstrating that they are not part of the heritage left by the African Muslims. Yet from a basis of heterodoxy, according to some, or heresy, according to others, one orthodox movement has emerged over the years, while others have continued to endorse unorthodox practices and beliefs. It is a paradox that the African American culture that has retained the least memory of its Muslim past is also the one in which Islam is the fastest growing religion.

Islam in the Americas has been the religion of some people of African origin in an almost uninterrupted manner for the past five hundred years.

Through the amazing determination of its enslaved practitioners, the religion took hold in the New World and was actively practiced.

Over the course of many centuries, African Muslim men and women wrote a story of courage, insuperable faith, fortitude, and fidelity to their culture, religion, and social values. Their achievements are not a proof that slavery in the Americas was somewhat lenient and accommodating. Even though some scholars have allowed themselves to be caught in a shameful game of "whose slave system was the best," or at least not the worst, slavery everywhere was a monstrous crime against the Africans and their children. If the Muslims succeeded in establishing far-ranging networks, forming strong communities, maintaining their intellectual stamina, and preserving their dignity and identity, they owed it to their solid sense of self, cultural self-confidence, organizational skills, discipline, frugality, and strong communality. They took advantage of whatever avenues they could find and used the contradictions and the cracks in the slave system to their benefit.

Although part of the African Muslims' legacy is tangible, much cannot be counted. Yet the intangible is probably the most inspiring. They pursued education at all costs, rejected limited and justifiable self-indulgence as a hindrance to advancement, insisted on preserving their physical integrity even in abject circumstances, and retained their identity in order to survive. While they were working inside as well as outside the system that exploited and attempted to dehumanize them, they also worked against it. The Muslims were the first to rebel; they played a major role in the only successful slave revolution and organized and led the most threatening slave uprising in urban America. Though individuals of different persuasions attained similar results, the Muslims were the only group that consistently, on a global scale, pursued these objectives with tenacity and achieved a high degree of success.

Their story also unveils some truths that have not been acknowledged. Much too often, the enslaved Africans are presented as uneducated peasants by some, kings and queens by others, and culturally "pristine" by all. The intellectual dimension of the deported populations is never taken into consideration. Yet the story of the African Muslims shows that there were school children, high-level students, scribes, scholars, poets, lawyers, judges, and teachers among the slaves who toiled on the American plantations. What they brought to the West was an authentic African culture that had absorbed a number of foreign elements over the course of many centuries and had, in turn, influenced the neighboring cultures in several ways. They also brought a passion for knowledge and self-improvement and a hunger for social and cultural respectability.

The African Muslims made decisions, exercised choices. They shaped their own world, re-created their culture as best they could, and insisted on keeping their identity. They did not attempt to appropriate what the white European culture was willing to give, nor did they reach out to Christianity. By the same token, they did not participate in the creolization process that commingled components of diverse African cultures and faiths with that of the slaveholders. By their dress, diet, names, rituals, Koranic schools, and imported religious items and books, they clearly indicated that they intended to remain who they had been in Africa—be it *emir*, teacher, *marabout, alfa, charno, imam*, or simply devout believer. Their education, social background, family history, personal choices, social connections, political convictions, and religious beliefs did not become irrelevant in the New World; on the contrary, they shaped their response to enslavement, defining how the Muslims lived it and reacted to it. The people they had been in Africa determined the people they were in the Americas.

The Middle Passage and enslavement were not an equalizing process that regurgitated a mass of men, women, and children with a set of similar attitudes and behaviors intended to help survival. Besides the realities of American slavery, the personal stories of the Africans, their ethnocultural backgrounds, their religions, and how and why they were shipped away constituted the criteria that defined and conditioned their new existence. There is little doubt that a teacher of Arabic grammar who had traveled to Egypt and Arabia and had made a conscious decision to participate in a religious war, whatever the outcome, responded differently to his enslavement than did a young man who had already been enslaved by somebody from another ethnic group in Africa, who was cut off from the ancestors' cult of his family, and who ultimately had been kidnapped for the American plantations on his way to the fields. The two men would have had quite different reactions to issues of adaptation, acculturation, conversion, identity, and preservation or re-creation of a beloved past.

To understand the communities of the African Diaspora, therefore, it is essential to search for the African story of the uprooted men and women who peopled the Americas, as evidenced by the study of the Muslims. To recognize the African Muslims and to delineate their contribution is indispensable if one is to make sense of some of the unexplained features of the cultures of the people of African descent in the New World.

Turbaned men and veiled women, their prayer beads around their necks, chopped cotton, cut cane, and rolled tobacco from sunup to sundown. Like other slaves, they were beaten, whipped, cursed, raped, maimed, and humiliated. They saw their families torn apart and their loved ones killed. In the midst of abuse and contempt, they continued to pray, fast, be charitable, read, write on the sand, help one another, sing their lonesome tunes, and display pride in themselves, their religion, and their culture.

The African Muslims may have been, in the Americas, the slaves of Christian masters, but their minds were free. They were the servants of Allah.

Notes

NOTES TO THE INTRODUCTION

1. Caesar Farah, *Islam* (Hauppauge, N.Y.: Barron's, 1994), 307.

NOTES TO CHAPTER 1

1. Joseph Dupuis, *Journal of a Residence in Ashantee* (London: Henry Colburn, 1824), part 2, chap. 8, p. xiv.

2. John O. Hunwick, "The Influence of Arabic in West Africa," *Transactions of the Historical Society of Ghana* (1964): 24.

3. Theophilus Conneau, *A Slaver's Log Book or Twenty Years' Residence in Africa* (Englewood Cliffs, N.J.: Prentice-Hall, 1976), 141.

4. Theodore Dwight, "Condition and Character of Negroes in Africa," in *The People of Africa: A Series of Papers on Their Character, Condition, and Future Prospects*, ed. Henry Schieffelin (New York: A. D. F. Randolph, 1871), 52–53.

5. Ibid.

6. Michael Crowder, *The Story of Nigeria* (London: Faber & Faber, 1973), 106–7.

7. Jean Baptiste Léonard Durand, *Voyage au Sénégal fait dans les années 1785 et 1786* (Paris: Dentu, 1807), vol. 1, 123.

8. Baron Roger, *Kélédor, histoire africaine* (Paris: Nepveu, 1828), xi.

9. Oskar Lenz, *Tombouctou, voyage au Maroc, au Sahara et au Soudan* (Paris: Hachette, 1887), vol. 2, 119.

10. Lamin Sanneh, *The Crown and the Turban: Muslims in West African Pluralism* (Boulder, Colo.: Westview Press, 1997), 148.

11. Gaspard Theodore Mollien, *L'Afrique occidentale en 1818* (1820; reprint, Paris: Calman Levy, 1967), 103.

12. Francis Moore, *Travels into the Inland Parts of Africa* (London: E. Cave, 1738), 30.

13. John Thornton, *Africa and Africans in the Making of the Atlantic World, 1400–1680* (Cambridge: Cambridge University Press, 1992), 87–88.

14. Moore, *Travels*, 30.

15. Ibid., 50.

16. Ibid.

17. Conneau, *Slaver's Log Book*, 69.

18. Carl Bernhard Wadstrom, *An Essay on Colonization, particularly applied to the Western Coast of Africa* (London: Darton & Harvey, 1794), part 2, 111.

19. Durand, *Voyage au Sénégal*, 125.

20. Paul Lovejoy, "Background to Rebellion: The Origins of Muslim Slaves in Bahia," *Slavery and Abolition* 15, 2 (August 1994): 164.

21. P. E. H. Hair, "The Enslavement of Koelle Informants," *Journal of African History* 6, 2 (1965): 199.

22. Philip Curtin, "Ayuba Suleiman Diallo of Bondu," in *Africa Remembered: Narratives by West Africans from the Era of the Slave Trade*, ed. Philip Curtin (Madison: University of Wisconsin Press, 1967), 40.

23. Wadstrom, *Essay on Colonization*, part 2, 91.

24. Allan Fisher, ed., *Slavery and Muslim Society in Africa: The Institution in Saharan and Sudanic Africa and the Trans-Saharan Trade* (London: C. Hurst & Co, 1970), 24–25.

25. Dixon Denham, *Narrative of Travels and Discoveries in Northern and Central Africa, in the Years 1822, 1823, and 1824* (London: John Murray, 1826), 149.

26. Orlando Patterson, *Slavery and Social Death* (Cambridge: Harvard University Press, 1982), 278–88.

27. Bernard Lewis, "The African Diaspora and the Civilization of Islam," in *The African Diaspora: Interpretative Essays*, ed. Martin Kilson (Cambridge: Harvard University Press, 1976).

28. Akbar Muhammad, "The Image of Africans in Arabic Literature: Some Unpublished Manuscripts." in *Slaves and Slavery in Muslim Africa*, ed. John Ralph Willis (London: Frank Cass, 1985), vol. 1.

29. Emily Ruete, *Memoirs of an Arabian Princess from Zanzibar* (New York: Markus Wiener Publishing, 1989)

30. Paul Edwards, ed., *Equiano's Travels* (1789; reprint, London: Heinemann, 1969), 126.

31. René Luc Moreau, *Africains musulmans* (Paris: Présence Africaine, 1982), 127.

32. Ibid., 128–29.

33. Ruth Mazo Karras, *Slavery and Society in Medieval Scandinavia* (New Haven: Yale University Press, 1988), 14–15.

34. Nize Isabel de Moraes, *A la découverte de la Petite Côte au XVIIe siècle* (Dakar: Université Cheikh Anta Diop, 1995), vol. 1, 111, 115, 117, 119.

35. Ibid., vol. 2, 358.

36. Ibid., vol. 2, 365.

37. As are 85 percent of the Guineans, 70 percent of the Malians, 60 percent of the Sierra Leoneans, and 50 percent of the Nigerians.

38. de Moraes, *A la découverte de la Petite Côte*, vol. 2, 358.

39. Jean Boulègue, *Le Grand Jolof XIIIe–XVIe siècles* (Bloir: Edition Façades, 1987), 136.

40. Max Portugal Ortiz, *La esclavitud negra en las épocas colonial y nacional de Bolivia* (La Paz: Instituto Boliviano de Cultura, 1977), 14–15.

41. It is an unpardonable sin in Islam to worship any being but God. Muhammad, being not divine but only a simple mortal, cannot be the object of devotional worship.

42. Rolando Mellafe, *La introducción de la esclavitud negra en Chile* (Santiago: Editorial Universitaria, 1984), 158–59.

43. Nicolas del Castillo Mathieu, *Esclavos negros en Cartagena y sus aportes lexicos* (Bogota: Instituto Caro y Cuerno, 1982), 159.

44. Scholars state that the Berbeci, or Berbesi, were Serer who were so called by the Europeans because their ruler was the "Bur Sine," or king of Sine. Yet the Serer were animists whereas the Berbeci were Muslims. The so-called Berbeci were Mandingo from Gabou who took over Sine, Salum, Uli, and Niani in south-central Senegambia.

45. Jaime Borja, "Barbarización y redes de indoctrinamiento en los negros cartageno XVII y XVIII," in *Contribución africana a la cultura de las Americas* (Bogota: Instituto Colombiano de antropología Colcutura, 1993), 249.

46. C. I. Ritchie, "Deux textes sur le Sénégal, 1763–1767," *Bulletin de l'I-FAN* 30, 1 (January 1968): 339.

47. Ibid., 352.

48. Ibid., 155.

49. Le Sieur Lemaire, *Les voyages du Sieur Lemaire aux îles Canaries, Cap-Vert, Sénégal et Gambie* (Paris, 1695), 100–101.

50. P. E. H. Hair, *Barbot on Guinea* (London: Hakluyt Society, 1992), 131.

51. Ibid., 107.

52. Moore, *Travels*; Curtin, "Ayuba Suleiman Diallo of Bondu"; Douglas Grant, *The Fortunate Slave* (New York: Oxford University Press, 1968).

53. Wadstrom, *Essay on Colonization*, part 2, 77.

54. Ibid., 112.

55. Charles Becker and Victor Martin, "Kayor et Baol: Royaumes sénégalais et traite des esclaves au XVIIIe siècle," in *La Traite des Noirs par l'Atlantique: Nouvelles approches* (Paris: Société française d'outre-mer, 1976), 285.

56. Ibid., 289.

57. Ibid., 286.

58. Pruneau de Pommegorge, *Description de la Nigritie.* (Amsterdam: Maradan, 1789), 102–3.

59. Wadstrom, *Essay on Colonization*, part 2, 112.

60. Conneau, *Slaver's Log Book*, 69.

61. Ibid., 70.

62. Cyrus Griffin, "Abduhl Rahahman, the Unfortunate Moorish Prince," *African Repository* (February 1828): 79–80.

63. Boubacar Barry, *Le royaume du Waalo, le Sénégal avant la conquête* (Paris: François Maspero, 1972), 216.

64. George Truman, *A Visit to the West Indies* (Philadelphia: Merrihew & Thompson, 1844), 109.

65. Roger, *Kélédor*, 66–67.

66. Ibid., 93–97.

67. Mungo Park, *Travels in the Interior Districts of Africa, Performed in the Years 1795, 1796, and 1797*, 2 vols. (London: John Murray, 1816–1817).

68. "Autobiography of Omar ibn Said, Slave in North Carolina, 1831," *American Historical Review* 30 (October 1924): 787–95; George Callcott, "Omar ibn Seid, a Slave Who Wrote an Autobiography in Arabic," *Journal of Negro History* (January 1954): 58–63.

69. Dupuis, *Journal of a Residence*, 245.

70. Richard Robert Madden, *A Twelve Months' Residence in the West Indies* (Philadelphia: Carey, Lea & Blanchard, 1835), 126–30.

71. A. Bivar, "The Wathiqat ahl al-Sudan: A Manifesto of the Fulani Jihad." *Journal of African History* 4, 2 (1961): 235.

72. Denham, *Narrative of Travels and Discoveries*, 170.

73. H. F. C. Smith, D. M. Last, and G. Gubio, "Ali Gazirmabe of Bornu," in Curtin, ed., *Africa Remembered*, 212.

74. Wadstrom, *Essay on Colonization*, part 2, 85.

75. Madden, *Twelve Months' Residence*, 126–30.

76. Richard Jobson, *The Golden Trade* (1623; reprint, Devonshire: E. Speight and Walpole, 1904), 97.

77. Madden, *Twelve Months' Residence*, 135.

78. Ibid., 126.

79. William Brown Hodgson, *Notes on Northern Africa, the Sahara and the Soudan* (New York: Wiley & Putnam, 1844), 74.

80. Colonel Malenfant, *Des colonies et particulièrement de celle de St Domingue* (Paris: Audibert, 1814), 215.

81. Captain J. Washington, "Some Account of Mohammedu Sisei: A Mandingo of Nyani-Maru on the Gambia," *Journal of the Royal Geographical Society*, no. 8 (1838): 449–54.

82. Jobson, *Golden Trade*, 98.

83. Allan Austin, *African Muslims in Antebellum America* (New York: Garland, 1984), 662.

84. Wadstrom, *Essay on Colonization*, part 2, 114.

85. Ibid., 77.

86. Carl Campbell, "John Mohammed Bath and the Free Mandingos in Trinidad: The Question of Their Repatriation to Africa 1831–38," *Journal of African Studies* 2, 4, (1975–1976): 467–95.

87. Truman, *Visit to the West Indies*, 108.

88. Joao Jose Reis, *Slave Rebellion in Brazil: The Muslim Uprising of 1835 in Bahia* (Baltimore: Johns Hopkins University Press, 1993).

89. Joseph Sturge and Thomas Harvey, *The West Indies in 1837* (1838; reprint, London: Dawsons of Pall Mall, 1968), 287.

90. Thomas Madiou, *Histoire d'Haïti* (1847; reprint, Port-au-Prince: Les Editions Fardin, 1981).

91. Campbell, "John Mohammed Bath," 486.

92. Madden, *Twelve Months' Residence*, 102.

93. Ibid., 126–36.

94. Park, *Travels*, 467–68.

95. "Autobiography of Omar ibn Said," (October 1924): 792–95; Dwight, "Condition and Character," 50.

96. Lovejoy, "Background to Rebellion," 161–62.

97. Rev. Schön, *Grammar of the Hausa Language* (London: Church Missionary House, 1862), 234.

98. Roger, *Kélédor*, 86.

99. Madden, *Twelve Months' Residence*, 129.

100. Charles Ball, *Fifty Years in Chains* (1837; reprint, New York: Dover Publications, 1970), 183–84.

101. de Pommegorge, *Description de la Nigritie*, 76.

102. Paul Erdmann Isert, *Letters on West Africa and the Slave Trade: Paul Erdmann Isert's Journey to Guinea and the Caribbean Islands in Columbia* (1788; reprint, London and Oxford: Oxford University Press, 1992), 175.

103. Ball, *Fifty Years*, 184.

104. Conneau, *Slaver's Log Book*, 82.

105. Mahommah Gardo Baquaqua, *Biography of Mahommah Gardo Baquaqua* (Detroit: Pomeroy & Co., 1854), 35.

106. Isert, *Letters on West Africa*, 176.

107. Roger, *Kélédor*, 96.

108. Baquaqua, *Biography*, 38.

109. Joseph Inikori and Stanley Engerman, eds., *The Atlantic Slave Trade: Effects on Economies, Societies, and Peoples in Africa, the Americas, and Europe* (Durham: Duke University Press, 1994), 6; Philip Curtin, *The Atlantic Slave Trade: A Census* (Madison: University of Wisconsin Press, 1969).

110. Michael Gomez, "Muslims in Early America," *Journal of Southern History* 60, 4 (November 1994): 682.

111. Paul Lovejoy, "The African Diaspora: Revisionist Interpretations of Ethnicity, Culture and Religion under Slavery," *Studies in the World History of Slavery, Abolition and Emancipation* 2, 1 (1997).

112. Curtin, *Atlantic Slave Trade*, 98.

113. Frederick Bowser, *The African Slave in Colonial Peru 1524–1650* (Stanford: Stanford University Press, 1974), 40–41.

216 | Notes to Chapter 1

114. Curtin, *Atlantic Slave Trade*, 192–97.

115. Ibid., 157.

116. Ibid., 158.

117. Ibid., 182.

118. Ibid., 247.

119. Ibid., 160.

120. Ibid., 207.

121. Paul Lovejoy estimates that at least 52.8 percent of the slaves from central Sudan deported to the Americas were Muslims ("Background to Rebellion," 167).

122. Edward Blyden, "Mohammedanism in Western Africa," in *The People of Africa*, ed. Schieffelin, 76.

NOTES TO CHAPTER 2

1. Allan Austin, *African Muslims in Antebellum America* (New York: Garland, 1984), 445–523.

2. Lydia Parrish, *Slave Songs of the Georgia Sea Islands* (1942; reprint, Athens: University of Georgia Press, 1992); Works Progress Administration (WPA), *Drums and Shadows: Survival Studies among the Georgia Coastal Negroes* (Athens: University of Georgia Press, 1986).

3. Gabriel Debien, *Les esclaves aux Antilles françaises XVIIe–XVIIIe siècles* (Pointe-à-Pitre: Société d'Histoire de la Guadeloupe, 1974), 254. "Gorée"—a slave depot off the coast of Senegal—must probably be read "Guinea." Guinea, during slavery, often referred to a vast territory that extended from present-day Guinea to as far south as Angola.

4. Jean-Baptiste Dutertre, *Histoire générale des Antilles habitées par les François.* (1667; reprint, Saint-Pierre, Martinique: Durieu et Leyritz, 1868–1869), 106.

5. Jean-Baptiste Labat, *Voyage aux îles de l'Amérique 1693–1705* (1722; reprint, Paris: Seghers, 1979), 203.

6. Debien, *Les esclaves aux Antilles françaises*, 266.

7. Mahommah Gardo Baquaqua, *Biography of Mahommah Gardo Baquaqua* (Detroit: Pomeroy & Co., 1854), 32.

8. Edwin A. Wallbridge, *The Demerara Martyr: Memoirs of the Rev. John Smith, Missionary to Demerara* (1848; reprint, New York: Negro Universities Press, 1969), 17.

9. Georges Raeders, *Le comte de Gobineau au Brésil* (Paris: Les Nouvelles Editions Latines, 1934), 75.

10. James Fletcher and D. P. Kidder, *Brazil and the Brazilians, Portrayed in Historical and Descriptive Sketches* (Boston: Little Brown, 1866), 136.

11. Richard Robert Madden, *A Twelve Months' Residence in the West Indies* (Philadelphia: Carey, Lea & Blanchard, 1835), 102.

12. Ibid., 136.

13. Ibid., 133.

14. Ibid., 133–34.

15. Ibid., 101.

16. He was a witness for the defense during the trial of the Africans who revolted on the *Amistad*.

17. Ralph Gurley, "Secretary's Report," *African Repository* (July 1837): 203.

18. "Autobiography of Omar ibn Said, Slave in North Carolina, 1831," *American Historical Review* 30 (July 1925): 787.

19. Austin, *African Muslims*, 41.

20. Charles Colcock Jones, *The Religious Instruction of the Negroes in the Southern States* (Philadelphia: Presbyterian Board of Publication, 1847), 51.

21. Joseph Sturge and Thomas Harvey, *The West Indies in 1837* (1838; reprint, London: Dawsons of Pall Mall, 1968), 287–88.

22. Harrison Hough, "Grégoire's Sketch of Angelo Solimann," *Journal of Negro History* 4, 3 (July 1919): 288.

23. Baron Roger, *Kélédor, histoire africaine* (Paris: Nepveu, 1828), 266.

24. Madden, *Twelve Months' Residence*, 135–36.

25. Ivor Wilks, "Abu Bakr al-Siddiq of Timbuktu," in *Africa Remembered: Narratives by West Africans from the Era of the Slave Trade*, ed. Philip Curtin (Madison: University of Wisconsin Press, 1967), 163–64n.

26. Roger, *Kélédor*, 136.

27. Douglas Grant, *The Fortunate Slave* (New York: Oxford University Press, 1968), 82.

28. Austin, *African Muslims*, 70.

29. Joseph Le Conte, *Autobiography* (New York: D. Appleton & Co., 1903), 29–30.

30. Charles Ball, *Fifty Years in Chains* (1837; reprint, New York: Dover Publications, 1970), 167.

31. WPA, *Drums and Shadows*, 121.

32. Ibid., 76.

33. Ibid., 141.

34. Ibid., 144.

35. Parrish, *Slave Songs*, 28.

36. Manoel Querino, *Costumes africanos no Brasil* (1938; reprint, São Paulo: Editora Massangana, 1988), 66.

37. Ball, *Fifty Years in Chains*, 22.

38. WPA, *Drums and Shadows*, 179.

39. Ibid., 161. "Hakabara" is a deformation of *akbar* ("great" in Arabic). The complete sentence must have been *Allahu akbar Muhammadu rasul-ullah*— "God is Great and Muhammad is his Messenger."

40. Ibid., 166.

41. Ibid., 165.

42. Gilberto Freyre, *The Masters and the Slaves* (Berkeley: University of California Press, 1986), 317.

43. Arthur Ramos, *As culturas negras no novo mundo* (1937; reprint, São Paulo: Companhia Editorial Nacional, 1979), 221

44. WPA, *Drums and Shadows*, 162, 194.

45. Melville Herskovits and Frances Herskovits, *Trinidad Village* (New York: A. Knopf, 1947), 88, 152.

46. WPA, *Drums and Shadows*, 162.

47. Ibid., 167.

48. Médéric Louis Elie Moreau de Saint Mery, *Voyage aux Etats-Unis de l'Amérique* (1798; reprint, New York: Doubleday, 1947), 307.

49. William Brown Hodgson, *Notes on Northern Africa, the Sahara and the Soudan* (New York: Wiley & Putnam, 1844), 69.

50. William Plumer, "Meroh, a Native African," *New York Observer*, January 8, 1863, 1.

51. Raymundo Nina Rodrigues, *Os Africanos no Brasil* (1932; reprint, São Paulo: Companhia Editora Nacional, 1976), 63.

52. Roger Bastide, *The African Religions of Brazil: Towards a Sociology of the Interpenetration of Civilizations* (Baltimore: Johns Hopkins University Press, 1978), 105.

53. Nina Rodrigues, *Os Africanos*, 60.

54. Querino, *Costumes africanos*, 71.

55. Nina Rodrigues, *Os Africanos*, 63.

56. Parrish, *Slave Songs*, 54.

57. Lorenzo Dow Turner, *Africanisms in the Gullah Dialect* (1949; reprint, New York: Arno Press/*New York Times*, 1969), 202.

NOTES TO CHAPTER 3

1. Daniel Littlefield, *Rice and Slaves: Ethnicity and the Slave Trade in Colonial South Carolina* (Urbana and Chicago: University of Illinois Press, 1991); Peter Wood, *Black Majority: Negroes in Colonial South Carolina from 1670 through the Stono Rebellion* (New York: Norton, 1974).

2. Gabriel Debien, *De l'Afrique à Saint Domingue*. Notes d'Histoire coloniale, nos. 221/222 (1982): 20.

3. Lorenzo Dow Turner, *Africanisms in the Gullah Dialect* (1949; reprint, New York: Arno Press/*New York Times*, 1969).

4. Jaime Borja, "Barbarización y redes de indoctrinamiento en los negros cartageno XVII y XVIII," in *Contribución africana a la cultura de las Americas* (Bogota: Instituto Colombiano de Antroplogía Colcutura, 1993), 249.

5. George Gardner, *Travels in the Interior of Brazil, 1836–1841* (1849; reprint, New York: AMS Press, 1970), 20.

6. Charles Ball, *Fifty Years in Chains* (1837; reprint, New York: Dover Publications, 1970), 108–9.

7. Colonel Malenfant, *Des colonies et particulièrement de celle de Saint Domingue* (Paris: Audibert, 1814), 232.

8. Shane White, "Slave Clothing and African-American Culture in the Eighteenth and Nineteenth Centuries," *Past and Present: A Journal of Historical Studies*, no. 148 (August 1995): 151.

9. James Alexander, *Transatlantic Sketches* (Philadelphia: Key & Biddle, 1833), vol. 1, 118.

10. Quoted in Vincent Monteil, *L'islam noir* (1964; reprint, Paris: Le Seuil, 1980), 359.

11. John Thornton, *Africa and Africans in the Making of the Atlantic World, 1400–1680* (Cambridge: Cambridge University Press, 1992), 231.

12. Works Progress Administration (WPA), *Drums and Shadows: Survival Studies among the Georgia Coastal Negroes* (Athens: University of Georgia Press, 1986), 162.

13. Ibid., 180.

14. Georgia Bryan Conrad, "Reminiscences of a Southern Woman," *Southern Workman* (May 1901): 252.

15. Jean Baptiste Debret, *Voyage pittoresque et historique au Brésil, 1816–1831* (Paris: Firmin Didot Frères, 1834).

16. WPA, *Drums and Shadows*, 179.

17. Ibid., 181.

18. George Callcott, "Omar ibn Seid, a Slave Who Wrote an Autobiography in Arabic," *Journal of Negro History* 39, 1 (January 1954): 62.

19. Wandalina Velez Rodrigues, *El Turbante bianco: Muertos, santos y vivos en la lucha politica* (Santo Domingo: Museo del Hombre Dominicano, 1982).

20. Harrison Hough, "Grégoire's Sketch of Angelo Solimann," *Journal of Negro History* 4, 3 (July 1919): 289.

21. Arthur Ramos, *O negro brasileiro* (São Paulo: Companhia Editorial Nacional, 1940), 84.

22. Carl Campbell, "John Mohammed Bath and the Free Mandingos in Trinidad: The Question of Their Repatriation to Africa 1831–38," *Journal of African Studies* 2, 4 (1975–1976): 467.

23. George Truman, *Narrative of a Visit to the West Indies in 1840–1841*. (Philadelphia: Merrihew & Thompson, 1844): 108.

24. Charles William Day, *Five Years' Residence in the West Indies* (London: Colburn & Co., 1852), vol. 1, 313.

25. Philip Curtin, ed., *Africa Remembered: Narratives by West Africans from the Era of the Slave Trade* (Madison: University of Wisconsin Press, 1967), 53.

26. Ibid., 53.

27. Fernando Ortiz, *La fiesta afro-cubana del "dia de reyes"* (Havana: Imprenta El Siglo XX, 1925), 6.

28. Newbell Puckett, *Folk Beliefs of the Southern Negroes* (1926; reprint, New York: Negro Universities Press, 1975), 203.

29. Melville Herskovits and Frances Herskovits, *Trinidad Village* (New York: A. Knopf, 1947), 27.

30. Professor and Mrs. Louis Agassiz, *A Journey in Brazil* (Boston: Ticknor & Fields, 1868), 83.

31. Gilberto Freyre, *The Masters and the Slaves* (Berkeley: University of California Press, 1986), 319.

32. Joao Jose Reis, *Slave Rebellion in Brazil: The Muslim Uprising of 1835 in Bahia* (Baltimore: Johns Hopkins University Press, 1993), 79.

33. Ibid., 84.

34. Gaspard Mollien, *L'Afrique occidentale en 1818* (1820; reprint, Paris: Calman Levy, 1967), 145.

35. Reis, *Slave Rebellion*, 105.

36. Ibid., 214.

37. Puckett, *Folk Beliefs*, 314.

38. WPA, *Drums and Shadows*, 179.

39. Pierre Verger, *Flux et reflux de la traite des nègres entre le Golfe de Bénin et Bahia de todos os Santos, du XVIIe au XIXe siècle* (Paris: Mouton, 1968), 328.

40. Manoel Querino, *Costumes africanos no Brasil* (1938; reprint, São Paulo: Editora Massangana, 1988), 66.

41. White, "Slave Clothing," 179–80.

42. *Gazette of the State of Georgia*, December 8, 1791.

43. Jean Fouchard, *Les marrons de la liberté* (Paris: Editions L'École, 1972), passim.

44. Reis, *Slave Rebellion*, passim; Paul Lovejoy, "Background to Rebellion: The Origins of Muslim Slaves in Bahia," *Slavery and Abolition* 15, 2 (August 1994): 176–80.

45. Donald Wood, *Trinidad in Transition: The Years after Slavery* (New York: Oxford University Press, 1968), passim; Campbell, "John Mohammed Bath," passim.

46. Richard Madden, *A Twelve Months' Residence in the West Indies* (Philadelphia: Carey, Lea & Blanchard, 1835), passim.

47. See *Louisiana Historical Quarterly* 8, 4 (October 1925): 628–31; 18, 1 (January 1935): 162; 18, 2 (April 1935): 297–330; 19, 2 (April 1936): 471–78.

48. WPA, *Drums and Shadows*, passim; Charles Joyner, *Down by the Riverside: A South Carolina Slave Community* (Urbana and Chicago: University of Illinois Press, 1984), passim.

49. Newbell Puckett, *Black Names in America: Origins and Usage* (Boston: G. K. Hall, 1975).

50. John Inscoe, "Carolina Slave Names: An Index to Acculturation," *Journal of Southern History* 49, 1 (February 1983): 533.

51. Turner, *Africanisms*, 40.

52. Michael Gomez, "Muslims in Early America," *Journal of Southern History* 60, 4 (November 1994): 696.

53. The family probably lived for a while in the French islands, on an island such as Saint Lucia, or in Trinidad, whose population speaks Creole or "patois," prior to being sent to the Bahamas. Patois is spoken in many Caribbean islands but not in the Bahamas. The women used words that have passed as being "African" but were actually French patois words. *Mosojo, diffy,* and *deloe,* meaning "bucket", "fire," and "water," are clearly the French *mon seau d'eau, du feu* and *de l'eau* (WPA, *Drums and Shadows*, 162). Also, Shad Hall mentions that his grandmother brought clay pots she had made in Africa—an impossibility, given the conditions of the trans-Atlantic slave trade. Those pots were probably made in the Bahamas. The grandson may have mixed her descriptions of where she actually lived with descriptions of Africa that she had gotten from her parents.

54. WPA, *Drums and Shadows*, 161.

55. William Brown Hodgson, *Notes on Northern Africa, the Sahara and the Soudan* (New York: Wiley & Putnam, 1844), 69.

56. Curtin, ed., *Africa Remembered*, 42

57. Allan Austin, *African Muslims in Antebellum America* (New York: Garland, 1984), 69.

58. Cyrus Griffin, "The Unfortunate Moor," *African Repository* (February 1828): 365.

59. Carlton Robert Ottley, *Slavery Days in Trinidad: A Social History of the Island from 1797–1838* (Port of Spain: Ottley, 1974), 59.

60. Charles Colcock Jones, *The Religious Instruction of the Negroes in the Southern States* (Philadelphia: Presbyterian Board of Publication, 1847), 138.

61. Edward Teas, "A Trading Trip to Natchez and New Orleans in 1822: Diary of Thomas Teas," *Journal of Southern History* 7 (August 1941): 388.

62. Gabriel Debien, *Les esclaves aux Antilles françaises XVIIe–XVIIIe siècles* (Pointe-à-Pitre: Société d'Histoire de la Guadeloupe, 1974), 173.

63. Terry Alford, *Prince among Slaves: The True Story of an African Prince Sold into Slavery in the American South* (New York: Oxford University Press, 1977), 59.

64. Curtin, ed., *Africa Remembered*, 44.

65. Ibid.

66. Frances Anne Kemble, *Journal of a Residence on a Georgia Plantation in 1838–1839* (1863; reprint, Athens: University of Georgia Press, 1984), 322.

67. Gomez, "Muslims in Early America," 698.

68. Reis, *Slave Rebellion*, 108.

69. Querino, *Costumes africanos*, 70.

70. Ibid.

71. Reis, *Slave Rebellion*, 110.

72. Esteban Montejo, *The Autobiography of a Runaway Slave*, ed. Miguel Barnet (New York: Pantheon, 1968), 38.

73. Reis, *Slave Rebellion*, 110.

74. Ball, *Fifty Years in Chains*, 21.

75. Austin, *African Muslims*, 268.

76. Conrad, "Reminiscences," 252.

77. Gomez, "Muslims in Early America," 701.

78. Lamin Sanneh, *The Crown and the Turban: Muslims and West African Pluralism* (Boulder, Colo.: Westview Press, 1997), 20.

79. Mungo Park, *Travel in the Interior districts of Africa, Performed in the Years 1795, 1796, and 1797*, 2 vols. (London: John Murray, 1816–1817), vol. 1, 479.

80. Nicholas Owen, *Journal of a Slave Dealer: A view of some remarkable Axcedents in the life of Nicholas Owen 1746–1757* (reprint, New York: Houghton Mifflin, 1930), 71.

81. Ball, *Fifty Years in Chains*, 219.

82. Agassiz, *Journey in Brazil*, 85.

83. Verger, *Flux et reflux*, 328.

84. John Matthews, *A Voyage to the River Sierra Leone in the Years 1785, 1786, 1787* (London: B. White, 1791), 96.

85. Alford, *Prince among Slaves*, 103.

86. Truman, *Narrative of a Visit*, 108.

87. Madden, *Twelve Months' Residence*, 140.

88. Alford, *Prince among Slaves*, 80.

89. Curtis Carroll Davis, *Chronicler of the Cavaliers: A Life of the Virginia Novelist Dr. William A. Caruthers* (Richmond: Dietz Press, 1953), 344.

90. Charles Lyell, *A Second Visit to the United States* (London: John Murray, 1849), 359.

91. Dr. Collins, *Practical Rules for the Management and Medical Treatment of Negro Slaves, in the Sugar Colonies* (1811; reprint, Freeport: Books for Library Presses, 1971), 36.

92. Madden, *Twelve Months' Residence*, 98.

93. Gardner, *Travels in the Interior*, 20.

94. Cyrus Griffin, "Prince the Moor," *Southern Galaxy*, June 5, 1828.

95. Austin, *African Muslims*, 474.

96. Ibid., 473.

97. Marina Wikramanayake, *A World in Shadow: The Free Blacks in Ante-*

bellum South Carolina (Columbia: University of South Carolina Press, 1973), 20–21.

98. Paul Barringer, *The Natural Bent* (Chapel Hill: University of North Carolina Press, 1949), 12.

99. Roger Bastide, *The African Religions of Brazil: Towards a Sociology of the Interpenetration of Civilizations* (Baltimore: Johns Hopkins University Press, 1978), 153.

100. Etienne Ignace, "La secte musulmane des Malés du Brésil et leur révolte en 1835," *Anthropos* 4, 1 (January 1909): 100.

101. Freyre, *Masters and Slaves*, 298.

102. Georges Raeders, *Le comte de Gobineau au Brésil* (Paris: Les Editions Latines, 1934), 74.

103. Ibid., 75–76.

104. Theophilus Conneau, *A Slaver's Log Book or Twenty Years' Residence in Africa* (1854; reprint, Englewood Cliffs, N.J.: Prentice-Hall, 1976), 88.

105. Clifton James, ed., *Life and Labor on Argyle Island* (Savannah: Beehive Press, 1978), 65.

106. Leslie Howard Owens, *This Species of Property: Slave Life and Culture in the Old South* (New York: Oxford University Press, 1976), 122.

107. Emilia Viotti da Costa, *Crowns of Glory, Tears of Blood: The Demerara Slave Rebellion of 1823* (New York: Oxford University Press, 1994), 195.

108. Truman, *Narrative of a Visit*, 109.

109. Ibid., 110.

110. Andrew Halliday, *The West Indies* (London: J. W. Parker, 1837), 321.

111. James Fletcher and D. W. Kidder, *Brazil and the Brazilians, Portrayed in Historical and Descriptive Sketches* (Boston: Little Brown, 1866), 135.

112. Raeders, *Le comte de Gobineau*, 75.

113. Reis, *Slave Rebellion*, 132–33.

114. Ibid., 131.

NOTES TO CHAPTER 4

1. Michael Johnson, "Runaway Slaves and the Slave Communities in South Carolina, 1799 to 1830," *William and Mary Quarterly* 38, 3 (July 1981): 437.

2. Gilberto Freyre, *The Masters and the Slaves* (Berkeley: University of California Press, 1986), 299.

3. Ibid., 299.

4. Theodore Dwight, "Condition and Character of Negroes in Africa." in *The People of Africa: A Series of Papers on their Character, Condition, and Future Prospects*, ed. Henry Schieffelin (New York: A. D. F. Randolph, 1871), 49.

5. Allan Austin, *African Muslims in Antebellum America* (New York: Garland, 1984), 561.

6. Richard Robert Madden, *A Twelve Months' Residence in the West Indies* (Philadelphia: Carey, Lea & Blanchard, 1835), 125.

7. Joao Jose Reis, *Slave Rebellion in Brazil: The Muslim Uprising of 1835 in Bahia* (Baltimore: Johns Hopkins University Press, 1993), 98.

8. William Brown Hodgson, *Notes on Northern Africa, the Sahara and the Soudan* (New York: Wiley & Putnam, 1844), 69.

9. "Autobiography of Omar ibn Said, Slave in North Carolina, 1831," *American Historical Review* 30 (October 1924–July 1925): 792.

10. Terry Alford, *Prince among Slaves: The True Story of an African Prince Sold into Slavery in the American South* (New York: Oxford University Press, 1977), 57.

11. Janet Duitsman Cornelius, *When I Can Read My Title Clear: Literacy, Slavery and Religion in the Antebellum South* (Columbia: University of South Carolina Press, 1992), 72.

12. Alford, *Prince among Slaves*, 89.

13. Jean Fouchard, *Les marrons de la liberté* (Paris: Editions L'École, 1972), 142.

14. Mungo Park, *Travels in the Interior Districts of Africa, Performed in the Years 1795, 1796, and 1797*, 2 vols. (London: John Murray, 1816–1817), vol. 1, 467–68.

15. Alford, *Prince among Slaves*, 103.

16. William Plumer, "Meroh, a Native African," *New York Observer*, January 8, 1863, 1.

17. Ralph Gurley, "Secretary's Report," *African Repository* (July 1937): 203.

18. Madden, *Twelve Months' Residence*, 133–34.

19. Georges Raeders, *Le comte de Gobineau au Brésil* (Paris: Les Nouvelles Editions Latines, 1934), 75.

20. Edward Bean Underhill, *The West Indies* (London: Jackson, Walford and Hodder, 1862), 46.

21. Carl Campbell, "John Mohammed Bath and the Free Mandingos in Trinidad: The Question of Their Repatriation to Africa 1831–38," *Journal of African Studies* 2, 4 (1975–1976): 467, 471.

22. Hodgson, *Notes on Northern Africa*, 69.

23. Works Progress Administration (WPA), *Drums and Shadows: Survival Studies among the Georgia Coastal Negroes* (Athens: University of Georgia Press, 1986), 179.

24. Lydia Parrish, *Slave Songs of the Georgia Sea Islands* (1942; reprint, Athens: University of Georgia Press, 1992), 28.

25. Harry Johnston, *The Negro in the New World* (1910; reprint, New York: Johnson Reprint Corp., 1969), 94–95.

26. Vincent Monteil, *L'Islam noir* (1964; reprint, Paris: Le Seuil, 1980), 343n.

27. John Oliver Killens, ed., *The Trial Record of Denmark Vesey* (1822; reprint, Boston: Beacon Press, 1970), 11.

28. Peter Wood, *Black Majority: Negroes in Colonial South Carolina from 1670 through the Stono Rebellion* (New York: Norton, 1974), 178.

29. B. G. Martin, "Sapelo Island's Arabic Document: The 'Bilali Diary' in Context," *Georgia Historical Quarterly* 78, 3 (fall 1994): 589–601.

30. Jeffrey Bolster, *Black Jacks: African American Seamen in the Age of Sail* (Cambridge: Harvard University Press, 1997).

31. Killens, ed., *Trial Record*, 70–71.

32. Madden, *Twelve Months' Residence*, 99.

33. Philip Curtin, "Ayuba Sulcyman Diallo of Bundu," in *Africa Remembered: Narratives by West Africans from the Era of the Slave Trade*, ed. Philip Curtin (Madison: University of Wisconsin Press, 1967), 52.

34. Maureen Warner Lewis, *Trinidad Yoruba: From Mother Tongue to Memory* (Tuscaloosa: University of Alabama Press, 1996), 27.

35. Raymundo Nina Rodrigues, *Os Africanos no Brasil* (1932; reprint, São Paulo: Companhia Editora Nacional, 1976), 56.

36. Reis, *Slave Rebellion*, 104–5.

37. Pierre Verger, *Flux et reflux de la traite des nègres entre le Golfe de Bénin et Bahia de todos os Santos, du XVIIe au XIXe siècle* (Paris: Mouton, 1968), 340.

38. Vincent Monteil, "Analyse des 25 documents arabes des Malês de Bahia (1835)." *Bulletin de l'IFAN* 29, 1–2 (1967): 88–98; Rolf Reichert, *Os documentos arabes do Arquivo do Estado da Bahia* (Bahia: Universidade Federal da Bahia, Centro de Estudos Afro-Orientais, 1970).

39. Nina Rodrigues, *Os Africanos*, 60.

40. Reichert, *Os documentos arabes*.

41. Roger Bastide, *The African Religions of Brazil: Towards a Sociology of the Interpenetration of Civilizations*, (Baltimore: Johns Hopkins University Press, 1978), 103.

42. Richard Jobson, *The Golden Trade* (1623; reprint, Devonshire: E. Speight and Walpole, 1904), 94.

43. Dwight, "Condition and Character," 51; Madden, *Twelve Months' Residence*, 99.

44. Edward Blyden, *Christianity, Islam and the Negro Race.* (1887; reprint, Edinburgh: Edinburgh University Press, 1967), 178.

45. George W. Ellis, "Islam as a factor in West African Culture." *Journal of Race Development* 2, 2 (October 1911): 114.

46. Raeders, *Le comte de Gobineau*, 75.

47. Mary Karasch, *Slave Life in Rio de Janeiro 1808–1850* (Princeton: Princeton University Press, 1987), 285.

48. Blyden, *Christianity*, 178.

49. Maximilien Radiguet, *Souvenirs de l'Amérique espagnole: Chili, Pérou, Brésil* (Paris: M. Levy, 1874), 138.

50. Cornelius, *When I Can Read*, 7–9.

51. Ibid., 3.

52. Verger, *Flux et reflux*, 328.

53. William Caruthers, *The Kentuckian in New York* (New York: Harper & Brothers, 1834), 147.

54. Edward Teas, "A Trading Trip to Natchez and New Orleans in 1822: Diary of Thomas Teas," *Journal of Southern History* 7 (August 1941): 387.

55. Colonel Malenfant, *Des colonies et particulièrement de celle de Saint Domingue* (Paris: Audibert, 1814), 212–13.

56. Joseph Sturge and Thomas Harvey, *The West Indies in 1837.* (1838; reprint, London: Dawsons of Pall Mall, 1968), 287. Yalla is the name given to God by the Senegalese. One may speculate that Yallah's Bay means "God's bay."

57. John Stewart, *View of the Island of Jamaica* (Edinburgh: Oliver & Boyd, 1823), 251.

58. William Brown Hodgson, *The Gospels written in the negro patois of English with Arabic characters by a Mandingo Slave in Georgia* (American Ethnological Society, October 13, 1857).

59. Edward Bean Underhill, *The West Indies* (London: Jackson, Walford and Hodder, 1862), 46.

60. Reichert, *Os documentos arabes*, n.p.

61. Austin, *African Muslims*, 515.

62. Hodgson, *Gospels*, 9.

63. Joseph Greenberg, "The Decipherment of the 'Ben-Ali Diary': A Preliminary Statement," *Journal of Negro History* 25, 3 (July 1940): 372–75.

64. Hodgson, *Gospels*, 9.

65. Marion Wilson Starling, *The Slave Narrative: Its Place in American History* (Washington, D.C.: Howard University Press, 1988), 311.

66. Ronald Judy, *(Dis)Forming the American Canon* (Minneapolis: University of Minnesota Press, 1993).

67. Jobson, *Golden Trade*, 63.

68. Nina Rodrigues, *Os Africanos*, 60.

69. Joseph Dupuis, *Journal of a Residence in Ashantee* (London: Henry Colburn, 1824), 142.

70. Thomas Edward Bowdich, *Mission from Cape Coast Castle to Ashantee* (London: John Murray, 1819), 272.

71. Antoine Le Page du Pratz, *Histoire de la Louisiane.* (Paris, 1758), vol. 1, 334. 3 vols.

72. Nicholas Owen, *Journal of a Slave Dealer: A view of some remarkable Axcedents in the life of Nicholas Owen, 1746–1757* (reprint, New York: Houghton Mifflin, 1930), 95.

73. Charles William Day, *Five Years' Residence in the West Indies* (London: Colburn & Co, 1852), 275.

74. Laura Porteous, "The Gri-gri Case," *Louisiana Historical Quarterly* 17, 1 (January 1934): 48–63.

75. Malenfant, *Des colonies*, 211.

76. Bastide, *African Religions of Brazil*, 103.

77. Nina Rodrigues, *Os Africanos*, 59.

78. Ibid., 41.

79. George Gardner, *Travels in the Interior of Brazil, 1836–1841* (1849; reprint, New York: AMS Press, 1970), 20.

80. Reis, *Slave Rebellion*, 89.

81. Nina Rodrigues, *Os Africanos*, 60.

82. Ibid.

83. Ibid.

84. Bastide, *African Religions of Brazil*, 120.

85. James Rodway, *History of British Guiana, from the year 1668 to the present time*, 3 vols. (Georgetown: J. Thompson, 1891–1894), vol. 2, 297.

86. Plumer, "Meroh," 1.

87. Ibid.

88. Alford, *Prince among Slaves*, 81.

89. For Job ben Solomon's story, see Curtin, "Ayuba Suleyman Diallo"; Francis Moore, *Travels into the Inland Parts of Africa* (London: E. Cave, 1738); Douglas Grant, *The Fortunate Slave* (New York: Oxford University Press, 1968).

90. Carl Bernhard Wadstrom, *An Essay on Colonization, particularly applied to the Western Coast of Africa* (London: Darton & Harvey, 1794), part 2, 114.

91. John Blassingame, ed., *Slave Testimony: Two Centuries of Letters, Speeches, Interviews, and Autobiographies* (Baton Rouge: Louisiana State University Press, 1996), 314–15.

92. Frank Rollin, *Life and Public Services of Martin R. Delany* (1883; reprint, New York: Arno Press/*New York Times*, 1969), 16–18.

93. For the complete story of Ibrahima abd al Rahman, see Alford, *Prince among Slaves*.

94. Slavery was officially abolished in the British colonies in 1834, a four-year period followed during which the former slaves became "apprentices." The effective date of Emancipation is therefore August 1, 1838.

95. Carlton Robert Ottley, *Slavery Days in Trinidad: A Social History of the Island from 1797–1838* (Port of Spain: Ottley, 1974), 58.

96. Campbell, "John Mohammed Bath," 481.

97. Ibid., 485.

98. Austin, *African Muslims*, 431.

99. Madden, *Twelve Months' Residence*, 136.

100. Ibid.

101. Ibid., 137.

102. Karasch, *Slave Life*, 219.

103. "Autobiography of Omar Ibn Said," *American Historical Review* 30 (July 1925): 793–94.

104. Madden, *Twelve Months' Residence*, 126.

105. Austin, *African Muslims*, 662.

106. Madden, *Twelve Months' Residence*, 129.

107. "Documents," *Journal of Negro History* 21, 1 (January 1936): 55.

108. See Curtin, ed., *Africa Remembered*, 162.

109. Madden, *Twelve Months' Residence*, 129.

110. Austin, *African Muslims*, 466.

111. Dwight, "Condition and Character," 48.

NOTES TO CHAPTER 5

1. J. A. Saco, *Historia de la esclavitud de la raza africana en el Nuevo Mundo*, (Havana, 1938), vol. 1, 65.

2. Françoise Mari, "À propos de la première révolte d'esclaves noirs au Nouveau Monde," *Bulletin de l'IFAN*, no. 164 (October 1979): 90–98. Complete text of Fernandez de Oviedo's description of the revolt published in 1549.

3. For this *cédula* and others, see Rolando Mellafe, *La introducción de la esclavitud negra en Chile* (Santiago: Editorial Universitaria, 1984), 158; Max Portugal Ortiz, *La esclavitud negra en las épocas colonial y nacional de Bolivia* (La Paz: Instituto Boliviano de Cultura, 1977), 14–15.

4. Jean-Baptiste Dutertre, *Histoire générale des Antilles habitées par les François*, 2 vols. (1667; reprint, Saint-Pierre, Martinique: Durieu & Leyritz, 1868–1969), vol. 1, 467–68 and 502–3.

5. Frederick Rodriguez, "Cimarron Revolts and Pacification in New Spain and the Isthmus of Panama" (Ph.D. Diss., University of Michigan, Ann Arbor, 1979), 151.

6. John Thornton, *Africa and Africans in the Making of the Atlantic World, 1400–1680* (Cambridge: Cambridge University Press, 1992), 285–86; Jack D. Forbes, *Africans and Native Americans: The Language of Race and the Evolution of Red-Black Peoples* (Urbana and Chicago: University of Illinois Press, 1993), 186–89.

7. Carlos Melendez and Quince Duncan, *El Negro en Costa Rica* (San José: Editorial Costa Rica, 1972), 18.

8. Frederick Bowser, *The African Slave in Colonial Peru 1524–1650* (Stanford: Stanford University Press, 1974), 251.

9. A. C. Saunders, *A Social History of Black Slaves and Freedmen in Portugal 1441–1555* (Cambridge: Cambridge University Press, 1982), 161.

10 Horses were not indigenous to the Americas but were introduced by the Europeans. The presence of the tsetse fly in most of Africa limited the population of horses there to the Sahelian region, where the fly did not exist.

11. A horse was worth between six and fifteen slaves.

12. Jean Boulègue, *Le grand Jolof XIIIe–XVIe siècle* (Blois: Edition Façades, 1987), 72.

13. Thornton, *Africa and Africans*, 298.

14. Juan de Castellanos, *Elegias de varones ilustres de Indias* (Madrid: M. Rivadeneyra, 1847), 48.

15. Jean Mongin, "Lettre à personne de condition," *Bulletin d'histoire de la Guadeloupe* (December 1984): 136.

16. Colonel Malenfant, *Des colonies et particulièrement de celle de Saint Domingue* (Paris: Audibert, 1814), 215.

17. Jean Fouchard, *Les marrons de la liberté* (Paris: Editions L'École, 1972), 405.

18. Ibid., 538.

19. Ibid., 496.

20. Thomas Madiou, *Histoire d'Haïti* (Port-au-Prince: Editions Fardin, 1981), 35.

21. Fouchard, *Les marrons*, 494–95.

22. Ibid., 495.

23. Ibid.

24. Ibid., 529.

25. John Matthews, *A Voyage to the River Sierra Leone in the Years 1785, 1786, 1787* (London: B. White, 1791), 69.

26. In addition to Boukman, there was a woman who has been described as a *mambo* (voodoo priestess) at Bois-Caiman. Her name was Cecile Fatiman, and she later became the wife of a president of Haiti. Her mother was an African and her father a Corsican. It is probable that her second name was Fatima, like that of Muhammad's favorite daughter, and she may have been a Muslim.

27. For details on the Muslim uprisings in Bahia, see Joao Jose Reis, *Slave Rebellion in Brazil: The Muslim Uprising of 1835 in Bahia* (Baltimore: Johns Hopkins University Press, 1993); Etienne Ignace, "La secte musulmane des Malés du Brésil et leur révolte en 1835," *Anthropos* 4, 1 (1909): 99–105; 4, 2: 405–15; Raymundo Nina Rodrigues, *Os Africanos no Brasil* (1932; reprint, São Paulo: Companhia Editora Nacional, 1976); Pierre Verger, *Flux et reflux de la traite des nègres entre le Golfe de Bénin et Bahia de todos os Santos, du XVIIe au XIXe siècle* (Paris: Mouton, 1968).

28. Reis, *Slave Rebellion*, 81.

29. Ignace, "La secte musulmane," 412.

30. Roger Bastide, *The African Religions of Brazil: Towards a Sociology of*

the Interpenetration of Civilizations (Baltimore: Johns Hopkins University Press, 1978), 104.

31. Reis, *Slave Rebellion*, 132.

32. Ibid., 217.

33. Manoel Querino, *Costumes africanos no Brasil* (1938; reprint, São Paulo: Editora Massangana, 1988), 72–73.

34. Nina Rodrigues, *Os Africanos*, 38.

35. Bastide, *African Religions of Brazil*, 106.

36. Verger, *Flux et reflux*, 326–27.

37. Reis, *Slave Rebellion*, 123.

38. Ibid., 90.

39. Ibid., 48.

40. Verger, *Flux et reflux*, 369.

41. Joseph Sturge and Thomas Harvey, *The West Indies in 1837* (1838; reprint, London: Dawsons of Pall Mall, 1968), 323.

42. Malenfant, *Des colonies*, 215.

43. Francis Moore, *Travels into the Inland Parts of Africa* (London: E. Cave, 1738), 204–5.

44. Ibid., 205–6.

45. Ibid., 207.

46. Ibid., 224.

47. Terry Alford, *Prince among Slaves: The True Story of an African Prince Sold into Slavery in the American South* (New York: Oxford University Press, 1977), 120.

48. Cyrus Griffin, "The Unfortunate Moor," *African Repository* (February 1828): 367.

49. Alford, *Prince among Slaves*, 158.

50. Allan Austin, *African Muslims in Antebellum America* (New York: Garland, 1984), 159.

51. Alford, *Prince among Slaves*, 111.

52. Richard Madden, *A Twelve Months' Residence in the West Indies* (Philadelphia: Carey, Lea & Blanchard, 1835), 132.

53. Ivor Wilks, "Abu Bakr al-Siddiq of Timbuktu," in *Africa Remembered: Narratives by West Africans from the Era of the Slave Trade*, ed. Philip Curtin (Madison: University of Wisconsin Press, 1967), 155.

54. Carlton Robert Ottley, *Slavery Days in Trinidad: A Social History of the Island from 1797–1838* (Port of Spain: Ottley, 1974), 58.

55. Ibid., 59.

56. Carl Campbell, "John Mohammed Bath and the Free Mandingos in Trinidad: The Question of Their Repatriation to Africa 1831–38," *Journal of African Studies* 2, 4 (1975–1976): 487–88.

57. Captain J. Washington, "Some Account of Mohammedu Sisei: A

Mandingo of Nyani-Maru on the Gambia," *Journal of the Royal Geographical Society*, no. 8 (1838): 449–54; Campbell, "John Mohammed Bath," 483–84.

58. Verger, *Flux et reflux*, 363.

59. For more details on the Brazilian repatriates, see ibid.

60. Ibid., 362.

61. James Fletcher and D. P. Kidder, *Brazil and the Brazilians, Portrayed in Historical and Descriptive Sketches* (Boston: Little Brown, 1866), 136, 607.

62. Richard Rathbone, "The Gold Coast, the Closing of the Atlantic Slave Trade, and the Africans of the Diaspora,"in *Slave Cultures and the Cultures of Slavery*, ed. Stephan Palmie (Knoxville: University of Tennessee Press, 1995), 57.

63. Ibid., 57.

64. John Duncan, *Travels in Western Africa in 1845 and 1846*, 2 vols. (London: R. Bentley, 1847), vol. 1, 185.

65. Elisée Reclus, *Africa*, 4 vols. (New York: D. Appleton & Co., 1895–1898), vol. 3, 316.

66. Pierre Verger, "Influence du Brésil au Golfe du Bénin," in *Bulletin de l'I-FAN*, no. 27, special issue, *Les afro-américains*, ed. Pierre Verger (1952): 20.

67. Lorenzo Dow Turner, "Some Contacts of Brazilian Ex-Slaves with Nigeria, West Africa," *Journal of Negro History* 27, 1 (January 1942): 65.

68. Michael J. Turner, "Les Brésiliens: The Impact of Former Brazilian Slaves upon Dahomey" (Ph.D. diss. University of Boston, 1975), 182–84.

NOTES TO CHAPTER 6

1. Joseph Inikori, "Africa in World History: The Export Slave Trade from Africa and the Emergence of the Atlantic Economic Order," in *General History of Africa*, vol. 5 (Berkeley: University of California Press, 1992), 104.

2. Paul Lovejoy, "Background to Rebellion: The Origins of Muslim Slaves in Bahia," *Slavery and Abolition* 15, 2 (August 1994): 161–62.

3. George Truman, *Narrative of a Visit to the West Indies, in 1840 and 1841* (Philadelphia: Merrihew & Thompson, 1844), 110.

4. Raymundo Nina Rodrigues, *Os Africanos no Brasil* (1932; reprint, São Paulo: Companhia Editora Nacional, 1976), 62.

5. Charles Ball, *Fifty Years in Chains* (1837; reprint, New York: Dover Publications, 1970), 165.

6. Lamin Sanneh, *The Crown and the Turban: Muslims and West African Pluralism* (Boulder, Colo.: Westview Press, 1997), 20.

7. Pierre Verger, *Flux et reflux de la traite des nègres entre le Golfe de Bénin et Bahia de todos os Santos, du XVIIe au XIXe siècle* (Paris: Mouton, 1968), 520.

8. Michael Gomez, "Muslims in Early America," *Journal of Southern History* 60, 4 (November 1994): 708.

9. Joseph Dupuis, *Journal of a Residence in Ashantee* (London: Henry Colburn, 1824), 163.

10. Mervyn Hiskett, "African Languages and Literatures." in *The Oxford Encyclopedia of the Modern Islamic World*, ed. John Esposition (London and Oxford: Oxford University Press, 1995), vol. 1, 40–41.

11. Elisée Reclus, *Africa* (New York: D. Appleton & Co., 1895–1898), vol. 3, 265.

12. Bernard Maupoil, *La géomancie à l'ancienne Côte des Esclaves* (1943; reprint, Paris: Institut d'Ethnologie, 1988).

13. Edison Carneiro, *Negros Bantus* (Rio de Janeiro: Civilizacao Brasileira, 1939), 37.

14. Arthur Ramos, *O negro brasileiro* (São Paulo: Companhia Editorial Nacional, 1940), 91.

15. Ibid., 89.

16. Ibid., 88–91.

17. Ibid., 75.

18. Ibid., 127.

19. Wandalina Velez Rodrigues, *El turbante blanco: Muertos, santos y vivos en la lucha politica* (Santo Domingo: Museo del Hombre Dominicano, 1982).

20. Odette Rigaud, "Vodou haïtien: Quelques notes sur ses réminiscences africaines," *Bulletin de l'IFAN*, no. 27 (1952): 236.

21. Leslie Desmangles, professor of Religion and International Studies at Trinity College, personal communication to the author, Hartford, Conn., April 14, 1997.

22. Odette Rigaud, "Le rôle du vaudou dans l'indépendance d'Haïti," *Présence africaine* 18–19 (February–May 1958): 55.

23. In slavery times, "Congo" referred to Bakongo, the people, and not to Congo the country.

24. Melville Herskovits and Frances Herskovits, *Trinidad Village* (New York: A. Knopf, 1947).

25. Ibid., 89.

26. George Eaton Simpson, *Black Religions in the New World* (New York: Columbia University Press, 1978), 102–3.

27. Lamin Sanneh, *The Jakhanke Muslim Clerics* (Lanham, Md.: University Press of America, 1989), 207.

28. Ramos, *O negro brasiliero*, 92–97.

29. Works Progress Administration (WPA), *Drums and Shadows: Survival Studies among the Georgia Coastal Negroes* (Athens: University of Georgia Press, 1986), 141, 145.

30. Ibid. 165, 174, 187.

31. Gomez, "Muslims in Early America," 709.

32. Etienne Ignace, "Le fétichisme des nègres du Brésil," *Anthropos* 3 (1908): 903.

33. Gilberto Freyre, *The Masters and the Slaves* (Berkeley: University of California, 1986), 316.

34. Mason Crum, *Gullah: Negro Life in the Carolina Sea Islands* (1940; reprint, New York: Negro Universities Press, 1968), 265.

35. Fernando Romero, *Quimba, fa, malambo, neque: Afronegrismos en el Peru* (Lima: Instituto de Estudios Peruanos, 1988), 236.

36. Ibid., 188.

37. William Bascom, "Yoruba Acculturation in Cuba," *Bulletin de l'IFAN*, no. 27 (1952): 166.

38. Maureen Warner Lewis, *Trinidad Yoruba: From Mother Tongue to Memory* (Tuscaloosa: University of Alabama Press, 1996), 178.

39. J. D. Elder, "The Yoruba Ancestor Cult in Gasparillo," *Caribbean Quarterly* 16, 3 (September 1970): 9.

40. Alan Lomax, *The Land Where the Blues Began* (New York: Bantam/Doubleday, 1993), 233.

41. George Washington Cable, "The Dance in Place Congo," *The Century* 31, 4 (February 1886): 196.

42. Carl Bernhard Wadstrom, *An Essay on Colonization, particularly applied to the Western Coast of Africa* (London: Darton & Harvey, 1794), part 2, 83.

43. Samuel Charters, *The Roots of the Blues: An African Search* (New York: G. P. Putnam's Sons, 1981), 125.

44. Paul Oliver, *Savannah Syncopators: African Retentions in the Blues* (New York: Stein and Day, 1970), 88.

45. Ibid., 186.

46. John Storm Roberts, *Black Music of Two Worlds* (New York: Praeger Publishers, 1972), 197.

47. Ibid., 213.

48. Lomax, *Land where Blues Began*, 276.

49. Frank Rollin, *Life and Public Services of Martin R. Delany* (1883; reprint, New York: Arno Press/*New York Times*, 1969), 16.

50. Dorothy Sterling, *The Making of an Afro-American: Martin Robinson Delany 1812–1885* (New York: Doubleday, 1971), 2–3.

51. Ibid., 3.

52. William McFeely, *Frederick Douglass* (New York: Norton, 1991).

53. John Blassingame, ed., *Slave Testimony: Two Centuries of Letters, Speeches, Interviews, and Autobiographies* (Baton Rouge: Louisiana State University Press, 1977), 457.

54. Toni Morrison, *Song of Solomon* (New York: New American Library, 1977), 307.

234 | Notes to Chapter 6

55. Richard Robert Madden, *The Island of Cuba; Its resources, progress, and prospects* (London: Gilpin, 1849), 237.

56. Allan Austin, *African Muslims in Antebellum America* (New York: Garland, 1984), 41.

57. Gwendolyn Midlo Hall, *Africans in Colonial Louisiana: The Development of Afro-Creole Culture in the Eighteenth Century* (Baton Rouge: Louisiana State University Press, 1992), 408.

58. A very condensed version has been published by Routledge (New York) in 1997.

59. Claude Andrew Clegg III, *An Original Man: The Life and Times of Elijah Muhammad* (New York: St. Martin's Press, 1997); Richard Brent Turner, *Islam in the African American Experience* (Bloomington: Indiana University Press, 1997).

60. Arthur Huff Fauset, *Black Gods of the Metropolis: Negro Religious Cults in the Urban North* (1944; reprint, Philadelphia: University of Pennsylvania Press, 1971); Albert Raboteau, "Muslim Movements," in *The Encyclopedia of Religion*, ed. Mircea Eliade (New York: MacMillan, 1987).

61. Clegg, *An Original Man*, passim; Eric Lincoln, *The Black Muslims in America* (Westport, Conn.: Greenwood Press, 1982).

62. Clegg, *An Original Man*, 68.

Select Bibliography

Adamu, Mahdi. "The Hausa and Their Neighbors in Central Sudan." In *General History of Africa*. Vol. 4. Berkeley: University of California Press, 1992.

Agassiz, Professor and Mrs. Louis. *A Journey in Brazil*. Boston: Ticknor & Fields, 1868.

Aguirre, Beltran Gonzalo. *La población negra de México: Estudio etnohistorico*. Mexico: SRA-CEHAM, 1981.

Alford, Terry. *Prince among Slaves: The True Story of an African Prince Sold into Slavery in the American South*. New York: Oxford University Press, 1977.

Austin, Allan. *African Muslims in Antebellum America*. New York: Garland, 1984.

"Autobiography of Omar ibn Said, Slave in North Carolina, 1831." *American Historical Review* 30 (October 1924–July 1925): 787–95.

Ball, Charles. *Fifty Years in Chains*. 1837. Reprint, New York: Dover Publications, 1970.

Baquaqua, Mahommah Gardo. *Biography of Mahommah Gardo Baquaqua*. Detroit: Pomeroy & Co., 1854.

Barringer, Paul. *The Natural Bent*. Chapel Hill: University of North Carolina Press, 1949.

Barry, Boubacar. *Le royaume du Waalo, le Sénégal avant la conquête*. Paris: François Maspero, 1972.

———. *La Sénégambie du XVe au XIXe siècle: Traite negrière, Islam et conquête coloniale*. Paris: L'Harmattan, 1988.

Bascom, William. *Yoruba Acculturation in Cuba. Bulletin de l'IFAN*, no. 27 (1952): 163–67.

Bastide, Roger. *Les Amériques noires*. Paris: Petite Bibliothèque Payot, 1967.

———. *The African Religions of Brazil: Towards a Sociology of the Interpenetration of Civilizations*. Baltimore: Johns Hopkins University Press, 1978.

Bilge, Barbara. "Islam in the Americas." In *The Encyclopedia of Religions*, ed. Mircea Eliade. New York: Macmillan Publishing Co., 1987.

Bivar, A. "The Wathiqat ahl al-Sudan: A Manifesto of the Fulani Jihad." *Journal of African History* 2, 2 (1961): 235–43.

Blyden, Edward. "Mohammedanism in Western Africa." In *The People of*

Africa: A Series of Papers on Their Character, Condition, and Future Prospects, ed. Henry Schieffelin. New York: A. D. F. Randolph, 1871.

———. "Mohammedanism and the Negro Race." *Methodist Quarterly Review* 29, 7 (January 1877): 100–27.

———. *Christianity, Islam, and the Negro Race*. 1887. Reprint, Edinburgh: Edinburgh University Press, 1967.

Bolster, Jeffrey. *Black Jacks: African American Seamen in the Age of Sail*. Cambridge: Harvard University Press, 1997.

Borja, Jaime. "Barbarización y redes de indoctinamiento en los negros cartageno XVII y XVIII." In *Contribución Africana a la cultura de las Américas*, ed. Astrid Ulloa. Bogota: Instituto Colombiano de Antropología Colcutura, 1993.

Boulègue, Jean. *Le grand Jolof XIIIe–XVIe siècle*. Blois: Edition Façades, 1987.

Bowser, Frederick. *The African Slave in Colonial Peru 1524–1650*. Stanford: Stanford University Press, 1974.

Brandon, George. *Santeria from Africa to the New World: The Dead Sell Memories*. Bloomington: Indiana University Press, 1993.

Bravman, René. *Islam and Tribal Art in West Africa*. Cambidge: Cambridge University Press, 1974.

Burton, Richard. *A Mission to Glegle, King of Dahome*. London: Tinsley Brothers, 1864.

Cable, George Washington. "The Dance in Place Congo." *The Century* 31, 4 (February 1886): 517–32.

Callcott, George. "Omar ibn Seid, a Slave who Wrote an Autobiography in Arabic." *Journal of Negro History* 39, 1 (January 1954): 58–63.

Cameron, Norman. *The Evolution of the Negro*. Demerara: Argosy Co., 1934.

Campbell, Carl. "John Mohammed Bath and the Free Mandingos in Trinidad: The Question of Their Repatriation to Africa 1831–38." *Journal of African Studies* 2, 4 (1975–76): 467–95.

Carneiro, Edison. *Religoes negras: Notas de etnografia religiosa*. Rio de Janeiro: Civilizacao Brasileira, 1936.

———. *Negros bantus*. Rio de Janeiro: Civilizacao Brasileira, 1939.

Caruthers, William. *The Kentuckian in New York*. New York: Harper & Brothers, 1834.

Castellanos, Juan de. *Elegias de varones ilustres de Indias*. Madrid: M. Rivadeneyra, 1847.

Charters, Samuel. *The Roots of the Blues: An African Search*. New York: G. P Putnam's Sons, 1981.

Clarke, Peter. *West Africa and Islam: A Study of Religious Development from the Eighth to the Twentieth Century*. London: E. Arnold, 1982.

Clegg, Claude Andrew III. *An Original Man: The Life and Times of Elijah Muhammad*. New York: St. Martin's Press, 1997.

Clifton, James, ed. *Life and Labor on Argyle Island: Letters and Documents of a Savannah River Rice Plantation 1833–1867.* Savannah: Beehive Press, 1978.

Collins, Dr. *Practical Rules for the Management and Medical Treatment of Negro Slaves, in the Sugar Colonies.* 1811. Reprint, Freeport, N.Y.: Books for Library Presses, 1971.

Conneau, Theophilus. *A Slaver's Log Book or Twenty Years' Residence in Africa.* 1854. Reprint, Englewood Cliffs, N.J.: Prentice-Hall, 1976.

Conrad, Georgia Bryan. "Reminiscences of a Southern Woman." *Southern Workman* 30, 5 (May 1901): 252–57.

Cornelius, Janet Duitsman. *When I Can Read My Title Clear: Literacy, Slavery, and Religion in the Antebellum South.* Columbia: University of South Carolina Press, 1992.

Crowder, Michael. *The Story of Nigeria.* London: Faber & Faber, 1973.

Crum, Mason. *Gullah: Negro Life in the Carolina Sea Islands.* 1940. Reprint, New York: Negro Universities Press, 1968.

Cuche, Denys. *Pérou nègre.* Paris: L'Harmattan 1981.

Curtin, Philip. *The Atlantic Slave Trade: A Census.* Madison: University of Wisconsin Press, 1969.

———, ed. *Africa Remembered: Narratives by West Africans from the Era of the Slave Trade.* Madison: University of Wisconsin Press, 1967.

Davis, Curtis Carroll. *Chronicler of the Cavaliers: A Life of the Virginia Novelist Dr. William A. Caruthers.* Richmond: Dietz Press, 1953.

Day, Charles William. *Five Years' Residence in the West Indies.* London: Colburn & Co., 1852.

Debien, Gabriel. "Origine des esclaves des Antilles." *Notes d'Histoire Coloniale,* no. 75 (1963).

———. *Les esclaves aux Antilles françaises XVIIe–XVIIIe siècles.* Pointe-à-Pitre: Société d'Histoire de la Guadeloupe, 1974.

———. *De l'Afrique à Saint-Domingue.* Notes d'Histoire coloniale, no. 221 (1982).

Debret, Jean Baptiste. *Voyage pittoresque et historique au Brésil, 1816–1831,* Paris: Firmin Didot Frères, 1834.

Denham, Dixon. *Narrative of Travels and Discoveries in Northern and Central Africa, in the Years 1822, 1823, and 1824.* London: John Murray, 1826.

Desmangles, Leslie. Personal communication to the author. April 14, 1997.

"Documents" (Abou Bekir Sadiki, alias Edward Doulan). *Journal of Negro History* (January 1936): 52–55.

Duncan, John. *Travels in Western Africa in 1845 and 1846.* 2 vols. London: R. Bentley, 1847.

Dupuis, Joseph. *Journal of a Residence in Ashantee.* London: Henry Colburn, 1824.

Durand, Jean Baptiste Léonard. *Voyage au Sénégal fait dans les années 1785 et 1786.* Paris: Dentu, 1807.

Dutertre, Jean-Baptiste. *Histoire générale des Antilles habitées par les François.* 1667. Reprint, Saint-Pierre, Martinique: Durieu et Leyritz, 1868–69. 2 vols.

Dwight, Theodore. "Condition and Character of Negroes in Africa." In *The People of Africa: A Series of Papers on Their Character, Condition, and Future Prospects,* ed. Henry Schieffelin. New York: A. D. F. Randolph, 1871.

Edwards, Paul, ed. *Equiano's Travels.* 1789. Reprint, London: Heinemann, 1969.

Elder, J. D. "The Yoruba Ancestor Cult in Gasparillo." *Caribbean Quarterly* 16, 3 (September 1970): 5–20.

Ellis, George W. "Islam as Factor in West African Culture." *Journal of Race Development* 2, 2 (October 1911): 105–30.

Falola, Toyin, ed. *Pawnship in Africa: Debt Bondage in Historical Perspective.* Boulder, Colo.: Westview Press, 1994.

Faria, Jose Luciano. *Presenca negra na america latina.* Lisbon: Prelo, 1971.

Fauset, Arthur Huff. *Black Gods of the Metropolis: Negro Religious Cults in the Urban North.* 1944. Reprint, Philadelphia: University of Pennsylvania Press, 1971.

Fisher, Allan, ed. *Slavery and Muslim Society in Africa: The Institution in Sahara and Sudanic Africa and the Trans-Saharan Trade.* London: C. Hurst & Co., 1970.

Fletcher, James, and D. P. Kidder. *Brazil and the Brazilians, Portrayed in Historical and Descriptive Sketches.* Boston: Little Brown, 1866.

Forbes, Frederick. *Dahomey and the Dahomans in the year 1849 and 1850.* London: Longman, Brown, Green & Longmans, 1851.

Forbes, Jack D. *Africans and Native Americans: The Language of Race and the Evolution of Red-Black Peoples.* Urbana and Chicago: University of Illinois Press, 1993.

Fouchard, Jean. *Les marrons de la liberté.* Paris: Edition L'Ecole, 1972.

Freyre, Gilberto. *The Masters and the Slaves.* Berkeley: University of California Press, 1986.

Gallaudet, Thomas. *A Statement with regard to the Moorish Prince, Abduhl Rahhahman.* New York: Daniel Fanshaw, 1828.

Gardner, George. *Travels in the Interior of Brazil, 1836–1841.* 1849. Reprint, New York: AMS Press, 1970.

Gemery, Henry, ed. *The Uncommon Market: Essays in the Economic History of the Atlantic Slave Trade.* New York: Academic Press, 1979.

Gomez, Michael. "Muslims in Early America." *Journal of Southern History* 60, 4 (November 1994): 671–710.

Grant, Douglas. *The Fortunate Slave.* New York: Oxford University Press, 1968.

Greenberg, Joseph. "The Decipherment of the 'Ben-Ali Diary': A Preliminary Statement." *Journal of Negro History* 25, 3 (July 1940): 372–75.

Griffin, Cyrus. "The Unfortunate Moor." *African Repository* (February 1828): 364–67.

———. "Abduhl Rahahman, the Unfortunate Moorish Prince." *African Repository* (May 1828): 77–81.

———. "Prince the Moor." *Southern Galaxy* (June 5, 1828).

Gurley, Ralph. "Secretary's Report." *African Repository* (July 1837): 201–7.

Hair, P. E. H. "The Enslavement of Koelle Informants." *Journal of African History* 6, 2 (1965): 193–203.

———. *Barbot on Guinea*. London: Hakluyt Society, 1992.

Hall, Gwendolyn Midlo. *Africans in Colonial Louisiana: The Development of Afro-Creole Culture in the Eighteenth Century*. Baton Rouge: Louisiana State University Press, 1992.

Halliday, Andrew. *The West Indies*. London: J. W. Parker, 1837.

Herskovits, Melville, and Frances Herskovits. *Trinidad Village*. New York: A. Knopf, 1947.

Hiskett, Mervyn. *The Sword of Truth: The Life and Times of the Shehu Usuman dan Fodio*. New York: Oxford University Press, 1973.

Hodgson, William Brown. *Notes on Northern Africa, the Sahara and the Soudan*. New York: Wiley & Putnam, 1844.

———. *The Gospels written in the negro patois of English with Arabic characters by a Mandingo Slave in Georgia*. Ethnological Society, October 13, 1857.

Hough, Harrison. "Grégoire's Sketch of Angelo Solimann." *Journal of Negro History* 4, 2 (1919): 281–89.

Hrbek, I., ed. *General History of Africa (Abridged Edition)*, vol. 3, *Africa from the Seventh to the Eleventh Century*. Berkeley: University of California Press, 1992.

Hunwick, John. "The Influence of Arabic in West Africa." *Transactions of the Historical Society of Ghana* (1964).

Ignace, Etienne. "La secte musulmane des Malés du Brésil et leur révolte en 1835." *Anthropos* 4, 1 (January 1909): 99–105; 2: 405–415.

Inikori, Joseph. "Africa in World History: The Export Slave Trade from Africa and the Emergence of the Atlantic Economic Order." In *General History of Africa*. Vol. 5. Berkeley: University of California Press, 1992.

Inikori, Joseph, and Stanley Engerman, eds. *The Atlantic Slave Trade: Effects on Economies, Societies, and Peoples in Africa, the Americas, and Europe*. Durham: Duke University Press, 1994.

Inscoe, John. "Carolina Slave Names: An Index to Acculturation." *Journal of Southern History* 69, 4 (November 1983): 527–54.

Institut Français d'Afrique Noire. *Les Afro-Américains*. Dakar: IFAN, 1952.

Isert, Paul Erdmann. *Letters on West Africa and the Slave Trade: Paul Erdmann Isert's Journey to Guinea and the Caribbean Islands in Columbia*. 1788. Reprint, London and Oxford: Oxford University Press, 1992.

Jobson, Richard. *The Golden Trade.* 1623. Reprint, Devonshire: E. Speight and Walpole, 1904.

Johnson, Michael. "Runaway Slaves and the Slave Communities in South Carolina, 1799 to 1830." *William and Mary Quarterly* 38, 3 (July 1981): 418–41.

Johnston, Harry. *The Negro in the New World.* 1910. Reprint, New York: Johnson Reprint Corp, 1969.

Jones, Charles Colcock. *The Religious Instruction of the Negroes in the Southern States.* Philadelphia: Presbyterian Board of Publication, 1847.

Joyner, Charles. *Down by the Riverside: A South Carolina Slave Community.* Urbana and Chicago: University of Illinois Press, 1984.

Karasch, Mary. *Slave Life in Rio de Janeiro 1808–1850.* Princeton: Princeton University Press, 1987.

Kemble, Frances Anne. *Journal of a Residence on a Georgia Plantation in 1838–1839.* 1863. Reprint, Athens: University of Georgia Press, 1984.

Killens, John Oliver, ed. *The Trial Record of Denmark Vesey.* 1822. Reprint, Boston: Beacon Press, 1970.

Kilson, Martin, ed. *The African Diaspora: Interpretative Essays.* Cambridge: Harvard University Press, 1970.

Koelle, Sigismund Wilhelm. *African Native Literature.* London: Church Missionary House, 1854.

———. *Polyglotta Africa.* London: Church Missionary House, 1854.

Labat, Jean-Baptiste. *Voyage aux îles de l'Amérique 1693–1705.* 1722. Reprint, Paris: Seghers, 1979.

La Traite des Noirs par l'Atlantique: Nouvelles approches. Paris: Société française d'outre-mer, 1976.

Lemaire, Le Sieur. *Les voyages du Sieur Lemaire aux îles Canaries, Cap-Vert, Sénégal et Gambie.* Paris, 1695.

Lenz, Oskar. *Tombouctou, voyage au Maroc, au Sahara et au Soudan.* Paris: Hachette, 1887.

Le Page du Pratz, Antoine. *Histoire de la Lousiane.* 3 vols. Paris, 1758.

Lewis, Maureen Warner. *Trinidad Yoruba: From Mother Tongue to Memory.* Tuscaloosa: University of Alabama Press, 1996.

Lincoln, Eric. *The Black Muslims in America.* Westport, Conn.: Greenwood Press, 1982.

Littlefield, Daniel. *Rice and Slaves: Ethnicity and the Slave Trade in Colonial South Carolina.* Urbana and Chicago: University of Illinois Press, 1991.

Lomax, Alan. *The Land Where the Blues Began.* New York: Bantam/Doubleday, 1993.

Louisiana Historical Quarterly, 1925–1940.

Lovejoy, Paul. "Background to Rebellion: The Origins of Muslim Slaves in Bahia." *Slavery and Abolition* 15, 2 (August 1994): 151–81.

———. "The African Diaspora: Revisionist Interpretations of Ethnicity, Culture and Religion under Slavery." *Studies in the World History of Slavery, Abolition and Emancipation* 2, 1 (1997). http://www.h-net.msu.edu.

———, ed. *Africans in Bondage: Studies in Slavery and the Slave Trade*. Madison: University of Wisconsin Press, 1986.

Lyell, Charles. *A Second Visit to the United States*. London: John Murray, 1849.

Madden, Richard Robert. *A Twelve Months' Residence in the West Indies*. Philadelphia: Carey, Lea & Blanchard, 1835.

———. *The Island of Cuba; its resources, progress, and prospects*. London: Gilpin, 1849.

Madiou, Thomas. *Histoire d'Haïti*. 1847. Reprint, Port-au-Prince: Editions Fardin, 1981.

Malenfant, Colonel. *Des colonies et particulièrement de celle de Saint Domingue*. Paris: Audibert, 1814.

Mari, Françoise. "À propos de la première révolte d'esclaves noirs au Nouve Monde (1522)" *Bulletin de l'IFAN*, no. 167 (October 1979): 90–98.

Martin, B. G. "Sapelo Island's Arabic Document: The 'Bilali Diary' in Context." *Georgia Historical Quarterly* 78, 3 (fall 1994): 589–601.

Mathieu, Nicolas del Castillo. *Esclavos negros en Cartagena y sus aportes lexicos*. Bogota: Instituto Caro y Cuerno, 1982.

Matthews, John. *A Voyage to the River Sierra Leone in the Years 1785, 1786, 1787*. London: B. White, 1791.

Maupoil, Bernard. *La géomancie à l'ancienne Côte des Esclaves*. 1943. Reprint, Paris: Institut d'Ethnologie, 1988.

Mazo Karras, Ruth. *Slavery and Society in Medieval Scandinavia*. New Haven: Yale University Press, 1988.

McFeely, William. *Frederick Douglass*. New York: Norton, 1991.

Melendez, Carlos, and Quince Duncan. *El negro en Costa Rica*. San José: Editorial Costa Rica, 1972.

Mellafe, Rolando. *La introducción de la esclavitud negra en Chile*. Santiago: Editorial Universitaria, 1984.

Mollien, Gaspard Théodore. *L'Afrique occidentale en 1818*. 1820. Reprint, Paris: Calman Levy, 1967.

Montejo, Esteban. *The Autobiography of a Runaway Slave*. Edited by Miguel Barnet. New York: Pantheon, 1968.

Monteil, Vincent. *L'islam noir*. 1964. Reprint, Paris: Le Seuil, 1980.

———. "Analyse des 25 documents arabes des Malés de Bahia (1835)." *Bulletin de l'IFAN* 39, 1 (February 1967): 88–98.

Moore, Francis. *Travels into the Inland Parts of Africa*. London: E. Cave, 1738.

Moraes de, Nize Isabel. *A la découverte de la Petite Côte au XVIIe siècle*. Initiations et Etudes Africaines 3 vols. Dakar: Université Cheikh Anta Diop, 1995.

Moreau de Saint Mery, Médéric Louis Elie. *Description topographique, physique, civile, politique et historique de la partie française de l'île de Saint Domingue*. 1797. Reprint, Paris: Larose, 1958.

———. *Voyage aux Etats-Unis de l'Amérique*. 1798. Reprint, New York: Doubleday, 1947.

Moreau, René Luc. *Africains musulmans*. Paris: Présence Africaine, 1982.

Nina Rodrigues, Raymundo. *Os Africanos no Brasil*. 1932. Reprint, São Paulo: Companhia Editora Nacional, 1976.

Oliver, Paul. *Savannah Syncopators: African Retentions in the Blues*. New York: Stein and Day, 1970.

Ortiz, Fernando. *Hampa afro-cubana: Los negros esclavos: Estudio sociologico y de derecho publico*. Habana: Revista Bimestre Cubana, 1916.

———. *Hampa afro-cubana: Los brujos negros*. Madrid: Editorial America, 1917.

———. *La fiesta afro-cubana del "dia de reyes."* Havana: Imprenta El Siglo XX, 1925.

Ortiz, Max Portugal. *La esclavitud negra en las épocas colonial y nacional de Bolivia*. La Paz: Instituto Boliviano de Cultura, 1977.

Ottley, Carlton Robert. *Slavery Days in Trinidad: A social History of the Island from 1797–1838*. Port of Spain: Ottley, 1974.

Owen, Nicholas. *Journal of a Slave Dealer: A view of some remarkable Axcedents in the life of Nicholas Owen, 1746–1757*. Reprint, New York: Houghton Mifflin, 1930.

Owens, Leslie Howard. *This Species of Property: Slave Life and Culture in the Old South*. New York: Oxford University Press, 1976.

Park, Mungo. *Travels in the Interior Districts of Africa, Performed in the Years 1795, 1796, and 1797*. 2 vols. London: John Murray, 1816–1817.

Parrish, Lydia. *Slave Songs of the Georgia Sea Islands*. 1942. Reprint, Athens: University of Georgia Press, 1992.

Patterson, Orlando. *Slavery and Social Death*. Cambridge: Harvard University Press, 1982.

Peytraud, Lucien. *L'esclavage aux Antilles françaises avant 1789*. Pointe-à-Pitre: Emile Desormeaux, 1973.

Porteous, Laura. "The Gri-Gri Case." *Louisiana Historical Quarterly* 17, 1 (January 1934): 48–63.

Plumer, William. "Mcroh, a Native African." *New York Observer*, January 8, 1863.

Pruneau de Pommegorge. *Description de la Nigritie*. Amsterdam: Maradan, 1789.

Puckett, Newbell. *Black Names in America: Origins and Usage*. Boston: G. K. Hall, 1975.

———. *Folk Beliefs of the Southern Negroes*. 1926. Reprint, New York: Negro Universities Press, 1975.

Querino, Manoel. *A Raca africana e os sues costumes*. 1940. Reprint, Salvador: Progresso, 1955.

————. *Costumes africanos no Brasil.* 1938. Reprint, São Paulo: Editora Massangana, 1988.

Raboteau, Albert. *Slave Religion: The "Invisible Institution" in the South.* New York: Oxford University Press, 1978.

Radiguet, Maximilien. *Souvenirs de l'Amérique espagnole: Chili, Pérou, Brésil.* Paris: M. Levy, 1874.

Raeders, Georges. *Le comte de Gobineau au Brésil.* Paris: Les Nouvelles Editions Latines, 1934.

Ramos, Arthur. *O negro brasileiro.* São Paulo: Companhia Editorial Nacional, 1940.

————. *As Culturas negras no novo mundo.* 1937. Reprint, São Paulo: Companhia Editorial Nacional, 1979.

Rathbone, Richard. "The Gold Coast, the Closing of the Atlantic Slave Trade, and the Africans of the Diaspora." In *Slave Cultures and the Cultures of Slavery*, edited by Stephan Palmie. Knoxville: University of Tennessee Press, 1995.

Reclus, Elisée. *Africa.* 4 vols. New York: D. Appleton & Co., 1895–1898.

Reichert, Rolf. *L'insurrection des esclaves de 1835 à la lumière des documents arabes des Archives publiques de l'Etat de Bahia (Brésil). Bulletin l'IFAN* 29, 1–2 (1967): 99–104.

————. *Os documentos arabes do Arquivo do Estado da Bahia.* Bahia: Universidade Federal da Bahia, Centro de Estudos Afro-Orientais, 1970.

Reis, Joao Jose. *Slave Rebellion in Brazil: The Muslim Uprising of 1835 in Bahia.* Baltimore: Johns Hopkins University Press, 1993.

Rigaud, Odette. "Vodou haïtien: Quelques notes sur ses réminiscences africaines." *Bulletin de l'IFAN*, no. 27 (1952): 235–38.

————. "Le rôle du Vaudou dans l'indépendance d'Haïti." *Présence africaine* 18–19 (February–May 1958): 43–67.

Ritchie, Carson. "Deux textes sur le Sénégal: 1673–1677." *Bulletin de l'IFAN* 30, 1 (January 1968): 289–353.

Roberts, John Storm. *Black Music of Two Worlds.* New York: Praeger Publishers, 1972.

Rodriguez, Frederick. "Cimarron Revolts and Pacification in New Spain and the Isthmus of Panama." Ph.D. diss., University of Michigan, Ann Arbor, 1979.

Rodway, John. *History of British Guiana, from the Year 1668 to the Present Time.* 3 vols. Georgetown: J. Thompson, 1891–1894.

Roger, Baron. *Kélédor, histoire africaine.* Paris: Nepveu, 1828.

Rollin, Frank. *Life and Public Services of Martin R. Delany.* 1883. Reprint, New York: Arno Press/*New York Times*, 1969.

Romero, Fernando. *Quimba, fa, malambo, neque: Afronegrismos en el Peru.* Lima: Instituto de Estudios Peruanos, 1988.

Ruete, Emily. *Memoirs of an Arabian Princess from Zanzibar.* New York: Markus Wiener Publishing, 1989.

Saco, J. A. *Historia de la esclavitud de la raza africana en el Nuevo Mundo.* Havana, 1938.

Sanneh, Lamin. *The Jakhanke Muslim Clerics.* Lanham, Md.: University Press of America, 1989.

———. *The Crown and the Turban: Muslims and West African Pluralism.* Boulder, Colo.: Westview Press, 1997.

Saunders, A. C. *A Social History of Black Slaves and Freedmen in Portugal 1441–1555.* Cambridge: Cambridge University Press, 1982.

Schön, Rev. *Grammar of the Hausa Language.* London: Church Missionary House, 1862.

Searing, James. *West African Slavery and Atlantic Commerce: The Senegal Valley 1700–1860.* Cambridge: Cambridge University Press, 1993.

Simpson, George Eaton. *Black Religions in the New World.* New York: Columbia University Press, 1978.

Starling, Marion Wilson. *The Slave Narrative: Its Place in American History.* Washington, D.C.: Howard University Press, 1988.

Sterling, Dorothy. *The Making of an Afro-American: Martin Robinson Delany 1812–1885.* New York: Doubleday, 1971.

Sturge, Joseph, and Thomas Harvey. *The West Indies in 1837.* 1838. Reprint, London: Dawsons of Pall Mall, 1968.

Tardieu, Jean-Pierre. *L'église et les noirs au Pérou: XVIe et XVIIe siècles.* Paris: L'Harmattan, 1993.

Teas, Edward. "A Trading Trip to Natchez and New Orleans in 1822: Diary of Thomas Teas." *Journal of Southern History* 7 (August 1941): 378–99.

Thornton, John. *Africa and Africans in the Making of the Atlantic World, 1400–1680.* Cambridge: Cambridge University Press, 1992.

Truman, George. *Narrative of a Visit to the West Indies, in 1840 and 1841.* Philadelphia: Merrihew & Thompson, 1844.

Turner, Lorenzo Dow. "Some Contacts of Brazilian Ex-Slaves with Nigeria, West Africa." *Journal of Negro History* 27, 1 (January 1942): 55–67.

———. *Africanisms in the Gullah Dialect.* 1949. Reprint, New York: Arno Press/*New York Times*, 1969.

Turner, Michael J. "Les brésiliens: The Impact of Former Brazilian Slaves upon Dahomey." Ph.D. diss., Boston University, 1975.

Underhill, Edward Bean. *The West Indies.* London: Jackson, Walford and Hodder, 1862.

Velez Rodrigues, Wandalina. *El turbante blanco: Muertos, santos y vivos en la lucha politica.* Santo Domingo: Museo del Hombre Dominicano, 1982.

Verger, Pierre. *Flux et reflux de la traite des nègres entre le Golfe de Bénin et Bahia de todos os Santos, du XVIIe au XIXe siècle.* Paris: Mouton, 1968.

Viotti da Costa, Emilia. *Crowns of Glory, Tears of Blood: The Demerara Slave Rebellion of 1823*. New York: Oxford University Press, 1994.

Wadstrom, Carl Bernhard. *An Essay on Colonization, particularly applied to the Western Coast of Africa*. London: Darton & Harvey, 1794.

Wallbridge, Edwin A. *The Demerara Martyr: Memoirs of the Rev. John Smith, Missionary to Demerara*. 1848. Reprint, New York: Negro Universities Press, 1969.

Washington, Captain J. "Some Account of Mohammedu Sisei: A Mandingo of Nyani-Maru on the Gambia." *Journal of the Royal Geographical Society*, no. 8 (1838): 449–54.

Willis, John Ralph, ed. *Slaves and Slavery in Muslim Africa*. London: Frank Cass, 1985.

Wood, Donald. *Trinidad in Transition: The Years after Slavery*. New York: Oxford University Press, 1968.

Wood, Peter. *Black Majority: Negroes in Colonial South Carolina from 1670 through the Stono Rebellion*. New York: Norton, 1974.

Works Progress Administration (WPA), Savannah Unit, Georgia's Writers Project. *Drums and Shadows, Survival Studies among the Georgia Coastal Negroes*. 1940. Reprint, Athens: University of Georgia Press, 1986.

Index

Abd al Rahman, Ibrahima: autobiography, 140; Bible, 112; capture, 25–26; diet, 87; family, 38, 180, 185; letters, 137, 139; literacy, 11, 123, 138; as Moor, 98; opinion of Christians, 95–96, 98; silent on Middle Passage, 41; as slaver enslaved, 12

Abu Bakr al Siddiq: autobiography, 140–44; Bible, 112; captivity, 41–43, 45; capture, 31; family, 35, 38, 68; in Jamaica, 55, 56; Koran, 113; letters, 96, 139; literacy, 108–9, 138; professional, 102; return to Africa, 169–70; studies, 35

Afonja, 33–34

Afrocentrism, 204

Ahmadiyah, 206

Ahmed Baba, 14–15

Ajami, 8, 124

Allah: *Al-Fatiha*, 123–24; Candomble, 187; incantation (Trinidad), 138; invocation (Middle Passage), 29; Jamaica, 124, 226n. 56; in pastoral letter in Jamaica, 139; Moorish Temple, 205–7; Nation of Islam, 207; *Shahada*, 49–50, 62, 187; Sufism, 5; in traditional religions, 186

Alms, 64–65, 191. See also *Saka; Sakara; Saraka*

Amari Ngone Ndella, 28–29

American Colonization Society, 166–68

Amistad, 202, 217n 16

Anna Moosa (Benjamin Cockrane), 38, 56, 96

Antigua, 29

Anti-Muslim legislation, 18, 145–47

Arabia, 14, 186

Arabic: in Africa, 6–8; autobiographies in, 110, 126, 139–44; Bibles in, 111–12; in Brazil, 56, 79, 119, 125–26, 139–40, 156–57, 176; books in, 36–37, 39, 56, 120–21, 140; in Georgia, 125–28; in Guyana, 133; in Jamaica, 108, 124–25, 138–40, 141–44; letters in, 55, 58, 115, 134–40, 165–69; in Maryland, 135; in Mississippi, 123, 137; in New Orleans, 124; in non-Muslim religions, 123–28; in North Carolina, 126, 134–35, 139, 141–44; in novel, 124; in Panama, 126; in revolts, 126, 133–34; in Saint-Domingue, 124, 133; in songs, 194; in South Carolina, 107; in Trinidad, 125, 139

Aprigio, 79, 118

Arouna, 38, 124

Ashanti, 6, 31, 186

Autobiographies by Muslims, 140; Africa in, 142, 144; austerity of, 143–44; emphasis on education in, 141–42; enslavement of authors in, 142–43; Islam in, 143; self-censorship in, 142, 144

Bahamas, 45

Bal, Suleyman, 27

Baol, 23–24, 28

Baquaqua, Mahommah Gardo: capture, 42–45, 203; on conversion, 53

Bath, John Mohammed: children, 180, 200; deported to Trinidad, 45; death, 174; diet, 87; dress, 77; letters, 138; and love of country, 172; nobility, 38; opinion of non-Muslim slaves, 87; repatriation efforts, 172–74

Beards, 81

Berbesi (Berbeci), 16, 20, 72, 213n. 44

Bibles, 56, 111, 112, 168

Bilali (Ben Ali), 35; descendants, 199; "diary," 115, 126–27; diet, 66, 89, 203; dress, 75; family, 65, 85–86, 180, 185; Koran, 114; and non-Muslims, 92–93; as Moor, 99; and prayers, 63; profession of faith, 50; professional, 92, 102

Bilali, Salih: capture, 36; children's names, 85–86; family, 65, 180; diet, 66, 87, 203; Koran, 114; literacy, 110; name, 84–85; professional, 102

Billo, Amadou, 13, 25

Bornu, 12, 14, 32, 35, 37, 111, 155

Boukman, 152–53

Bouna, 30, 36, 55

Brazil: children of Muslims in, 181; circumcision, 91; conversions, 53–54; freedom associations, 104–5; funeral rites, 192; gris-gris, 131, 193–94; Islam in other religions, 200; Islamic diet, 90; Islamic dress, 75, 77–80; Koranic schools, 118, 120; Korans, 113–15; *marabouts,* 35, 38, 121; Muslims and Christians, 95, 101–2; pilgrimage, 68; polygamy, 91; prayers, 62, 64; Ramadan, 64, 67; religious writings, 125–26; revolts, 153–63; Yoruba religion, 186

Bundu, 8, 30, 166

Candomble, 181, 185–87, 198

Catholicism: and African religions, 181, 184, 185; in Brazil, 53; evangelization in Africa, 16–17; evangelization in America, 49; in French West Indies, 50–52; Inquisition, 147–48; and Islam in Americas, 18, 49, 146–48

Cédula. See Anti-Muslim legislation

Charno, 124

Children (Muslim): in Koranic schools, 7, 36; literacy, 110, 181–82; turn to other religions, 180, 181, 182

Chile, 45, 130, 146–47

Circumcision, 4, 90

Clothing: in Africa (Islamic), 44, 74–75; Islamic in Americas, 76–80, 192; of clerics, 77, 132; dress codes, 74; headgear, 75–76, 78, 188, 192; and identity, 81–82; influence of Islamic in Americas, 76, 78–79; Muslims and western, 74–75; Islamic and "hoodoo," 78; nudity, 44, 73; retention of, by slaveowners, 73; and revolts, 79–80, 155–57; of slaves, 72–74; of women, 75, 78–79; as sign of Islamic faith, 81; as sign of recognition, 81–82

Colombia, 20, 52, 200

Color prejudice: absent in African slavery, 14; in Islam, 13; in Americas, 15, 97–102

Conversion: and Catholicism, 17, 49–50, 54; interdiction of new converts in Spanish colonies, 146; and Islam, 4, 10, 13; and Protestantism, 50, 54–55; pseudoconversions, 54–58; reconversions, 58, 172, 177; refusal of, by Muslims, 17, 51–53, 57, 146

Costa Rica, 147

Crime (enslavement for), 9–11

Cuba, 33, 58; gris-gris, 193; Mandingo, 91, 200; Mina, 200; music, 194; Muslims, 48; Nupe, 194; professional slaves, 102; returnees from, 172; revolts, 147; Santeria, 179, 185–86, 188; Tapa, 194

Dahomey (Benin), 10, 42; returnees to, 174, 176–77; Voodoo, 188

Daughters of the Dust, 202

Delany, Martin Robinson, 136, 199

Dhikr, 5, 64, 159, 195

Diet: alcohol, 66, 87–88, 191; *halal* meat, 89–90, 192; pork, 87–88; and self-control, 90

Djibirilu, 115, 184

Dominican Republic, 76, 146, 188

Douglass, Frederick, 199

Egypt, 5, 31, 39

Equiano, Olaudah, 14, 140

Fard, Wally, 200, 206

Ferreira, Paulo Jose, 177

Free Mandingo Society/Free Mohammedan Society: affirmation of faith, 138; debt question, 172, 173; failure to return to Senegambia, 174; and Islamic networks, 104, 173; letters to King and Queen of England, 138, 173; literacy, 139; and maintenance of faith, 104; opinion about non-Muslim slaves, 87;

orthodoxy, 173; ownership, 104, 172; redemption of Muslims, 104; rejection of alcohol, 87; repatriation efforts, 138–39, 172–74; solidarity, 104; success of some at repatriation, 104

Free Muslims, 103–4; and associations, 104–5; in Bahian revolt, 155; in Brazil, 104–5; and Koranic schools, 119, 121; role of Islam in freedom, 105–6; in Trinidad, 104. *See also* Free Mandingo Society/Free Mohammedan Society; *and individual Muslims*

French West Indies, 52, 80. *See also* Guadeloupe; Martinique; Saint Christopher; Saint-Domingue

Fulani: in Brazil, 100, 115, 153; contribution to Gullah, 72; in Guinea, 24, 37, 46; indentured laborers, 118; in Nigeria, 32; in Puerto-Rico, 171; in Saint-Domingue, 72, 148; in Senegal, 8, 16, 19–20, 26; returnees, 176; in United States, 26, 98. *See also* Abd al Rahman, Ibrahima; Bilali (Ben Ali); Bilali, Salih; Job ben Solomon (Ayuba Suleyman Diallo); Yarrow Mahmout

Funeral rites: in Brazil, 192; in Islam, 193; in Sea Islands, 164, 193; in Trinidad, 191

Futa Jallon, 8, 10, 24–27, 30, 38, 168

Futa Toro, 8, 20–21, 26–30, 79

Gambia, 10, 37, 165, 172, 196

Gazirmabe, Ali Eisami, 33, 44–45

Georgia, 35–36, 47, 82, 171. *See also* Sea Islands

Ghana (Gold Coast), 10, 30–31, 176

Gilofo, Pedro, 147

Gobir, 31, 31

Gorée, 23–24, 29, 43

Grenada, 65, 118, 191

Gris-gris: in Africa, 4, 36; in Americas, 35; in Bahia, 119, 131–33, 193; brought from Africa, 130; description of, 128–29; in Latin America, 130; in Louisiana, 130–31; and Mandingo, 130; and non-Muslims, 129, 131; purpose of, 130–31; in Saint-Domingue, 131, 151, 153; survival, 193; in revolts, 131–32; in Trinidad, 130

Guadeloupe, 48, 51, 118

Guiana (French), 48, 118

Guinea, 7, 11, 18, 35, 51, 216n. 3

Gullah, 68, 72, 84, 201

Guyana, 118, 133

Haiti: Revolution, 150–53; influence of Revolution, 163. *See also* Hispaniola; Saint-Domingue

Halaou, 150

Harvesttime, 192–93

Hausa: in Nigeria, 31, 34, 38, 42, 46; in Brazil, 34, 81, 100, 153–55, 158; indentured, 118; in Jamaica, 124; in Saint-Domingue, 72; returnees, 176

Hispaniola, 18, 20

Ibrahima Sori, 24–25

Illiteracy, 107–8

Ilorin, 33–34

Indentured laborers, 117–18, 183–84, 198

Indians, 145, 147

Islam: in Africa, 4; and African religions, 4–5; democratic, 20, 162; and European colonization, 41; fear of, in Spanish colonies, 147–48; galvanizing force, 162; Islamic world, 5–6; literacy, 6; in Muslims' life, 159; numerology in, 133, 159, 194; organizing force, 161–62; orthodox, 67, 69–70, 90, 179, 184–85, 206–7; and peasant resistance, 20, 41; prestige of, 187; and race, 13–14; in revolts, 158; and slavery, 10–15; unifying force, 20, 30, 33–34, 48, 71–72, 104–6, 132, 189–90

Islamic networks: in Brazil, 68, 115, 120, 122, 139–40; in Jamaica, 59; and sailors, 116, 172; in Sea Islands, 114–16; in Trinidad, 104, 173

Israel, 63, 75, 81, 114

Jamaica: Africans, 48; Arabic writing in, 125, 139, 141; clerics, 35; indentured laborers, 118; Korans, 113; maroons, 163–64; Muslims, 55–57; nobility, 38

Jihad: clerics in, 39–40; in Central Sudan, 12, 31–33, 153, 162–63; rules, 159; in Senegal, 19, 20–22; uprising in Bahia, 158

Job ben Solomon (Ayuba Suleyman Diallo): capture, 11–12, 36–37; diet, 87–89; dress, 77; faith, 50; family, 40, 164–65, 180; freedom, 136; Koran, 117; letters in Arabic, 135–36, 139; literacy, 138; name, 82; prayers, 60; return to Senegal, 164–66
Jolof: empire, 1, 19–20, 148; kingdom, 20, 27–28

Kaba Mohammed (Caba), 35, 55–56, 58–59, 139
Kane, Abdel Kader, 27–30, 171
Kanem, 5–6, 32
Kano, 7, 14, 31
Karamoko Alfa, 24
Kayor, 20–21, 23–24, 27, 28–30
Kebe, Lamine: on Africa, 144; capture, 36; family, 40; Koranic teacher, 7, 120; letters, 139; return to Africa, 171; warrior, 39
Kélédor: capture, 29, 42, 44–45; faith, 59; return to Senegal, 171
Khalwa, 5, 159
Kidnappings, 9, 11, 15, 34, 36–37, 40
Koki and Pir, 27, 30
Kong, 30–31, 35, 167
Koran: among slaves, 56, 110–16, 125, 181; in Brazil, 55, 113–15; by heart, 8, 14, 40, 117, 121; indentured laborer and, 118; and Islamic networks, 115–17; in Jamaica, 113; and literacy, 6, 7; by Noble Drew Ali, 205; in Peru, 121; procured by Christians, 113; in Pulaar, 25; and race, 13; recitation of, 5, 159, 195–98; in Sea Islands, 114; treatment of slaves in, 14; in Trinidad, 114; in United States, 113; women reading, 7, 40; written by Benjamin Larten, 117; written by Job ben Solomon, 117
Koranic law, 4; in Brazil, 121; and manumission, 13; and slavery, 8–15; and unbelievers, 10–12
Koranic schools: in Africa, 7–8, 25, 27, 36, 181; in Americas, 121; in Bahia, 118–20, 161; books in, 120; girls in, 7; and Islamic networks, 122; non-Muslims in, 7; numbers of, 7–8; organization of, 122; in Rio, 120; slates in, 119; writing exercises in, 119–20

Koranic teachers: in Africa, 31; in Bahia, 79–80, 118–19; in Guinea, 120; and kidnappings, 36; Lamine Kebe, 7, 39, 120; in autobiographies of Muslims, 141; in Rio, 121; in Saint-Domingue, 124; in Trinidad, 174

Ladinos, 17
Liberia, 166–68
Licutan, 38, 67, 105, 156–57
Literacy: in Africa, 6–8; in Americas, 107–12; children and, 110, 181; end of Arabic literacy in Americas, 182, 189; in European languages, 122; and freedom, 134–36, 138; preservation of, 109–12; of Muslims, whites on, 107–9; in Rio, 114. *See also* Arabic
London, 125
Louisiana, 71, 130–31, 200, 203

Macandal, 38, 150–51, 153
Macumba, 188
Maghreb, 5–6, 37, 39
Maguina, Mohammedou, 174
Makumba, Samba: beard, 81; capture, 28; dress, 77; on children of Muslims, 181; and Free Mandingo Association, 104; nobility, 38; opinion of Christians, 96; professional, 102
Mala Abubakar, 133
Malés, 4, 100, 156, 159, 181, 187–88, 194
Mali (western Sudan), 7–8, 14, 38, 51
Mandinga, Antonio, 147
Mandingo: in Brazil, 100, 115, 187; in Colombia, 200; contribution to Gullah, 72; in Cuba, 79, 91; in Futa Jallon, 24, 26, 152, 196; in Georgia, 125; in Hispaniola, 148, 150; in Jamaica, 97, 125; indentured laborers, 118; and literacy, 8; in Mexico, 47; and music, 196–97; and occult, 130–31, 187; in Peru, 47, 121; in Saint-Domingue, 47, 151; in Senegal, 16, 19–20; as slave dealers, 11; traders, 37–38, 48, 95; in Trinidad, 172–74. *See also* Abu Bakr al Siddiq; Anna Moosa (Benjamin Cockrane); Bath, John Mohammed; Delany, Martin Robinson; Free Mandingo Society/Free Mohammedan Society; Kaba Mo-

hammed (Caba); Macandal; Maguina, Mohammedou; Makumba, Samba; Rainsford, William; Sisei, Mohammedu
Marabouts: in Africa, 7; *Amistad,* 202; in Bahia, 119, 131–32; dress, 76–77; in French West Indies, 18, 51, 149; healers, 188; during Middle Passage, 44; mobility, 35–36, 39; in Peru, 121; in Rio, 121; in Saint-Domingue, 151; and shout, 190; in Trinidad, 76–77, 114, 125; warriors, 31, 151–54; wars in Senegal, 20–22, 27–30. *See also* Grisgris; Koranic teachers
Maroons: in Africa, 26; in Brazil, 162; Muslim and cavalry, 148; in Jamaica, 163; in Saint-Domingue, 150–52; in Spanish America, 145, 148–49, 154
Martinique, 47, 118, 147
Maryland, 60, 135, 164. *See also* Job ben Solomon (Ayuba Suleiman Diallo); Yarrow Mahmout
Mecca, 5–6, 39, 69, 190
Memory of Muslims: and Afrocentrism, 204; in art, 201–2; in Americas, 198; and "Black Muslims," 205–7; in Christianity, 204–5; in scholarly works, 200–203; in United States, 198–203; in West Indies, 198, 200
Mexico, 20, 47, 146–47
Middle Passage: baptism before, 52; branding, 43; food for, 25, 27; description by Muslims, 41–42; fear of, 21, 43; feelings about, 45; forced entertainment during, 44; nudity, 44; revolt during, 24; suicide, 29, 44
Mina, 47, 54, 104–5, 139–40, 175–76
Mississippi, 80, 196–97. *See also* Abd al Rahman, Ibrahima; Samba
Mmadi Make (Angelo Solimann), 57, 77
Mohammed Abdullah, 68, 95, 104, 122
Mohammed Ali ben Said, 37, 68, 141, 144
Mohammedou Maguina, 38, 174
Montserrat, 118
Moorish Temple, 205–7
Moors: and *marabouts'* war, 20; and Moorish Temple, 205; *Moros y Christianos,* 149; Muslim slaves as, 98–100, 104, 140, 204; in Spain, 17; and slave trade, 26–27
Morenos, 76, 188

Moriscos, 146
Morocco, 5, 38, 137, 170
Mosques, 62, 68, 157, 177
Muhammad, 4; illiterate, 6; black companions of, 13; descendants of, 6, 76, 151, 170; incantation to, in Trinidad, 138; as Jesus, 57; letter about, in Jamaica, 139; Moorish Temple, 207; names of family and companions, 83; Nation of Islam, 207; warrior, 39, 49–50, 213n. 41
Muhammad, Elijah, 199, 203, 206–7
Music and songs: Arabic words in, 194; blues, 196–98; Central African, 195; in Peru, 194; Sufi, 195; rice cake song, 194; in Trinidad, 194
Muslims/non-Muslims relations, 92, 93; Africans' opinion of whites, 94–95; Muslims' opinion of Christians, 94–97; Muslims' opinion of non-Muslim blacks, 92; Muslims/whites relations, 95; non-Muslim blacks' opinion of Muslims, 91–92, 189; whites' opinion of Muslims, 97–102, 109

Nafata, 32
Nago (Yoruba): in Brazil, 91, 115, 153–55, 158, 177, 188; civil war, 33–34; religion, 33, 186, 188; in Saint-Domingue, 72
Names: "basket-names," 83–84; day-names, 84; ethnic, 84; and identity, 82, 85–86; Islamic in Americas, 83–84, 150, 201, 203; of native-born children, 85–86; transformation of Islamic, 82; and religious identification, 87; using two, 82, 86
Nasir al Din, 20–22, 27, 30
Nation of Islam, 206–7
Ndiaye, Lamine, 165, 171
Nigeria (central Sudan): enslavement of Muslims, 11, 12; Jihad in, 31–33; Muslims from, in Bahia, 153–63; nobility deported from, 38; Oyo civil war, 33–34; returnees to, 174–76; Yoruba, 112
Noble Drew Ali (Timothy Drew), 205–7
North Carolina, 30, 47, 134–35, 140–41. *See also* Omar ibn Said
Nupe, 33, 46

Obatalla, 186

Old Lizzy Gray, 57
Omar ibn Said: autobiography, 140–44;
  and Bible, 112; captivity, 41; capture,
  30; dress, 76; faith, 50, 56; family, 180;
  Koran, 113; literacy, 110, 138; name,
  82–83; pilgrimage, 68; and Ramadan,
  66; warrior, 39; writings, 126, 134, 139
Oyo, 33–34

Panama, 126, 147
Paraiso, Souleiman, 176–77
Pawning, 9, 21, 27, 38
Peru: Africans, 45, 47; anti-Muslim legisla-
  tion, 146; Arabic in songs, 194; fear of
  Islam, 147; Koranic teaching, 121;
  Mandingo, 121, 130; Muslims, 20; re-
  volts, 147
Pilgrimage, 56; and shout, 68–69, 190–91
Polygamy, 4, 90–91
Prayers: Islamic integrated in other reli-
  gions, 189–90; in mosques, 62; number
  of, in Americas, 62–63; public, 60–62;
  prayer beads, 63–64; prayer mat, 63;
  secret, 60
Professional slaves, 102–3, 152
Proselytism (Muslim) 147, 182–84
Protestantism: and North American slaves,
  204–5; and conversion of Muslims,
  55–57; and slavery, 50, 54; and proselytism in Africa, 167–68, 171
Puerto Rico, 29, 146, 148, 171

Qadiriyah, 5, 20, 27, 30–31

Rainsford, William, 96
Ramadan, 64, 66–67, 159
Recaptives, 130, 183–84
Redemption (of slaves), 11–13, 38, 104,
  135–37, 165, 167–70
Religious writing: al-Fatiha, 123–24;
  "Ben-Ali Diary," 126–28; gospels, 125;
  other *surah*, 124–25; and revolt in
  Bahia, 126; and the lot of the slave, 126
Return to Africa: Abu Bakr al Siddiq,
  169–70; and African Colonization Soci-
  ety, 166; and Catholicism, 177; to cen-
  tral Sudan, 175–77; from Cuba, 172; to
  Dahomey, 174–77; and Free Mandingo
  Society, 172–74; to Gold Coast, 176;
  Ibrahima abd al Rahman, 58, 167–69;

Job ben Solomon, 164–66; Kélédor,
  171–72; Muslims wanting to, 164, 172;
  and reconversion, 58, 177; after revolt
  in Bahia, 174–77; to Senegal, 58,
  171–72; western view of, 170–71
Revolts: in Africa, 26; in Bahia, 153–63;
  by Denmark Vesey, 163; in Guyana,
  133–34; in Hispaniola, 145–46,
  148–49; Muslim factor in, 151–53,
  158–63; in Saint-Domingue, 151–53,
  163; in Spanish America, 20, 147
Rings, 80
Roots, 201
Rumfa, 7

Saint Christopher, 149, 150
Saint-Domingue: ethnic groups, 72; impor-
  tation of Africans, 145; literacy in, 124;
  marabouts, 36, 131, 150–53; maroons,
  150–53; Muslims, 47; Muslims in syn-
  cretic religions, 200; nobility, 38; oc-
  cult, 131, 150–53; revolts, 145–46,
  150–53, 163; Senegalese, 29, 47; slave
  dress, 73; Voodoo, 179, 185, 189–90,
  198. *See also* Boukman; Kélédor;
  Macandal; Tamerlan
Saint-Louis, 20–21, 23, 26, 29–30
Saint Lucia, 118, 221n. 53
Saint Vincent, 118
Saka, 64, 65, 180
Sakara, 65, 191
Samba, 26, 82, 85
Santeria, 179, 185–86, 198
Saraka, 65–66, 191–92, 194
Sea Islands: Africans, 61; alms, 65–66;
  "Ben-Ali Diary," 127; clerics, 35–36,
  50; diet, 89; dress, 75; funeral rites,
  164; harvesttime, 192; Korans, 110,
  113; memories of Islam, 183, 198;
  Muslims, 61–62; Muslim/non-Muslim
  relations, 92; prayer beads, 63; prayers,
  61–61; Ramadan, 66; shout, 68–69. *See
  also* Bilali (Ben Ali); Bilali, Salih; Israel
See (Sy), Shaykh Sanna, 126
Senegal: family name in Louisiana, 200;
  loas, 190; music, 197; people from, in
  West Indies, 51, 97; returnees to, 58,
  172; slavery in 10–11. *See also* Baol;
  Bundu; Gorée; Jolof; Futa Toro; Kayor;
  Koki and Pir; Saint-Louis; Walo

Senegambia, 7, 30–31, 47, 203
Sharif/Shurfa, 6, 76, 151, 170, 206
Shout, 68–69, 190, 193
Sierra Leone, 26, 37, 47–48, 115, 152, 166, 196
Sisei, Mohammedu, 36, 174
Slave systems: in Africa, 8–15; in Americas, 13, 15; in Arab countries, 13–14; in Europe, 16; in Islam, 10–15
Slave trade: caravans, 26, 29, 42–43; in Europe, 16–17; to Europe, 15; Muslims against, 20–21, 24–26, 27–30, 32, 40; Muslims involved in, 12, 14, 21, 24–25, 41; Muslims victims of, 20–21, 24, 26, 28–29, 41; role of firearms in, 22–23, 25; and spread of Islam, 20, 40–41; numbers, 45–48; sex ratio, 40; slave dealers victims of, 12, 36–38
Sokoto, 8, 34, 176
Song of Solomon, 202
Soninke/Sarakhole, 46–47. *See also* Kebe, Lamine
Sorcery, 11, 130, 147, 188
South Carolina, 45, 47, 61, 71, 99, 163
S'Quash, 99, 102
Sufism, 5, 150, 159, 195
Surinam, 74
Syncretism, 184–94. *See also* Candomble; Macumba; Traditional religions; Voodoo

Takrur, 4
Tamerlan, 36, 124, 164
Timbo, 7, 13, 24–26, 35, 37, 63, 168
Timbuktu, 8, 141, 170
Torodo revolution, 26–30
Traders, 36–38, 115–16
Traditional religions: 4–5; conversion, 51–52; followers enslaved by Muslims, 12–14, 21, 24–25; Islam and, 185–86, 204; Muslims enslaved by followers of, 20–21, 24, 26, 28–29
Trinidad: Arabic in songs, 194; children of Muslims, 181; Free Mandingo Society, 138–39, 172–74; gris-gris in, 130; Islamic features in religion, 190, 200; Is-

lamic dress, 77–78; Korans, 113–14, 118, 125; nobility, 38; recaptives, 130; *Sakara*, 191; shout, 68. *See also* Bath, John Mohammed; Maguina, Mohammedou; Makumba, Samba; Sisei, Mohammedu
Tubenan revolution (*marabouts'* war), 20–21
Tubman, Harriet, 200
Tukulor, 19, 26, 47, 148, 200. *See also* See (Sy), Shaykh Sanna

Usman dan Fodio: and female literacy, 7; events in Bahia, 153, 158–59, 162–63; *Jihad*, 31–33, 39, 144

Vai, 46, 72
Vesey, Denmark, 163
Voodoo, 152–53, 189–90

Walo, 19–21, 26, 28
Wars: in Jolof empire, 19–20; role of Europeans in, 22–23; for gaining slaves, 22–23; Islamic, 39–40; political, 23–24, 33–34; prisoners as slaves, 9; religious, 24–25, 30–31
Wolof: cavalry, 148; contribution to Gullah, 72; in Costa Rica, 147; indentured laborers, 118; in Louisiana, 47, 196, 200; music, 196; Muslims, 14, 16; in Portugal, 147; revolts, 24, 145–46, 148; in Saint-Domingue, 18; in Spain, 17; in Spanish colonies, 20
Women: and alms, 65, 66; aristocracy, 40; concubines, 9, 15; dress, 75, 78–79; kidnapping of, 40; marriage, 91; literacy, 6–8; mothers and wives, 40; number in slave trade, 40, 179–80; polygamy, 91; prayers, 59; returnees, 171, 176; and revolt in Bahia, 80, 155, 157, 160

Yarrow Mahmout: diet, 87; dress, 78; prayers, 60; no descendants, 180
Yaya, 150
Yunfa, 31–32

About the Author

A writer specialized in African affairs and the history of people of African descent, SYLVIANE A. DIOUF has written extensively for international publications and scholarly journals.

She holds a Doctorate in Human Sciences from the University of Paris 7 Denis Diderot. After having resided in various countries in Africa and Europe, she now lives in New York.